LOOKING FOR
HUMBOLDT

&

SEARCHING FOR GERMAN FOOTPRINTS
IN NEW MEXICO AND BEYOND

ERIKA SCHELBY

For Frederick

CONTENTS

LIST OF FIGURES

9. *page 78. Alexander von Humboldt, pencil and ink drawing by Frédéric Christophe de Houdetot, Berlin 1807.* Wikimedia Commons, File: Alexander von Humboldt 1807 225-91-1-PB.jpeg, 186x240 pixels

10. *page 102. The Battle of Cerro Gordo.* Wikimedia Commons, File: Battle of Cerro Gordo depicted in Coffin's Building the Nation, 1883,jpg. 394x480 pixels

11. *page 105. Plucked, or The Mexican eagle before the War! The Mexican eagle after the War!* Published May 15, 1847 in Yankee Doodle, v. 2, no.32. Library Of Congress, Prints and Photographs. http://www.loc.gov/pictures/item/2002695264/

12. *page 116. Map of the Santa Fe Trail.* United States National Park Service-Map, Robert McGinnis illustration. Wikimedia Commons: File Map of Santa Fe Trail, 2012., 320x203 pixels

13. *page 143. Manifest Destiny: "Spirit of the Frontier,"* painting by John Gast, 1872. Columbia, representing America, light from the East. Wikimedia Commons, File: Ameican progress. JPG. Pixels 390x289.

14. *page 158. Native Americans in the Valley of the Colorado River by Balduin Möllhausen, 1861.* Original in The British Library. Wikimedia Commons: File: Möllhausen (1861) 2.012 Eingeborene im Thale des Colorado (2) jpg, 320x212 pixels.

15. *page 161. Valley of the Rio Pecos at La Cuesta, after a painting by Balduin Mölhausen, 1853,* Whipple Report. National Park Service: Kiva, Cross, and Crown. https://www.nps.gov/parkhistory/online

16. *page 175. Rio Colorado of the West, map by F.W. Egloffstein. United States Office of Explorations and Surveys, 1858.* Library of Congress. https://www.loc.gov/item/79692915

17. *page 187. Soldier Guarding Interned Navajos at Bosque Redondo, circa 1864.* Google search: images

18. *page 196. Al Sieber with Apache Scouts, photo by J.C. Burge, 1870's. Wikimedia Commons.*

19. *page 203. The Apache Kid.* Google search: images.

1

A Question and A Quest

On seeing a Detailed Map
I noticed the empty space
Where there is no map,
Only the theater of man and myth,
The land of the unicorn
And less lovely beasts
Trying to corral him.

—*Antonio Mares*
(Gonzales-Berry, 1989, p. 277)

Coming from the east, a plane approaches the Sandia Mountains like a surfer riding to the crest of a wave. Depending on the winds, there is usually a pronounced lift across the top of the range before the aircraft begins its gliding descend to the rift valley below. Seeing this vast, rolling plateau for the first time from the air made me wonder if we were landing in Central Asia. Was this Tibet or Afghanistan? What else could look so empty, remote, and austere?

That was then, years ago. Seen from the bird's eye perspective, the lay of the land hasn't changed. What has changed is my perception. Various newcomers to New Mexico have long constructed interpretations that suited their requirements. These versions, born from particular imaginations, were garnished with fact and then used to wrap the locale and the locals in either the exotic finery or the humble garments of their day.

I also arrived as a newcomer—all the way from the other side of the pond. To make a home along the Rio Grande, I had to look, listen, pull back the layers of history, put things in a frame of reference, and fill in some of the empty spaces. This book is a record of doing this. It's called *Looking for Humboldt*. In choosing the title, I had my tongue firmly in cheek. Here in the United States, there are mountains and rivers, towns and schools, mines, and even a calypso band named after Alexander von Humboldt. But, with rare exceptions, the people I asked didn't know who Humboldt was, or that he was a man who played, at least indirectly, a role in the story of New Mexico. It was the Prussian who put Santa Fe on the map and then shared that map with Thomas Jefferson and members of his cabinet.

Looking for Humboldt soon became a game I played. At first, I asked friends and acquaintances, and then even strangers. Before long, I queried

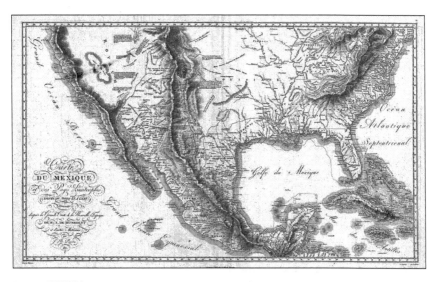

FIGURE 1. *Seminal map by Alexander von Humboldt of New Spain, with today's Mexico, the American Southwest, and the Southern U.S.*

everyone I ran into. Humboldt was unknown. Why? That became the question and the quest.

This book is not a formal history, but an informal, selective, and personal one. History is a terribly large subject. It is as big as life, and even with the best of intentions and the greatest of skills, one has to confront the twin dangers of painting a large canvas devoid of detail, or of cutting the whole into small slices that will no longer show the context within a bigger picture. I hope to find a path between these pitfalls. My sampling will be respectful of facts and sources, but, at the same time, it should wiggle like a radiation-detecting Geiger counter in the presence of humbug.

The book leaps through time and inspects some of New Mexico's many connections to the larger world as seen through a different pair of glasses and the eyes of a late German arrival. The great waves of immigration from Western Europe to the United States ended more than a century ago in the 1890s, and what followed was only a trickle. It amuses me to think that I am but one of the sentient droplets within that thin stream.

Many books have been written about New Mexico and the Southwest. And so, as I set out to add another contribution to this rich lore, I felt it would be best to use a navigational tool that could help me find a way through regions that were, at least to me, largely uncharted: The device that serves as a compass through *terra incognita* while looking for Humboldt is a tale. It comes from Umberto Eco's essay collection *Serendipities*.

Unicorns, Eco tells us, were part of the medieval European tradition and, consequently, people were convinced that these gentle creatures existed. To be sure, no one had seen a unicorn lately, but believers moved around this hurdle by assuming that the fabulous beasts lived exclusively in exotic countries. So, when Marco Polo traveled to China, he was up-to-date on the latest infotainment about faraway countries, and he was certainly, among other things, on the lookout for unicorns. Sadly, he didn't see a single one. But at last, already on his way home, he observed animals that looked similar to unicorns. They had a horn on their heads just above their noses. Yet they were black, not white. They were also massive, and had none of the elegance and graceful strength one expected of them. (The military tank had not been developed back then, but if it had, perhaps Marco would have compared this animal to a tank.) In any event, the great traveler accepted the creature seen in Java as the unicorn. Actually, it was the rhinoceros.

> "We cannot say that Marco Polo lied," Eco (1988) concluded (p. 54).
>
> He told the simple truth, namely, that unicorns were not the gentle beasts people believed them to be. But he was unable to say he had found new and uncommon animals; instinctively, he tried to identify them with a well-known image. Cognitive science would say [that] he was determined by a cognitive model. He was unable to speak about the unknown but could only refer to what he already knew and expected to meet. He was a victim of his background books (Eco, 1988, pp. 54–55).

So was Columbus. So are we all.

Therefore, as I set out on my own journey—looking for Humboldt, searching for traces of things German in New Mexico and beyond—I will pay close attention to the last wonderful sentence in Eco's essay. I typed it and then taped the printout to the side of my computer as a constant reminder: "The real problem of a critique of our own cultural models is to ask, when we see a unicorn, if by any chance it is not a rhinoceros" (Eco, 1988, p. 75).

2

Faultline of Empires

The difference between colonial Mexico
and the English colonies was immense.

> —*Octavio Paz,*
> *The Labyrinth of Solitude*

Solitude is un-American.

> —*Erica Jong*

Living in New Mexico sometimes leaves me with the feeling of sitting on a tectonic plate that pushes lightly but persistently against the massive rest of North America. The cause for such a low-key seismic grumbling isn't geological like that of the San Andreas Fault in California. Instead, the slight local friction is historical, legal, social, and cultural. The land here was the northern frontier of the former Spanish empire in America, and it remains a region where two worldviews, two world systems, and two different ways of looking at life come together. The strong third component—that of the Native Americans—adds additional levels of intricacy. New Mexico's stance is of happily comprising three cultures: Native American, Hispanic, and Anglo. Hereabouts, the term *Latino* is seldom used, and the term *Anglo* apparently makes all the rest of us palefaces honorary Anglo-Saxons.

New Mexico's blending of cultures is real enough. We get along and, as far I am concerned, appreciate each other. Yet, if you look a little closer, you will notice fine fissures and fractures. How did they develop? What do they mean? How deep and how far back do you have to go to find out?

The rivalry between Spain and England goes back almost to the start of the European explorations, conquests, and expansions across the Americas. The U.S. is an English-speaking country that pays far more attention to one side of the story. But I am interested in well-rounded tales, and when one half of it isn't told properly or when it is omitted once too often, my ears perk up. What is more, we have heard much about the word *Eurocentric*, and I wonder what that is all about. Both Britain and Spain are part of Europe, but how can something be Eurocentric when a large part of Europe's history is excluded or told in a way that would baffle many in the so-called Old World? Is the history of the British Isles used as a North American surrogate for the story of the European continent? And how did Americans slip into the role as inheritors of British versions of the past, especially since they—as British colonies—fought a revolutionary war to gain their independence from the motherland? A friend of mine has a funny little quip about our Anglophilia. More than once I have heard him say *once a colonial, always a colonial.*

Acquaintances and friends are usually incredulous when I mention that Germany and New Spain had the same Habsburg ruler back during the 1540s when Francisco Vásquez de Coronado traveled north to explore new land, *la Tierra Nueva,* for the first time. Hardly anyone had ever considered such a double monarchy. So I give a little laugh and change the subject. Anyway, according to the Muster Roll of February 1540, among Coronado's men was the 22-year-old German bugler, Juan Fioz, from Worms, the city where Martin Luther defied the same emperor Coronado served. The young man had an unusual (probably adapted) name for someone from the Rhineland, but nevertheless, he must have been the first German to set foot on what was to become the northernmost province of New Spain and later part of the United States.

Like others, I had paid no attention to an esoteric New Mexico-German connection until I saw a piece of information in the September 4, 2000, issue of Forbes. To be sure, news about long-dead Spanish kings and Holy Roman Emperors of the German Nation (full official name since the 15th century) are about as common as tidings from the far side of the moon, especially in the U.S. business or mainstream press. But here it was: "Charles V rules!" proclaimed Forbes, always impressed with chief executive officers that pack a punch.

The magazine proceeded to list European museum exhibits honoring "the former ruler of the Western world" on the 500th anniversary of his birth. The birthday offered a nice round number: 1500. Renaissance. Reformation. Printing Press. Advancing Turks. Voyages of Exploration. Lifetime of the glorious Francis I in France and the vigorous Henry VIII in England. All of Europe in the ferment of turbulent change. Beginning of the modern era. Charles, though, was born in a quiet place: in chivalrous, prosperous Renaissance Ghent, then part of Burgundian Flanders and today a handsome city in Belgium.

Forbes listed the exhibits: "*The Art of Silverware and Jewels in the Spain of Charles the V*" was shown in La Coruna; "*Portraits of the Royal Family*" could be seen in Ceres. Toledo presented the show *"Carolus,"* and Barcelona exhibited "*Catalunya and the Spanish Empire.*" There was also a display of *"The Tapestries of Charles V"* at the Cultural Centrum in Mechelen, Belgium. But what Forbes overlooked in its "ruler of the western world" trumpet solo was the most ambitious, comprehensive, and dazzling show of the anniversary year 2000: *Emperor Charles V (1500–1558)—Europe's Power and Weakness"* (Codart, 2009).

This exhibit's title didn't pair power with strength or wealth. It appropriately combined the opposites of power and weakness, and that in itself indicates a certain contemporary European way of looking at things. Assembled through the cooperative efforts of four countries with Habsburg ties—Austria, Belgium, Germany, and Spain—the show displayed paintings by Titian, Duerer, Leoni, Cranach, and Seisenegger, among others, and sculptures, jewels, a splendid crown, tapestries, armor, swords, scientific instruments, books, and rare documents from various museum collections and archives. Many items had never been shown before. Special attention was given to technological advances in the fields of mining, botany, astronomy, medicine, and to the navigation that would propel Europe toward the modern age. The show opened in Ghent and then traveled on to Bonn, Vienna, and Toledo.

Charles V (Charles I of Spain) inherited extensive Habsburg lands from his European family. His father was Philip, Duke of Burgundy; his mother was Joanna (later called "*la loca*"), daughter of Ferdinand and Isabella of Aragon and Castile; his grandfather was Maximilian I, German king and Holy Roman Emperor. Just nineteen years old, Charles was elected as HR emperor on June 28, 1519. Traditionally, the election and the coronation were two different events. In 1530, Charles became the last emperor to be crowned by a pope. Some say he was Europe's last emperor, period. Just for the fun of it, let's present a garland of his honors and titles:

> Charles the Fifth, by the grace of God, Roman emperor, ... king in Germany, Castile, Aragon, Leon, and both Sicilies, Jerusalem, Hungary, Dalmatia, Croatia, Navarre, Granada, Toledo, Valencia, Galicia, Mallorca, Seville, Sardinia, Cordoba, Corsica, Genoa, Algarve, Algericas, Gibraltar, the Canary and Indian Islands, the mainlands across the Ocean Sea, etc.; archduke of Austria, duke of Burgundy, Lorraine, Brabant, Styria, Carinthia, Carniola, Limburg, Luetzenburg, Geldern, Calabria, Athens, Neopatras, and Wuerttemberg, etc.; count of Habsburg, Flanders, Tirol, Goricia, Barcelona, Artois, Burgundy, count palatine of Hainault, Holland, Zeeland, Pfirdt, Kyburg, Namur, Roussillon, Ceretano and Zutphen, landgrave of Alsace, margrave of Burgau, Oristani, Gotiani, Holy Roman Imperial prince of Swabia, Catalonia, Asturias, etc., master of Frisia, of the Wendish March, of Portenau, Biscay, Molina, Salins, Tripoli, Malines, etc. (Gress, 1998, p. 245).

That is quite a laundry list for the king of the Spaniards and the Germans, who was the elected Holy Roman Emperor during the years when the entrepreneurial Hernan Cortés entered the capital city of the Aztecs on November 8, 1519, without an initial authorization from the Spanish crown for the conquest of Mexico. To compensate for his lack of permission, Cortés wrote letters—the legally required *cartas de relación*—to the Spanish court explaining his actions. News about Charles' 1519 election as HRE reached Cortés within a few months. (The election was supported by substantial financial campaign funds from the Fugger banking firm in Augsburg, Germany. As in today's United States, elections had grown expensive by that time). Adjusting quickly, the conqueror of the Aztecs wrote his Second Letter addressed to the new emperor. He explained how busy he was, and he shrewdly compared Mexico with Germany:

> I have not acquainted Your Majesty with all that has happened since. God knows how much this has troubled me; for I wished Your Highness to know all the things of this land, which, as I have already written in another report, are so many and of such a kind that one might call oneself the emperor of this kingdom with no less glory than of Germany, which, by the Grace of God, Your Sacred Majesty already possesses (Pagden, 1986, p. 48).

Well, not exactly. The emperor did not "possess" Germany. He ruled with the estates. Among them were the free imperial cities with their extensive rights and distinct voices. The empire was not a centralized entity, but a federative one. This seems to contradict the popular view that all empires must be sinister, as shown in the movie *The Empire Strikes Back*. In fact, Rome had been both a republic and a growing empire. Its name was *"imperium populi Romani,"* the empire of the Roman people. And paradoxically, the Christian empire of the West with its Holy Roman Emperor was called *"respublica christiana"*—the Christian republic.

J. H. Elliott explained that the lengthy Cortés letter should be read, "as it was written, not as an accurate historical narrative but as a brilliant piece of special pleading, designed to justify an act of rebellion" (Pagden, 1986, p. xx).

The defiance was directed against the governor of Cuba, Diego Velázquez, who had wanted to dispatch Cortés on nothing more than a trading mission.

But back to the outline of events: Charles V was King of Spain and Germany, and Holy Roman Emperor when:

- In April of 1521, the German Martin Luther refused to retract his teachings at the famous Diet of Worms, saying: "Here I stand. I cannot do otherwise. God help me. Amen." It was curtain up for the Reformation.
- The Spaniard Bartolomé de Las Casas fought for the legal and human rights of the native population in the Americas and contributed unwittingly, through the harsh criticism voiced against his own countrymen's conduct, to the English-Dutch propaganda campaign of the anti-Spanish "Black Legend." Subtly, or not so subtly, it remains with us even today, nearly five hundred years later. We will return to it in a while.
- Francisco Vasquez de Coronado, born in Salamanca and only 30 years old, led a north-bound expedition of approximately 300 soldiers on horseback and on foot, 1000 allied Mexican Indians from Tlaxcalan, a few married women, and food on the hoof—a herd of livestock—to New Mexico and as far north as Kansas. From 1541–1542, Coronado searched for the golden Cities of Cibola but found no precious metals like his fellow conquistadors in Mexico and Peru. Instead he found the Zuni pueblos, the Great Plains, and huge buffalo herds. Water was scarce. Horses died. His men endured hardships. Accurate information was difficult to obtain. The various Indian peoples he encountered during the expedition all spoke different languages. Coronado was forced to dispatch advance and exploration parties to search the region. They roamed through much of today's American Southwest, became the first Europeans to visit the Hopi villages, the sky city of Acoma, the Grand Canyon, the Colorado River, and the pueblos of Taos and Pecos. Coronado himself probably spent two miserable winters at the pueblo of Tiguex on the Rio Grande, near the future settlement of Albuquerque. The expedition force soon exhausted the hospitality

and the food supplies of the village. There was enough to eat for the locals, but not enough to provision a visiting army. Native people began to die. As is often the case with uninvited or occupying troops, the local welcome was guardedly friendly until deprivation increased and the situation got out of hand. On October 20, 1541, Coronado wrote to Charles V from his winter camp, which may well have been at the Pueblo of Tiguex, located once only a few miles from the place where I now live and write. The letter, or account, was detailed and remarkably levelheaded. It reported, among other things, on the physical appearance of the Pueblo Indians.

> "The people here are large. I had several of them measured, and found that they were 10 palms in height; the women are well proportioned and their features are more like Moorish women than Indians."

3

Nurturing the Black Legend

The **Black Legend** (in Spanish, *La Leyenda Negra*) is a style of nonobjective historical writing or propaganda that demonizes the Spanish Empire, its people, and its culture in an intentional attempt to damage its reputation.

—*Wikipedia*

Various craftsmen participated in constructing and refining the anti-Spanish Black Legend. One of the most industrious contributors was the 17th-century Dominican friar Thomas Gage. I stumbled by chance on material about this man and his remarkable career in the colonial city of Antigua, Guatemala. This was in the mid-90s shortly after the civil war.

Gage had lived in *Santiago de los Caballeros de Guatemala* (as Antigua was then called with full flourish) from 1627–1629, and then spent a number of years as a village priest. In the century before him, Bartolomé de Las Casas had also lived in Antigua, at least for a while. The Captaincy General of Guatemala was much larger back then. It included Mexico's Chiapas, where Las Casas was appointed as bishop, and Honduras, El Salvador, Nicaragua, Costa Rica, and a portion of what became Panama.

Today, the city of Antigua retains a lovely and haunted 18th century atmosphere under the watchful eyes of the three attending volcanoes—Agua, Fuego with its plume of smoke, and Acatenango. The town stands on dangerous ground. In 1773, much of it of was destroyed by a series of earthquakes. The survivors fled. The stately ruins of palaces, churches, monasteries, convents, and the university fell into a long sleep. It lasted well into the 20th century.

As for Thomas Gage, he managed to return to London where he published an "I was there" eyewitness account titled *The English-American his Travail by Sea and Land: or a New Survey of the West India's.* The year was 1648. The timing was excellent. The book became a bestseller.

The 16th and the 17th centuries did not yet enjoy the benefits of full-fledged ministries of propaganda, although the fundamentals were certainly in place. Accordingly, the propagandistic benefits of Gage's book were quickly recognized and exploited. In the 1650s, the Black Legend was already a century old and Las Casas, with his passionate condemnation of Spanish behavior in the Americas, had ironically helped to launch it. Especially influential had been his book *A Short Account of the Destruction of the Indies.* Written in 1542, it was a shorter version of his monumental *The Apologetic History of the Indies.* It contained exaggerations, contradictions, horror stories, and engravings showing atrocities in progress. Intended for a popular audience, the *Short Account* became a crowd pleaser throughout Europe.

As it turned out, pictures produced by skilled craftsmen with the help of the new printing press embedded images of Spanish cruelty deeply in the public mind. Back then this was done through prints—today, we do it with photographs, video, film, and fancy computer graphics.

The most prolific and famous illustrator was Theodor de Bry. Biographies call him either Dutch, or Belgian, or German. He was born in 1528 as a citizen of the Holy Roman Empire in Liege, later a town in the independent Netherlands, and much later, a city in Belgium. Belgium didn't exist back then, so let's call him a European.

Trained as a goldsmith and engraver, de Bry, a Protestant, fled religious strife by moving to the free imperial city of Strasbourg, and in 1586 to England. He returned to Germany in 1589 and set up shop in Frankfurt. *History of the Indies* was published in 1590, became enormously popular, and shaped the

FIGURE 2. *Engraving by Theodor de Bry, from Las Casas: A Short Acount of the Destruction of the Indies 1552.*

European imagination about native peoples and 'Indians' for a long time to come. Earlier, in the 1570s and 1580s, de Bry also read and then illustrated editions of the *Short Account* by Las Casas. He had never traveled in the Americas, yet his prints circulated widely and spread visual Black Legend propaganda all across Europe.

And so it was that, both in word and picture, the Black Legend, or *La Leyenda Negra*, systematically disparaged the character, reputation, and achievements of the Spanish people for centuries. It is an example of historically stereotyping a population on a collective scale. The result is then used as a tool of foreign policy. Just like *The Short Account* by Las Casas, so the tale by Thomas Gage was soon successful, and numerous translations were made. The book came out in French in 1676, when France was planning to extend her power overseas against the Spanish; this French edition was reprinted at least eight times between 1677 and 1821 (Rosengarten, 1988, p. 1). There were also German, Dutch, and Spanish editions. The *New American Magazine* in Woodbridge, New Jersey, printed Gage's book in a shortened serial format in 1758.

The sensational aspects of the tract were heightened because Englishmen, even if they were Catholic friars, were prohibited from traveling in Spanish America or the Indies—as these regions were called at the time. Gage had boarded a Spanish ship in Cadiz, hid himself in an empty biscuit barrel during a search by Spanish authorities, escaped discovery, and sailed for the Indies. According to Frederic Rosengarten, the friar who abandoned the Catholic faith and became a fanatical antipapist when he returned to his homeland after an absence of twenty years, "gave his Protestant readers in England exactly what they wanted to read" (Rosengarten, 1988, p. 1). Gage described how the Spanish oppressed the wretched Indians, while the Spaniards themselves were often "portrayed as lazy, lecherous, degenerate, and deceitful" (Rosengarten, 1988, p. 3).

For twelve years, the English friar had likewise enjoyed such a degenerate (translation: easy and comfortable) life among his flock of Maya villagers. Indeed, he lived well, learned native languages, and acquired the considerable fortune of about nine thousand Spanish-American silver dollars, which he secretly exchanged for easily portable assets of pearls and precious stones. Thus prepared, Gage fled Guatemala one night in December of 1636. He traveled for many days, first on muleback and then on a frigate headed from Puerto Limón to Porto Bello (Portobelo), Panama. There he boarded another ship, which was soon seized by a Dutch man-of-war. The pirates robbed Gage of nearly his entire fortune. He now had only a few well-hidden coins and some books left.

Back in England, Gage saw it as his duty to promote the liberation of Guatemala and of other kingdoms in the West Indies from evil Spanish rule. Victory, he observed, would be easy because "military defenses were weak and soldiers careless and negligent." The ex-friar was apparently unaware of the duplicity found in the dedication of the first edition of *The English-American Traveler*. He suggested that Indian subservience to English overlords would be a good thing:

> No question but the right or title to those countries [New Spain] appertains to the natives themselves, who, if they shall willingly and freely invite the English to their protection, what title so ever they have in them no doubt but they may legally transfer it or communicate it to others (Rosengarten, 1988, p. 3).

Oliver Cromwell was pleased with Gage's efforts and with their influence on public opinion. The Dominican friar had recanted his former beliefs in London's St. Paul's Church on August 28, 1642. His bathos-rich sermon was published with the title

> *"Tyranny of Satan, Discovered by the teares of a Converted Sinner,* by Thomas Gage, formerly a Romish Priest, for the space of 38 years, and now truly reconciled to the Church of England."

An ingredient of this reconciliation was a freshly fanned Puritan passion and the testimony against a former schoolmate, Father Thomas Holland, who was hanged, drawn, and quartered for treason at Tyborn on December 12, 1642. Two other Catholics, Father Arthur Bell and Father Peter Wright, were likewise executed based on the testimony given by Gage. Being a Catholic was no longer politically correct. In the England of the time it was treason, and the punishment for it was death.

After his conversion, the honorable Thomas Gage lived well once more. He was rector of St. Leonhard's Church at Deal in Kent when Oliver Cromwell decided that the time was right for taking some real estate away from Spain. No, not Guatemala—such an ambitious conquest could lead to serious supply problems. Cromwell wished to invade the islands of Hispaniola and Jamaica instead. Since Gage was now regarded as the leading authority on

Spanish America, the Lord Protector of England commissioned him to prepare a report. The finished document was titled *Observations on the West Indies*. Once more, Gage predicted an easy victory for the British "since the Spaniards were so decadent and feeble; furthermore, great wealth could be obtained with relatively little effort" (Rosengarten, 1988, pp. 28–29).

Gage was appointed chaplain for the campaign. The fleet sailed from Portsmouth on December 20, 1654 with 60 ships and 6,000 men under the joint command of General Venables and Admiral William Penn. With Cromwell's approval, most of the men had been impressed, so the conquering army contained many "common cheats, thieves, cutpurses, and such like persons" (Christianson, 1998, p. 14).

The attempted 'liberation' of Hispaniola had failed. Local anti-Spanish guides didn't show up, so the invaders sailed on and captured Jamaica without much difficulty. But then the troubles started. The joint commanders, Venables and Penn, quarreled, and many men of the expeditionary force perished from fever or starved to death. In early 1656, Gage's luck finally ran out: he too fell ill and died. To justify the conquest of Spanish Jamaica, an English edition of Las Casas had been published in the same year of 1656. The translator was Cromwell's nephew. Illustrations by De Bry showed the most gruesome atrocities committed by the Spaniards and made the most of Protestant propaganda. The island remained the largest British colony in the West Indies for about three hundred years.

I don't know if Thomas Gage is buried on Jamaica, but I visited recently and took a look around. Today the hinterland appears to be widely impoverished and distressed. I felt embarrassed as a tourist going on a rafting trip through tropical forest, and later as someone who had permission to enter a heavily guarded prosperity zone, an enclave of opulent jewelry and international brand-name shops reserved for visitors from the far and beyond. On the outside of this zone were the locals staring in, and I was warned by the shepherd—oops, guide—not to venture beyond the boundaries of this shopping oasis, which had to be protected by armed security officers from the island's own population. It reminded me of the former luxury shops behind the Iron Curtain where you could buy anything the West had to offer, as long as you had Western currency, which honest locals couldn't earn or obtain.

A few of the images and conversations will stay with me: the exhausted soil of the countryside; the half-starved cows, each one alone and tied to a stake with rope on a piece of nearly barren ground; the bad roads; and the faces, some of them soft and beautiful with large quiet eyes, others animated and defiant, and none of them white. The young female guide who drove with us in a van to the interior spoke an impeccable British English. The landmarks she pointed out were a plain metal warehouse here or a plain metal assembly plant there. These were the most wonderful buildings imaginable— they provided jobs.

I didn't ask about a minimum wage. Not even slightly historical sights deserved the guide's attention or our own, and perhaps that was as it should be. She was obsessed with private, well-paved roads that sometimes branched off from the potholed public road or the dirt track the van used. Occasionally we could see a fine large house at the end of one of those long, private driveways.

"Do you see this road?" the guide would ask repeatedly. "This is how rich people construct something exclusively for their own comfort."

She grew agitated about this single feature of private road building for the purpose of providing access to lone mansions. I wondered at the time what good a mile or two of smooth private road would do if you had to travel to it over many miles on a bad and bumpy public one. Even the rich people had to do that. But logic had nothing to do with it: The fine roads leading to the isolated fine houses were symbols, such as the enclaves of luxury shops glittering behind a barrier of guns. Surely it was this which upset our well-educated young guide. In any case, the island, at least the part I saw of it, was like an undeclared penal colony. It was like a place from which you cannot escape. This is my own subjective notion, and I can't claim more. But on the other hand, I have seen many other places with much poverty. Not one of them resembled this one.

—

Another diligent Black Legend construction worker and enthusiast for taking big bites out of the Spanish Empire was Daniel Defoe of *Robinson Crusoe* fame. In a letter written on July 23, 1711 to his mentor Robert Harley, he outlined a *"Proposall for Seizing, Posessing, and Forming an English Collony in the kingdome of Chili in the South Part of America"* (Healey, 1955, p. 346). Like Gage, Defoe argued that the natives would cooperate with their new masters because the Spaniards were cruel and had a tyrannical temper. English colonialism would be good, while the Spanish variety was unquestionably bad.

Harley, Earl of Oxford and soon also Lord Treasurer, created the South Sea Company to restore the shaky faith in public credit. It had taken a beating during the War of the Spanish Succession.

As authorized by an act of Parliament, the newfangled stock company took England's entire national debt on its shoulders. In exchange, the government agreed to an annual payment of six percent or £568,279 10s for a number of years, and granted a trade monopoly in Spanish America to the South Sea Company. As Alexander Pope said: "Hope springs eternal in the human breast"; in this case, everyone in Britain knew about the gold and silver riches Spain transported home from the Americas, and many hoped to get rich.

Philip V of Spain, however, must have remembered generations of English pirates feasting on Spain's treasure-laden ships, so he was not terribly eager to open the ports of Mexico, Chile, or Peru to English traders. True, the war ended with the 1713 Peace of Utrecht, but the contract that the South Sea Company was able to get was the money-losing *assiento* of shipping and selling "4,800 'piezas de Indias.'" (Reed, 1999). Such a pieza was a black slave, in good condition, at least 58 inches tall. What other trade occurred with Cartagena and Vera Cruz didn't amount to much. Undeterred, the company continued financial speculations on an unprecedented scale. Much of England—rich or otherwise—gambled with South Sea Company stock. Ballads were sung, poems written, caricatures printed, and traffic jams endured: the stock-buying public choked London's 18th century Wall Street, the Exchange Alley.

This one is from Jonathan Swift:

Subscribers here by thousands float,
And jostle one another down,
Each paddling in his leaky boat,
And here they fish for gold and drown.

A frenzy for starting joint-stock companies broke out: they boomed and perished as quickly as lightning. What Charles Mackey wrote in 1841 about one adventurer's business plan sounds somehow familiar to us in our own era of financial scandals: "A company for carrying on an undertaking of great advantage, but nobody to know what it is." (Mackey, 1841, p.33). Well, the bubble burst, and the English language acquired a new word for a worthless, unstable, and unsound project—at least, that this how my trusty old Brewer's (Dictionary of Phrase and Fable) defines it.

With Robert Harley and England so preoccupied, nothing came of Defoe's proposal to liberate Chile, but he didn't give up. In his 1724 fictional book *A New Voyage Round the World,* he turned directly to the reading public with the attempt to sell his version of a reversed conquest in South America. Like someone walking on a path already established by others, the author firmly exploited well-known Black Legend stereotypes: Spaniards were bloodthirsty, proud, greedy for gold, and licentious. Being a Spaniard and being a barbarian were one and the same thing. As happens with such tales, the Black Legend had grown ever more gruesome with the telling. English translations embellished and enhanced the 16th century rhetoric of Las Casas. This was wonderful for one's self-image, for one's expansionist appetite, and for the rising tide of English nationalism, while it provided, at the same time, the opportunity to bash Spain's "conquest of the earth" (Hanke & Fernandez [Eds.], 1954, p. 234).

For all that, the hunger for gold was certainly not a specifically Spanish national characteristic. The English liked treasure just as much. The Spanish had been luckier in Mexico and South America, which motivated English buccaneers to attack their ships and steal as much as they could.

There are about 35,000 surviving pages of one of Europe's earliest newspapers in the Vienna National Library. These Fugger News-Letters reproduced tidings from agents and correspondents placed throughout the known and expanding world after their initial delivery to the Fugger merchant firm and banking house in Augsburg, Germany. Usually this news was often reliable, and written in various languages. The following sample is dated:

> From Rome, the 8th day of April, 1596
> Letters from the Spanish Court, dated the 8th day of March, report the arrival in Seville of three galleons laden with two million gold pieces ... In Porto Rico, five Spanish ships have run against two English vessels and captured one of these. When informed by the sailors that Drake with the rest of them was not far away, two of the Spanish ships again returned to Porto Rico. The other three were overtaken by Drake and burnt, whereupon they made bold to land near that spot. The inhabitants, however, put up resistance and killed about four hundred of his men, the French buccaneer, Zacaria, being among the number. Drake thereupon sailed for the Indies (Matthews, 1959).

As Anthony Pagden (1995) observed, "The argument that the British would be welcomed by the Native Americans as liberators, as Raleigh claimed to have been by the inhabitants of Guiana, became a staple of the propaganda war waged against the Spaniards, and on behalf of almost every British colonization project" (p. 88). A 1689 English edition of Las Casas also emphasized Catholicism as one of the evils:

> Popery truly display'd in its bloody colours: or, A Faithful narrative of the horrid and unexampled massacres, butcheries, and all manner of cruelties, that hell and malice could invent, committed by the popish Spanish party on the inhabitants of West-India (Hanke & Fernandez, 1954, p. 241).

—

How fortunate it is that the future United States eventually provided a constitutional separation of church and state. Nevertheless, it was apparently impossible to nominate or elect a Catholic prior to 1960, when John F. Kennedy became President. After tasting from the witches' brew of ancient propaganda, it will be refreshing to consider English writing of a different type. After all, not every Englishman spent his days bashing the Spanish competition. Richard Steele, for example, had the grace to amuse readers with the follies and weaknesses of his own countrymen. The sparkling little satire about Inkle and Yarico was published in the March 13 issue of *The Spectator* in 1711. The essay begins with an episode from the battlefield of the sexes. To comment on the habitual hypocrisy of men and the often unfairly disparaged character of women, an English lady of Steele's acquaintance relates the adventures of a traveling young Englishman, Inkle, who meets the Indian maiden, Yarico, in the wilds of America:

In June of 1647, young Inkle, 20 years old and the third son of a noteworthy citizen, sails on the ship *Achilles* to make his fortune. His education had emphasized the arts of gain, the mastery of numbers, a quick grasp of profit and loss, control of natural impulses, and a sharp eye for his own interests. He was, in other words, a young gentleman with a 17th century type of MBA. He wasted no thoughts on the common good and was a perfectly clever and businesslike young gent who strode into the world equipped with a thatch of curly yellow hair, strong limbs, and considerable vigor.

There is some trouble during the voyage. The ship drops anchor near a shore. A party of sailors and Mr. Inkle search inland for provisions. The strangers are attacked by native warriors. Most are killed, but our hero escapes by fleeing deep into the forest. There he meets the maiden, Yarico. Love at first sight, life in a hideout, the pleasures of Eden. For several months, the girl gives freely and helps to protect and maintain Inkle's life. One day she spots another English ship, signals at night, and the lovers succeed in joining the crew bound for Barbados.

The minute Inkle enters English territories in his return to civilization, he has second thoughts. Being frugal and sensible, the young man seeks to recover his financial losses. So he promptly sells Yarico as a slave to a Barbadian merchant, "notwithstanding," wrote Steele, "that the poor girl, to incline him to commiserate her Condition, told him she was with Child by him. But he only made use of that information, to rise in his Demands upon the Purchaser." So much for Mr. Inkle and his attention to the business bottom line. Jonathan Swift, who was alive in merry old England or maybe in Ireland during this time, made a little verse that provides a fitting comment.

> So, Naturalists observe a Flea
> Hath smaller fleas that on him prey;
> Und they have smaller fleas to bite 'em,
> And so proceed, ad infinitum (Swift, 1733. v. 8).

4

Roman Law and Common Law

There is no such thing as a specially favoured nation on
earth ... There cannot, therefore, be any order of rank ... The
culture of *man* is not the culture of the European, it manifests
itself according to place and time in *every* people.

—JOHANN GOTTFRIED HERDER
*Letters on the Advancement of
Humanity, 1793–1797*

One of my acquaintances announced the other day that she's a coyote.
(No, she's not the sort of coyote that smuggles Mexicans across the
U.S. border and sometimes abandons them in the desert). Her father is
Scandinavian, Alice tells me, and her mother is Hispanic. She hasn't had the
chance to start digging for roots in Norway yet, but knows that her maternal
grandmother's family has lived in northern New Mexico for eight generations.
Her grandfather, on the other hand, was a wetback.

She laughs, and then says: they don't use that word any longer. But I heard
it as a child. It makes me angry that even Hispanics in our state called new
arrivals from the other side of the border with such a derogatory term—wetback. To those who are unfamiliar with the term, it means people who swim,
wade, or paddle across the Rio Grande from Mexico to the U.S.

Why does Alice call herself a coyote, however jokingly? The habit of labeling children of mixed Hispano-Anglo ancestry as "coyotes" began in the late nineteenth century. Prior to the annexation of the Southwest by the United States, the same term was used for children of mixed Indian-Spanish parentage.

Alice and I talk about hierarchy, pecking order, race, and class. She isn't sure why New Mexicans use the term "Hispano" instead of "Latino." She tells me that it all started some 3000 years ago, when the Phoenicians called Spain "Hispalis," and the people who lived there were the "Hispani." The Romans went along, and eventually the place morphed into Hispania. Today, however, there is a great deal of diversity among the Hispanics and Latinos. They live in many countries.

Alice tells me that she took far more college history courses than required for her science degree. She found oral history projects especially fascinating. She interviewed her grandmother in Santa Fe, and recorded it all on tape. She also interviewed a frail ninety-year-old Taos woman with a crisp mind, and several other aged Hispanics. There is still so much more out there. Alice says that she has barely scratched the surface. Soon, these old people will be gone, and their knowledge goes with them. She would like to continue with the recording, but has little free time. Before we part, I ask her about Humboldt. She has never heard about him, her, or it. Because we are friendly with each other and she is a curious young woman, she promises to look him up. So here we go, looking for Humboldt.

Frankly, the identity business can be a bit confusing. There are large numbers of Latinos who are Mexicans, Guatemalans, Brazilians, Peruvians, etc., etc. They call themselves Americans. They say America is a continent, not a country. Some people abroad play with this, and tease United States citizens. They call them "USAians" or "'Merkins." *Merkins* is a droll term. It reminds me of Smurfs. Anyway, foreigners point out that the first man who realized that this long hunk of a land mass wasn't India, but a continent unknown to Europe, was Amerigo Vespucci. This happened in 1502, four years before Columbus died. Soon thereafter, in 1507, the German cartographer Martin

Waldseemueller (pretty name, meaning "miller of the forest lake") produced a map, one that for the first time showed a separate western hemisphere and a separate Pacific Ocean. He also named it *America,* and printed the new name on it, in honor of Amerigo Vespucci. This map is often called America's birth certificate. Waldseemueller explained his selection of the name as follows:

> Inasmuch as both Europe and Asia received their names from women, I see no reason why any one should justly object to calling this part Amerige [from the Greek *ge* meaning *land of*], i.e. the land of Amerigo, or America, after Amerigo, its discoverer, a man of great ability (qtd. in Boorstin, 1985, p. 253).

Kretzmann (2001) reported, "The first map to use the name America is coming to the Library of Congress." The price for the 494-year-old map was $10 million. Said James H. Billington, the Librarian of Congress: "This map, giving our hemisphere its name for the first time, will be the crown jewel of the library's already unparalleled collection of maps and atlases."

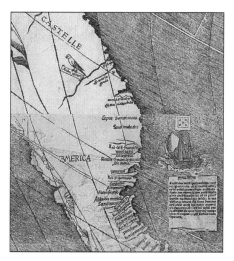

FIGURE 3. *America's Birth Certificate: Martin Waldseemüller's map showing the name AMERICA, 1507.*

The newswire article did not mention the creator of the map, Martin Waldseemueller.

The library had tried for decades to buy the map from the owner, Prince Johannes of Waldburg-Waldegg. But that was not possible, because the document is legally listed as a protected cultural property. Export is strictly prohibited. In the end, however, the German government engineered an unusual exception and allowed the sale to the Library of Congress. A formal wall display of the twelve map panels will be installed at the library's Jefferson Building across from the capitol in Washington. Yet the sale of the map created some unhappiness in Germany. Leading newspapers, among them the *Frankfurter Allgemeine Zeitung*, criticized the government's actions. One scholar called the sale of protected national cultural property immoral, and wondered if the Library of Congress lacked a sense of shame.

In any event, after 1507, the name "America" took hold quickly. It had a feminine ending like the names of the other known continents: Asia, Europa, Africa. From then on, this one was America, whether north or south.

Sitting on a perch near the New Mexican fault line, I listen to Octavio Paz. "New Spain committed many horrors," he says, "but at least it did not commit the gravest of all: that of denying a place, even at the foot of the social scale" (Paz, 1961, pp. 102–103). According to Paz, there were no pariahs in Iberian America. No matter how wretched life was for many, they too belonged to a living social order. Such an inclusive order "was cruelly denied to the Indians by the Protestants of New England" (Paz, 1961, p. 102).

This, perhaps, is one of the keys to understanding. For Calvinists, only the elect could be saved by God. Catholics, on the other hand, believed that God desired the salvation of all humans. Calvinists were convinced that God died only for the elect, whereas Catholics believed that Christ died for all men. New England Calvinists envisioned the exclusion of those to whom God's grace was denied: Native Americans, for example. The Amerinds were unbelievers and had no status under the law. Their property, and "even their persons, were forfeit to the first 'godly' person with the capacity to subdue them" (Pagden, 1995, p. 75). The Puritans of New England aimed to create

Cities on the Hill. These utopias were planned as their very own cities. They should contain no aliens. Accordingly, Charles II's charter to settle Carolina places Native Americans in the general category as "other enemies, pirates, and robbers: persons who are to be displaced, not incorporated" (Pagden, 1995, p. 37). These old colonial plans for the cities of the elect seem to be related to the "gated communities" which punctuate the U.S. landscape today. Maybe we still dream about "Cities on the Hill."

Spaniards, in contrast, argued for the inclusion of native populations. Among the more intriguing Iberian activities were handwringing, soul-searching, and humanitarian-philosophical debates, all in the midst of a bold and ruthless conquest. This is a bit unusual, to say the least. It's difficult to think of other conquerors stopping in their tracks because there were worries in high places about the legality and ethics of their doings. Indeed, some of the best minds in Spain struggled with profound questions, asking: Are these Indians human? Do they have a soul? And if so, why do we treat them in such an inhumane manner? Can they be converted to Christianity by coercion, or do they have to accept the faith voluntarily? Should the Indians elect the emperor Charles, as it was done in Europe? And finally, what right do we have to claim this so-called New World for Spain in the first place? The Dominican Padre Francisco de Vitoria published lectures held at the University of Salamanca: *De Indis* in 1537 and *De Jure Belli* in 1538. Both questioned the Crown's legal right of conquest and possession of the Indies. Amazing, such a freedom of speech and such a lack of censorship, and the courage to challenge emperors and kings!

And, yes, the Spanish were aware that the Americas were new only to them. They had scholars who quoted from the ancient texts. Domingo de Soto, for example, used a line from Lucan: "Arabs, you have come to a world unknown to you" (Pagden, 1995, p. 54). It was thus for the Spanish: they had come to a world unknown to them, but it was most familiar to the Aztecs, the Maya, the Inca, and the various Native American peoples north of the Rio Grande.

All this Spanish questioning led to a grand debate on political theory; religion; the nature and size of empires; the legality of the expansion based on the papal Bulls of 1493; the role of the Church; Roman law derived from the great codification by the Emperor Justinian in the sixth century; the unjust or the legitimate rule over infidels; the issues of slavery and forced labor; and much more. The Spanish jurist Francisco de Vitoria wrote extensively about such matters, and in doing so uncovered the bedrock of international law: might does not make right. These issues were fully covered in 1551, during the famous debate in Valladolid between Bartolomé de Las Casas and Juan Ginés de Sepúlveda.

A few years earlier, the New Laws of 1542 had pleased Las Casas. They had the potential of putting an end to the inhumanities inflicted on the native populations. They reformed and extended the judicial system; introduced labor laws which, for example, regulated how much any Indian could be asked to carry; and they gave freedom to all but a small number of Indian slaves. If these laws had worked out as written on paper within one generation, the Indians would have gained the same rights as the Spanish. But the colonists reacted in disbelief. They were the ones who had to deal with the hardships on the frontier. Settlers in Peru threatened revolt against the crown, and so, over time, these laws were repealed or watered down. Nevertheless, they belong to the historical record. They document a gallant effort.

Today, when people discuss the dismal results of western colonialism and expansionism, one often hears that the past can't be judged by the standards we now have at the start of the 21st century. We talk a great deal about human rights even if they are violently abused all around us and across the globe. Some of us may say that men back then didn't know any better. Others will point out that the invaders were brutal, and not yet enlightened or fully civilized despite the encouragements provided by the European Renaissance. Such talk just makes me feel apprehensive.

⁓

In 1520, the German artist Albrecht Duerer visited Brussels and saw the first display of Mexican art in Europe. Hernan Cortés had sent the materials to Charles V. Duerer's father was a goldsmith and had taught the skills of engraving to his son, who was full of admiration for the finely crafted gold and silver objects in the exhibit, and recorded his impressions in a memorandum book: "Throughout my life I have seen nothing that made my heart so joyful as these things. Among them are wonderful works of art, and I marveled at the subtle intellect of men in foreign lands" (Steck, 1981, p. 48).

Charles V himself was no benighted backwoodsman either. Diego Valadés, the first native-born citizen of New Spain to publish a book in Europe (*Rhetorica Christiana,* 1579), described the emperor's pleasure at Valladolid, where he and a group of courtiers watched a large Aztec troupe of dancers, musicians, and singers perform for an entire morning.

In any event, it is doubtful that humans of the Middle Ages or the Renaissance had lower standards or insufficient intellects compared to those of our time. I am not terribly impressed with our own standards. Meanwhile, the fact that Spain combined conquest with a search for justice and legality stands out as surprising. The country searched for justifications and understanding. I would not dream of deciding how much of this was spin doctoring in the contemporary sense, and how much of it was based on genuine concern. Yet the record itself is clear in showing that Spain, in the 16th century, engaged in a major battle over fundamental human rights. Aristotle's theory of natural slavery was well known at the time. The Greeks with their democracy had held slaves, and Aristotle had argued that some groups of people were natural slaves, bound to a life of endless labor. Las Casas would have none of it. The scope and content of the debates pointed far into the future and focused at the same time on legacy and Christian and Roman law for the support of specific arguments.

I was in my twenties when I saw a play by Reinhold Schneider, a member of the Catholic resistance during the Third Reich: *Las Casas vor Karl V* (Las Casas Before Charles V.) The details are forgotten but the voices, quality, and, above all, the essence of a dramatic intellectual struggle, remain vivid. When I read a relevant text today, the spotlights from the play still go on, illuminating the stage and the actors, bringing the set to a glow, putting life into the controversy.

Charles V was king of Spain and Holy Roman Emperor. How can one explain this specific old emperor business? It is difficult to talk about this with American friends and acquaintances. If you mention the Holy Roman Empire hereabouts, a somehow pre-conditioned negative reaction sets in immediately. Most people ignore that the much-touted 'Western civilization' formed itself during the 10th to the 14th centuries. How else could such goodies as the Renaissance, science, the Reformation, and the beginning of the modern era come about? How could they spring up suddenly, out of nowhere, from the Dark Ages?

Yet even the nicest people tend to sneer a bit, repeating Voltaire's wisecrack that the Holy Roman Empire was neither holy, nor Roman, nor an empire. It's like a reflex. I can also rely on a reflex, but usually repress the impulse to open my mouth, restraining myself instead from pointing out that the Bill of Rights remains a splendid document despite the fact that many people in the newly created United States of America were neither equal, nor free. Many were slaves, others were seen as "savages," or dismissed as the working poor. Somewhat later, deprived persons were labeled as members of the dangerous (pauper) classes, while during the second decade of our 21st century, they were sometimes described as the precariat.

Strange as it sounds, important phases of "our" civilization are nearly unknown to most persons in the USA. Voltaire was right with his quip about the Holy Roman Empire—if you are willing to dismiss some 800 to 1000 years of earlier history with a flip of your tongue. It is also true that during Voltaire's 18th-century Spain was below its peak and Germany had deteriorated into a patchwork quilt of mini-states due to the Reformation, religious conflict, and the disaster of the Thirty Years' War.

—

After his ceaseless activism for the political and religious unity of the western world, Charles V abdicated in 1556. He had voluntarily split his empire and gave the Austrian lands and the imperial honor to his brother Ferdinand I, hoping that he would be able to defend Hungary and Austria against the advancing Ottoman Turks. Charles left Spain and her possessions in the New World to his son Philip II. The connection between Spain and Germany came to an end. There were now two branches of the Habsburg family: one centered in Spain, and the other in Austria. As for the Holy Roman Empire, it had gradually dried up to a husk after the harvest. Napoleon dispatched the old thing for good in 1806. The age of the nation states, with their mutual testiness, suspicion, and egotism, was about to evolve.

Regardless of the American tendency to ignore the foundation building of the medieval centuries in question, they were of crucial importance. Dismissing this time period is like cutting the heart and guts out of continental Europe. Maybe this old stuff is of no consequence to the young United States, but it certainly has historical significance for Spanish America, and thereby for New Mexico, which used to be a part of it. I live here; that's why I am interested. Without some understanding of the basics about these centuries, it will be difficult to gain some insight into the Lebensgefuehl (feeling for life) and the legal traditions of Hispanics and Latinos.

In my wanderings through the state along the faultlines of history, I came across very old remnants of culture. Examples are shreds of Roman law, traces of (Germanic) mining law and customs, and patterns of social life. Perhaps details from the life of an exiled poet can help. He could not return home to his beloved Florence under threat of execution: he was Dante Alighieri. The reason for the death sentence was that Dante was politically on the losing side. It is both ironic and somehow logical that a writer driven from his home wrote the *Monarchia* (Monarchy; written between 1310–1314), a political essay in Latin that contains the perfect vision and the longing for a Christian Europe under the guidance of unifying law. Dante believed that the monarchy (empire) was the best form of government, and that it was necessary for keeping the peace. He lived in tempestuous times and was a passionate defender of the lawful empire. God gave the spiritual power to the pope, and the political power to the emperor, and that was that.

To Dante it was evidently necessary for the welfare of the world for there to be a Monarchy, or single Princedom, which men called Empire.

These ideas, and the concept of continuity between the pagan and the Christian Roman Empire, were already well established by the fifth century. At that time, St. Augustine of Hippo suggested to the historian and theologian Paulus Orosius that he write a first universal history, which covered antiquity plus the Christian centuries. It was then believed that there were four great empires in history: Babylon in the East, Rome in the West, with Carthage in North Africa, and Macedonia (Greece) occupying the intermediate stages. This view was widely accepted back then, just as our ideas of the free market economy, of democracy, or even such oddities as Francis Fukuyama's thesis on "The End of History" have been entertained during our time.

The desire for continuity fused the Roman legacy with the new Christian world, and both belonged to one of the four empires possible on earth. No wonder the Holy Roman Empire was seen as important for centuries. We can dismiss it, but that may only be a sign of ignorance or, as C. S. Lewis put it, of "chronological snobbery." By this he meant a mode of thinking that assumes that only the new can be true. Whatever the case, for a thousand years or so the Holy Roman Empire was more or less in tune with the spirit of the times, or Zeitgeist, and it was matched to the worldviews of a relatively new and vigorous religion.

No, Dante's *Monarchia* was not a model for tyranny. It was an intellectual-political structure as beautiful and soaring as the great Gothic cathedrals of Europe. These buildings of grace and strength required the work and dedication of generations, and without the faith of communities over a long period of time, their completion would have been impossible. These ambitious buildings were as delicate as they were stable, and they endured, and lasted. It required the unprecedented destructiveness of the 20th century to reduce some of them to ruins.

The concepts of the universal *respublica christiana*, the Christian republic, envisioned a brotherhood of God and men for the good of the community.

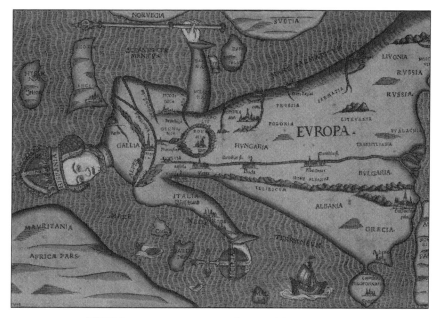

FIGURE 4. *Europe as Queen, or the respublica christiana,*
made in 1588 in Hannover by Heinrich Bünting.

It was never achieved, and when it came close here and there, it endured only for limited amounts of time. It is easy to scoff at the idea and the dream of this Christian Europe, but so what? The point is respect, and perhaps admiration, for human aspiration. Just as the Constitution and the Bill of Rights grew out of the Enlightenment, so the idea of a universal community of humans grew from the synthesis of Roman law and Christian belief.

If you grew up in Europe, you didn't have to be a pious person to absorb the essence of these old times from the cathedrals. I am not even a Catholic, but that doesn't stop me from reading the language of the churches. They are made of idea and spirit carved in stone. You tend to understand through osmosis, and hardly notice that certain cultural elements are bred into the bone and into consciousness without the use of words.

When I was a child, these messages were present and strong, especially in those half-broken churches that had been bombed during World War II by the Christian allies. I remember distinctly what I saw and felt in Cologne's severely damaged cathedral.

—

The office of Holy Roman Emperor was the highest worldly position available. It was desirable, so much so that both Henry VIII of England and Francis I of France competed with the future Charles V (so named after the election) for the title, despite the fact that they had no dynastic claims.

Charles V lived a life in the saddle, constantly traveling from one corner of crisis-plagued Europe to the next. "Some say that I wish to be Monarch of the world," he protested to Pope Paul III in 1536, "but my thoughts and deeds prove that the contrary is true" (qtd. in Pagden, 1995, p. 42).

Charles was Catholic, a word derived from the Greek *katholicos*. It means all-inclusive or universal, and accordingly he strove to defend what was valuable within an older order against the uncertainties and dynamics of a just-forming new Protestant order. It was an almost impossible job. He was the emperor, but he was not above the law. The legal traditions demanded attention: questions about just title to new lands and about the rights of the indigenous populations in the Americas had to be dealt with. Looking back-ward, the 16th-century Spanish concern appears to be perplexingly modern, and a starting point which eventually led to today's international (and widely dishonored) humanitarian law. In the process, Spanish advocates defended the rights of conquered foreign peoples against a growing colonialism that would permit descent into exclusion, slavery, and racism. It is noteworthy that the other rising colonial powers at the time—the English and Dutch, and eventually the French—were not exceedingly bothered by ancient legal traditions or the human rights of various natives. After the Reformation was victorious in two of these countries, the old "popish" learning was simply ignored or discredited. Regardless of how history will evaluate Charles V's deeds, Europe's last emperor will certainly remain the highest-placed player in what Lewis Hanke called "the Spanish struggle for justice" (qtd. in Pagden, 1995, p. 56).

⌒

The 1542 New Laws for the Indies had been pro-Indian. Here are a few excerpts from the original legal document:

Charles by divine clemency Emperor ever august, King of Germany . . .

We have commanded persons to assemble of all ranks . . . with some of our Council to discuss and treat of the things of most importance . . . the which have been maturely debated and consulted upon in the presence of me the King . . . and Finally having taken the opinion of all, we resolved on commanding to enact and ordain the things contained below.

Whereas one of the most important things in which the Audiencias are to serve us is in taking especial care of the good treatment of the Indians and preservation of them.

Item, We ordain and command that from henceforward for no cause of war nor any other whatsoever, though it be under the title of rebellion, nor by ransom nor in other manner can an Indian be made a slave.

Because report has been made to us that owing to the pearl fisheries not having been conducted in a proper manner, deaths of many Indians and Negroes have ensued, We command that no free Indian be taken to the said fishery under pain of death, and that the bishop and the judge who shall be at Venezuela direct what shall seem most fit for the preservation of the slaves, . . . both Indians and Negroes, and that the deaths may cease. If, however, . . . the risk of death cannot be avoided, . . . let the fishery of the said pearls cease, since We value much more highly (as is right) the preservation of their lives than the gain which may come to us from the pearls (Stevens, 1893, pp. iii–xvii).

There is much more in the document, for example, this labor-law detail: Indians must not carry burdens that endanger their health and life, and they must not be forced into such labor against their will and without being paid. Violators, without regard to rank and status, shall be severely punished.

The historian Daniel J. Boorstin evaluated the situation well when he wrote:

> The public climax of Las Casas' struggle provided a spectacle unique in the history of colonization. On April 16, 1550, Charles V, impelled by Las Casas' doubts and accusations, ordered that conquests in the New World be suspended and not be resumed until his theologians had agreed on a just way of proceeding ... For a while this order was strictly enforced ... policed by the friars against the impatient protesting colonists. The moral grandeur of this effort—the ruler of a vast empire refusing to use his power until he was fully satisfied that he was using it justly—would be overshadowed by the brutality of the frontline conquistadors (Boorstin, 1985, p. 632).

5

Passages

Everything is huge, dimensions so vast
there is no need to seek significance.
—*Simon J. Ortiz (1994, p. 75)*

It is not for want of trying, but I don't quite understand why the Spaniards, and later the Americans, were hungry for so much land—and grandiose, but mostly arid land, at that. Much of New Mexico belongs to the Upper Sonoran life zone, with elevations between 4,500 and 6,500 feet. The desert land here is not like in Death Valley or the Sahara. Our dry landscapes have vegetation in various shades of green, gray, and brown. Still, six of the seven life zones on Earth are found here, and the terrain climbs from 2,840 to 13,160 feet. Generally, the higher the elevation, the greener it gets. Near the top of the mountains, the trees are tall and the air is cool and during the winter months a thick snow layer covers the range. Yet to grow things we have to cling to the valleys and canyons along the rivers, and we maintain an oasis culture wherever there is a bit of precious water. Only some areas rely on large-scale agriculture based on aquifer irrigation.

Almost 500 years have passed since the first Europeans explored the regions north of the Rio Grande, yet at the beginning of the 21st century cities, towns, roads, and infrastructure—all the elements of development—still look somehow incidental in New Mexico. They sit like temporary tattoos on the rough skin of the land. Granted, some of these surface embellishments have a terrible potency, but that is part of the local incongruity. There are indeed good reasons for naming Interstate 25—running south from Colorado through New Mexico—the 'Atomic Highway.' Both the population and the high-tech activities are clustered along this road, while the rest of the state remains almost empty, at least to an eye accustomed to the crowded continent of Europe or America's coasts. New Mexico's population density is about 13 souls per square mile, and the state is larger than West Germany was prior to the fall of the Berlin Wall and unification. But New Mexico had only about 1.8 million inhabitants, while the old Federal Republic I left had more than 62 million. I tell myself such numbers. They can help me to put things in perspective.

In other, more crowded parts of the world, people are used to living with antiquities, architecture, and artifacts from the past. These things are part of the cluttered human landscape. The old and the new are interwoven. But not here. Here you can see, feel, touch, and smell the skin of the planet without the clothing of construction put upon it by inexhaustible human activity. Perhaps that is why the impact of Chaco Canyon is immediate: You recognize that man is, or a few men are, alone and vulnerable in such an environment. The works of humans do not drown in a multitude, or seek shelter behind the comforting skirts of long-lasting civilizations, or perform as cogs in the machinery of state. Even if there is conflict, it is on a small human scale set against a vast wild canvas.

Chaco Canyon is my pre-Columbian place of choice, but whenever I want to see a manifestation of the comings and goings, conquests and passages, advances and retreats that New Mexico has experienced since the arrival of the first Europeans, I visit El Morro, the headland, the fortress-like bluff, the rock of ages and the cliff of inscriptions. It displays about 2000 carved graffiti. It is a history book written in stone.

Trade routes and pathways for travel through largely unpopulated regions are much older than modern national borders or networks of roads. Located on the ancient Cibola-Zuni trail, a path connecting the Rio Grande pueblos with the Laguna, Acoma, and Hopi Indian villages, El Morro was an essential rest stop and a campsite first for the pre-Columbian peoples, later for the European explorers, soldiers, friars, settlers, and finally for the American surveyors, soldiers, miners, settlers, and traders.

Today the monolith sits dreaming into the stillness of the Zuni Mountains in an out-of-the way area of western New Mexico near the Ramah Navajo Reservation. The railroad, and eventually the interstate highway, bypassed the old trail and made it obsolete.

Getting to the rock is captivating enough. After dealing with the heavy traffic on Interstate 40, we bypassed the perfectly-shaped volcanic cone of Mount Taylor (11,301 feet high) and the town of Grants, which is known for its former uranium mining. We then headed south and west on State Road 53. At once, the world grew quiet. There was seldom another car in sight. Mormon farmers and missionaries founded a few communities in the vicinity during the 1870s and 1880s, among them the village of Ramah, which is now one of the smaller Navajo Reservations west of El Morro.

One Hispanic rancher breeds and preserves the small, spirited Spanish Barb horses near the village. Originally from the Barbary Coast of North Africa, these were the resilient ponies that crossed the Atlantic in the belly of galleons, endured the harshest conditions, and managed to carry the Spaniards through the unexplored immensity of the (horse-less) Americas. Once upon a time there were dog-sized ancestors of the horse in America, but they long ago died out. Serving the conquerors well, the imported Barb horse couldn't be kept from the Indian warriors for long. It soon changed the way things were done. But, as the fortunes of the Spanish empire declined gradually, so did the survival chances of the sturdy little horses. In the end they were killed like the buffaloes or turned into dog food for the pets of a growing urban population. Then some people remembered their deeds and their endurance, and they began to rescue the breed.

Before long we were traveling along the ragged edges of El Malpais (badlands) National Monument, a wilderness of black lava flows, volcanic spatter cones, lava tube caves, a chain of thirty craters, bat caves, sandstone bluffs, a sandstone arch going back to the age of the dinosaurs, pre-historic petroglyphs, and old-growth trees. The fields of lava are from 2,000 to 300,000 years old. Brochures call this "The Land of Fire and Ice." Close to Road 53 is the Ice Cave, a collapsed lava tube with aged layers of blue-green ice and a constant temperature of 31 degrees Fahrenheit. The ice doesn't melt even if the outside summer temperature exceeds 100 degrees. Evidence of past fireworks are on display at the Bandera Crater. It is 10,000 years old, 1,200 feet wide, and 800 feet deep. Visitors can hike up to it.

Occasionally people still disappear in the gnarled terrain of the badlands. Just steps from the trail, the sharp-edged lava surface can slice methodically through shoes and skin. Hikers may break bones or fall into crevices and sinkholes.

I am not sure where the first Europeans crossed the watershed of the Continental Divide in this area, yet we—comfortably protected in a car—did the same to reach our destination. From this point on, rivers run towards the Pacific Ocean. The road now sliced through the Zuni Mountains. Geologists call the formation a dome. Much has happened here in the course of earth time. Sea after sea covered the land; sediments accumulated; uplifts folded them; dinosaurs roamed through the region; and erosion did its patient work until the softer layers of shale were carved away. The dome collapsed. Only the harder Jurassic sandstone remained standing on the edges, and it now forms a chain of prominent cliffs ringing the valley. It is shaped much like a crown. I was tickled to find out that the geologic term Jurassic was coined by Alexander von Humboldt.

So here we were, riding through a Jurassic Park to El Morro. The inscription rock was made a National Monument in 1906, some years before New Mexico overcame its prolonged territorial status and advanced to being a U.S. state. Seen from a viewing stop about a mile away, the big cliff sits on its haunches against a deep blue sky. As children we used to decipher imaginary beings in the clouds, and while viewing the rock the habit comes back: I can see that the outline of El Morro resembles the Sphinx. The stillness here is so intense, it seems to make a sound. It sings.

We picked up a printed guide and walked for half a mile up to an elevation of 7,200 feet. The base of the bluff wears a skirt of purple sage, Ponderosa pine, piñon trees, and the tall yuccas. There is a pleasing story written on one of the descriptive signs placed along the path. It tells of the symbiosis between the gorgeous yucca and the humble yucca (*Tegeticula*) moth. The yucca's tall white blooms are a characteristic feature in the desert Southwest. Travelers braving the harsh conditions and big distances of these mesas and high plateaus honored the plant with various names: Spanish Dagger, Adam's Needle, or the Lord's Candlestick. Eventually, scientists found out that each yucca species among dozens has one sole pollinator: a specific species of the yucca moth. It's a sophisticated relationship of live and let-live. I wish human societies would function lastingly like that, instead of fostering the horrid Social Darwinism they've invented.

Anyway, after the moth species mates in spring, the female collects sticky pollen from a yucca, flies to another plant, lays a number of her eggs in the flower's ovary, and coats the stigma with pollen. This cross-pollinates and fertilizes the flower so it can grow the seeds, which will feed the little baby caterpillars from the moment they hatch. The mothermoth leaves a pheromone on the egg-hosting yucca which will announce that this womb is occupied. Amazingly, there are never enough little caterpillars to eat all the seeds. A number of the seeds survive to start new yucca plants, while the grown caterpillars leave their childhood host, go underground to become cocoons, and break out to the sun as newlyborn moths the next spring. And so the cycle of collaborative life continues.

─

The trail now winds itself along vertical walls of fawn-colored sandstone. They are up to 230 feet high in most places, and smooth as polished marble. What

43

a writing surface! Panels of prehistoric petroglyphs were probably incised or stone-hammered by the Anasazi, and others by the people of A'ts'ina. Preserved are images of human hands, bear tracks, mountain sheep, and various geometrical symbols.

A'ts'ina was a barely accessible 875-room pueblo built on top of the bluff. Notches and footholds led up to the ruins. They are visible in a few places along the sheer walls. Researchers believe that a severe, long-lasting drought forced the population of the San Juan area to abandon the classic pre-Columbian center of the pueblo civilization at Chaco Canyon. Perhaps life became hard and dangerous in the course of the migrations, forcing humans to live like eagles, for example, on top of the cliff at A'ts'ina, but nevertheless close to a precious source of water that apparently never failed.

It is this good, sweet water that makes El Morro so special. It falls from the top during the brief rains of late summer and the melting snows of winter into the catchment area of a natural rock bowl. Protected by an overhang, it is a lovely shaded spot. When full, the pool is about 12 feet deep. No wonder man and animal were invariably drawn to this oasis: there was no other source of water for 30 miles around.

Paso pór aquí [passed by here] ... so begins the oldest (1605) Spanish inscription, and many others start the rite of passage with the same words.

They passed by here and recorded their wanderings on stone, humans from different cultures, different continents and countries, speaking different languages, and having different goals. Many of their carved calling cards are executed with calligraphic elegance in the style of their time. Some of the inscriptions were left by persons known to history, others were chiseled by the unknown. There are even a few poems, and a joke.

One message dated July 29, 1620, was phrased in the richly ornamented language of the Spanish baroque, probably carved by Governor Eulate of New Mexico, or New Spain as it was called then. It praised his majesty the king with courtly bombast "as a most Christian-like gentleman extraordinary and gallant soldier of enduring and praised memory." Someone with wit or a grudge apparently disagreed and tried to remove the word 'gentleman' by

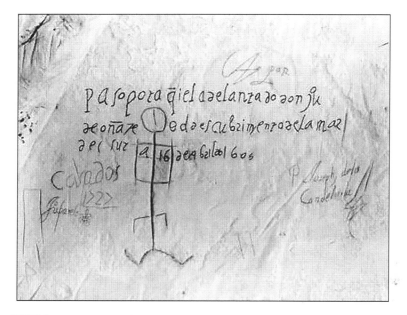

FIGURE 5. *Inscription at El Morro: Governor Don Juan de Oñate passed by here, from the discovery of the Sea of the South [Pacific] on the 16th of April, 1605.*

scratching it out. We don't know when, but it was done prior to 1849 and the 'passing by' of the first English-speaking military expedition. It traveled in the opposite direction, from the north to south and west. Lt. J. H. Simpson, an army engineer, and R. H. Kern, an artist, stopped at El Morro, inspected the assorted graffiti, and left their own dated September 17th-18th, 1849. Kern wrote on the wall that he copied many of the messages. The one with the scratched out 'gentleman' was among them.

As we have seen, fifteen years before the English Pilgrims landed at Plymouth Rock, the first Spanish governor of New Mexico left his message on stone. Translated from the Spanish, it reads: "Passed by here the Governor Don Juan Oñate, from the discovery of the Sea of the South on the 16th of April, 1605" (Southwest Parks, 1994).

Oñate was returning from the Sea of Cortés (or Gulf of California) with a party of thirty men. Other Spaniards had traveled the route before him, and so had he, stopping at El Morro for the first time on December 13, 1598, but without leaving an inscription on that occasion. Much more writing was done by the poet-historian of this expedition, Gaspar Pérez de Villagrá. In 1610, he published the first book dealing with an area of the future United States, the epic *Historia de la Nueva Mexico*. Separated for a period from his companions, Villagrá found the life-saving water hole at El Morro and described in verse how he flung himself into it "blinded and burning with thirst" (Southwest Parks, 1994).

Oñate, a Basque nobleman, was wealthy. He had married a granddaughter of Cortés and a great-granddaughter of the Aztec emperor Montezuma. His family owned one of the richest silver-mines in Mexico, so he spared no expense for the expedition to *El Norte*. The more than 200 settler families traveled supplied with tools, seeds, necessities, and above all with horses and livestock of various kinds to make the task of settlement possible.

Yet 87 eventful years after 1598, years during which the first Spanish settlers struggled to survive in an unforgiving land, the temporarily united Pueblo Indians staged a successful revolt. "Your god is dead," the rebels cried in 1680, while proceeding to kill many of the colonists and missionaries. The survivors fled south, away from New Mexico and the territory of today's United States.

Lessons had to be learned. Twelve years later, a returning and wiser governor, accompanied by "the Hundred Gentlemen Soldiers from Spain," also left this announcement on soft stone: "Here was the General Don Diego de Vargas, who conquered for our Holy Faith, and for the Royal Crown, all of New Mexico at his own expense, year of 1692" (Southwest Parks, 1994).

At his own expense? Indeed, these officially authorized expeditions, or *entradas,* were privately financed by one or several individuals for an anticipated return of investment sometime in the future. Oñate, for example, was a member of the so-called "silver aristocracy," and used the family fortune gained from silver mining for the exploration and settlement of El Norte. The enterprising explorers hoped to find gold and silver like in Mexico or Peru. But, regardless of their desires, they couldn't just march off to explore and lay claim (as Cortés had daringly done it in the beginning) without going through a whole legalistic process of securing official permission. Furthermore, at the end of the enterprise they had to go through an evaluation, or even an investigation. Some of Oñate's actions, for example, led to various accusations and his resignation of the governorship in 1607. His guilt was established on some of the charges. Disgraced and banished from New Mexico for life, he returned to Spain, where he died in 1626 (New Mexico History.org.)

I am astonished about the contrast in procedure: in our USA, the authorities—including politicians and military men—make serious mistakes, but rarely, if ever, commit a crime, and particularly no war crime.

Scratched into the rock below the de Vargas message are three names: Williamson, Holland, and Udell. The tide had turned—these men belonged to the first group of pioneers from the United States who tried to reach California on this—for them—new land route. The gold rush was on, and John Udell wanted to search for his children out West. He recorded the party's adventures in a journal. After losing their goods, animals, and the lives of several fellow travelers in an attack by Mojave Indians, Udell and his 64-year-old wife turned around and walked back for hundreds of miles through wilderness and desert. They passed El Morro and finally reached Albuquerque in November of 1858. They used the winter months to recover from near-starvation and promptly undertook the same hazardous journey once more in 1859, this time under the protection of Lt. Edward F. Beale. The trip was successful. It is said that Udell lived happily ever after in California, and that he reached a ripe old age.

The leader of the immigrant group in which Udell traveled was a German, L.J. Rose, who also left his graffiti on a wall at El Morro. Born in Germany, he moved to New Orleans in 1830, then grew fairly wealthy as a merchant in Iowa, and was wounded during the Mojave attack, as reported by Udell. But somehow Rose survived, recovered, and made his way to Los Angeles despite it all (Southwest Parks, 1998).

As for Lt. Beale, a military officer who made six land journeys from ocean to ocean prior to 1851 and his resignation from the service, he had already gained local notoriety in 1857 when he led a caravan of twenty-five camels and seven mule-drawn wagons through Albuquerque, past El Morro, and all the way to California. Congress was not amused about a subsequent request for one thousand camels. No funding was forthcoming. Beale's successful test drive of a real caravan across the arid expanse of the West remained an experiment.

6
Mining Freedom

It is complained that some sellers and buyers of the shares
in mines are fraudulent. I concede it. But can they deceive
anyone except a stupid, careless man, unskilled in mining matters?

— *Gregorius Agricola, De Re Metallica*
1556, Book I

Humboldt predicted the importance of mining for New Mexico. I had
that in mind during our little explorations throughout the state. Visiting
a few ghost towns and decaying mining camps was part of getting to know
New Mexico, and my husband was a willing and cheerful companion. At first,
I had no clue that this would lead me to several other German connections.
It started with Humboldt, continued with Georg Bauer (*Gregorius Agricola*),
and then led to the mining engineer who became a U.S. president—Herbert
Hoover. Next it leaped to something called 'Germanic mining freedom' and
at last, as the frosting on the cake, pointed to the birthplace of the dollar in
the Erzgebirge (Ore Mountains) of Germany.

Rock hounding was a favorite activity, and so was visiting the old Kelly
Mine in the Magdalena Mountains. Huddled high against a hillside, Kelly is
a splendidly spooky place. The smells of rust and sage are pervasive. During
the last quarter of the 19th century, the mine became very productive, but now

it sleeps among abundant debris. It still has a large dilapidated head-frame, a few foundations, and a heartbreakingly simple little church. Someone keeps that one whitewashed and in repair.

A dirt road goes up to the mine from the tiny cow town and former mining camp of Magdalena. As the car climbed up trailing a cloud of dust like a comet, I watched for the face of Maria Magdalena. If you search carefully, you can see her oversized profile outlined by rock formations and vegetation on the flank of the mountain to your right. And there it was, just as the Spaniards had imagined it first. They called it Our Lady of Magdalena. They peopled the vast and lonesome land of El Norte with beloved beings, and infused it with the spirit of their longing, just as Native Americans have done it for many centuries in their own way.

Later, legends grew up around the face on the rock. Miners found lead, silver, copper, gold, and smithsonite in the district. The work was hard and the living wild. But, according to the tales, there was never a murder committed on that mountain, and even the Apaches didn't kill an enemy if he could flee to the protection of Magdalena's face (McKenna, 1936/1969).

As I scrambled across the tailings hunting for specimens of azurite, quartz, and the aqua-green smithsonite, my mind wandered. I have always liked rocks. As children, my sisters, my brother and I searched various outcroppings for fossils and beach-combed for amber during our vacations along the Baltic Sea. I had a fairly large collection of such treasures as a kid: ancient insects embedded in golden pieces of fossilized resin, sea urchins turned to stone, ammonites neatly encased in rich black slate. All this was later lost in the postwar migration and relocation from east to west.

There were mines in the heart of Germany. We lived there when I was a young child. Our father pointed them out to his two eldest daughters and even took us on a tour deep into the belly of a mountain. I couldn't recall names or the precise location of this childhood tour into the underworld on the afternoon I spent in the New Mexico ghost town—but instead, Humboldt came to mind. The associations that memory makes! In a flash, I recalled that he had started his career in mining. It was a hot topic and a hot technology at the time. Without mining's solid foundations, the following industrializations would have been impossible.

When Francisco Vasquez de Coronado led his expedition into the unknown lands of the north, he wanted to discover precious metals, and, above all, gold. His hopes were disappointed. On 20 October 1541, he wrote to his emperor Charles V from the vicinity of today's Albuquerque. The natives, he reported, had given him a piece of copper that an Indian wore around his neck. No other metals had been seen or found during the expedition. But 163 years later, in 1803, German scientist and explorer Alexander von Humboldt remarked: "The wealth of the world will be found in New Mexico" (qtd. in Christiansen, 1974, p. 1).

Some say that the Prussian aristocrat was "New Mexico's first [mineral] promoter" (Museum of New Mexico, n.d., p. 1). And, while there was hardly any mining activity in the state at the beginning of the 1800s, by 2012 New Mexico produced about $ 2.8 billion per year, primarily from coal, copper, gold, silver, molybdenum, and potash mines. The industry employs nearly 7000 people. In addition, uranium mining was big during the Cold War.

After New Mexico became a territory of the United States in the mid-1800s, prospecting and mining activities increased rapidly. Consequently, the state is riddled with some 10,000 abandoned mines, and in addition with about 1900 natural caves. One would think that the land should look like a Swiss cheese, but that is not the case. Many of the mining scars left on the land are small and hidden. Before new technology became available, miners used to swing 4-pound hammers 50 times per minute to drive chisels into the rock. The hole was then filled with dynamite and blasted. The ore had to be shoveled into carts. It was backbreaking work somewhere in the wilderness.

Still, the old mines can be dangerous: In the last ten years, at least 10 people were killed during visits to these deserted places. The authorities closed 40 mines in the late 1990s, but that is just a tiny percentage of the total. New Mexico also has its uranium mines, some of which remain untended. In addition, since 2003 the government has supported plans for the drilling of thousands of new natural gas wells on public land in the San Juan Basin of northwestern New Mexico. The area already has 18,000 such wells, which are relatively inconspicuous, but cause considerable pollution. As of 2010, the State was the second largest natural gas producer in the United States. The new drilling plans face environmental protests and legal challenges.

In neighboring Nevada, which has a Humboldt mine, the Humboldt River, the Humboldt Range, the Humboldt Sink, and a Humboldt Wildlife Management Area, contaminants are monitored. Of Nevada's many mines, at least 16 are in the Humboldt River Basin. They go down deeper than the water tables. Pit lakes have formed in the open holes in the ground, and they draw precious water from the river. In arid Nevada, the water needs to be returned to the aquifer. An organization named Great Basin Mine Watch in Reno, Nevada, defines this as "the process of removing groundwater from around a mine that extends below the water table" (GreatBasinMineWatch. org, 2002).

—

Alexander von Humboldt was born in 1769 and educated together with his older brother Wilhelm by private tutors drawn from circles of the Berliner Enlightenment around Moses Mendelssohn. The boys were raised by their Huguenot mother at *Schloss Tegel*, located a few miles from the Prussian capital.

Humboldt continued his studies in Goettingen, at Germany's most liberal university. It was also a leading school in the natural sciences. Here, the student wrote his first book based on mineralogical observations in the field. He walked and hiked a lot. Many nature lovers did this at the time.

From Goettingen, the budding scientist moved to Hamburg, where he attended a commercial college or 18th century version of a business school. There he prepared himself well for his future tasks. He studied finance and Spanish. Completing his formal education at the School of Mines in Freiberg, Saxony, he was subsequently appointed to the post of *Bergassessor* within the Prussian Department of Mines. Successful from the start, he revitalized old gold mines in the *Fichtel Gebirge* and submerged himself in ambitious research focused on reducing the risks for miners from accidents, explosions, and occupational diseases. He was a hands-on guy, and not someone who shied away from danger or risk. To know, observe, and measure required that he go down into the shafts himself. He analyzed gases and developed, in the course of his work, breathing equipment and a safety lamp, both useful in protecting the health and the lives of miners.

In 1796, after the death of his mother (his father, an officer in the Army of Frederick the Great, had died when Alexander was ten), Humboldt came into a substantial inheritance and decided to leave his employment. He was only 27 years old and held the title of supervisor-in-chief. This was just one level below the highest rank available in the Department of Mines—that of minister.

Free to pursue his own plans, and now financially independent, Humboldt began to travel throughout Europe. He collected ideas; interacted with the best minds of the time; was a frequent guest at the Berlin salons of Henriette Herz and Rahel Levin Varnhagen; viewed natural history collections; hiked with Georg Foster—a participant in Cook's second circum-navigation of the world—in England; and spent time at Jena, where he met Goethe and his closest circle. Visits in Weimar followed.

Goethe told Karl August, Duke of Saxe-Weimar, about Humboldt. The young man, he reported, "is a true cornucopia of natural science. His company is very stimulating and interesting indeed. You couldn't learn as much from books in a week as he teaches you in an hour" (Botting, 1973, p. 38).

In turn, Humboldt was strongly influenced by Goethe and said that "being with him was like being equipped with new organs" (qtd. in Botting, 1973, p. 39). Years later, Swiss-born Albert Gallatin, U.S. Secretary of the Treasury, shared an impression similar to that of Goethe. At first he was a little put out by Humboldt's rapid conversation in German, French, Spanish, and English, but in the end mentioned that he "was really delighted, and swallowed more information of various kinds in less than two hours than I had for two years in all I had read or heard" (qtd. in Botting, 1973, p. 181).

In any case, for Ralph Waldo Emerson, Humboldt was "one of those wonders of the world … who appear from time to time, as if to show us the possibilities of the human mind, the force and the range of the faculties, a universal man" (qtd. in Botting, 1973).

That was hindsight. In real time, the up-and-coming universal creature arrived in Paris and met the botanist Aimé Bonpland, his future research assistant and friend. From France, the two men traveled to Madrid, where Humboldt was received by the soon-to-be-toppled King Carlos IV. Humboldt impressed the king with his Spanish language fluency, enticed him with expertise on mining, which could benefit Spain, and succeeded in obtaining royal permission and passports for travel in Latin America from the secretary of state and from the Council of the Indies (qtd. in Botting, 1973, p. 62).

These documents enabled him and Bonpland to explore Spanish-America without restrictions. So, from 1799–1804, the pair did just that, and in an extraordinary fashion. Simon Bolivar would eventually call Humboldt "the discoverer of the New World, whose wisdom has done more good to America than all the conquistadors put together" (Schwarz, n.d., para. 1). Well, perhaps that was rather hyperbolic, and perhaps not even a compliment, considering the deeds of the Spanish conquerors, but a sober Charles Darwin also praised Humboldt as the "greatest scientific traveler who ever lived" (Darwin, 1839/1962).

At the very least, the baron was certainly the first explorer of the Western Hemisphere who set out to concentrate on research, and he was the best equipped, carrying books, balances, compasses, microscopes, telescopes, cyanometers, eudiometers, thermometers, chronometers, magnetometers, sextants, quadrants, and much else with him on this trip. The financial details of the long and uncertain journey had all been arranged by banker friends in Berlin and Madrid. The exploring scientist paid for everything out of his own pocket. He made his will. And there is a note from him, written to his friend Freiesleben (a nice name: translated, it means "free life" or "liberated life") on board the corvette Pizarro shortly before she sailed for Havana:

In a few hours we sail round Cape Finisterre. I shall collect plants and fossils and make astronomic observations. But that's not the main purpose of my expedition. I shall try to find out how the forces of nature interact upon one another and how the geographic environment influences plant and animal life. In other words, I must find out about the unity of nature (qtd. in Botting, 1973, p. 65).

The unity of nature was his thing.

⁓

Covering the travels, discoveries, and scientific research of Humboldt and Bonpland in South-America is not within the scope of this book. Let's just say that the men traveled 6,000 miles by canoe, on foot, or on horseback, much of it in extremely difficult and unexplored territory.

They were almost overwhelmed by a sense of wonder, spiced up by hardship and danger. In Indian canoes, the explorers struggled with the Great Cataracts of the Orinoco River, with primeval rainforests, spoiled provisions, bugs and beasts, hunger, and extreme humid heat. Days of rest and recreation in Cuba restored their spirits and their strength after these lowland adventures. As soon as they felt better, they promptly set sail for South America again and now resumed their investigations on the high ground—in the Andes. The pair hiked and climbed various peaks and investigated the avenue of volcanoes in Ecuador. Humboldt was often unwell as a child, yet here he ascended Chimborazo (20,561 feet) almost to the summit.

Reaching a height of 19,280 feet without oxygen, ropes, or any of the modern equipment contemporary mountaineers now rely on, the pair set the world's mountain climbing record for the next 30 years. The French balloonists who thrilled onlookers with the first spectacles of human flight could not match such a height for lack of oxygen. In any case, the scientific work based on the material, samples, and measurements, (for example: 60,000 plants were collected) would keep Humboldt busy for decades, consume his fortune, and eventually fill the lavishly illustrated 30 volumes of his *Voyage aux Regions Équinoxiales du Nouveau Continent.*

But before the two men returned to Europe, Humboldt and Bonpland spent a year in Mexico, researching the richest and most advanced country of Spain's American dominions virtually from top to bottom, from the rim of volcanoes to the deepest mines. Endorsed by the Spanish king and then welcomed by the Viceroy Don José de Iturrigaray in Mexico City, Humboldt received a special permit and letters of introduction that opened doors to archives, institutions, offices, universities, mines, plantations, laboratories, and provincial governors in Mexico.

Such openness shown to a foreigner was unprecedented and generous. At the time, the laws of New Spain were written against inquisitive persons who might come in to collect intelligence. Schemes for the liberation of the Spanish colonies, which, according to the advocates of the Black Legend, could lead to happier days under British overlords, were apparently well remembered. British pirates and privateers were not forgotten either. But, as in other cases of slamming the doors shut, this closing a country off to the world didn't work—at least not for long.

There is a small story attached to the survival of the original passport given to Humboldt by New Spain's viceroy in Mexico City: It was counted as lost in World War II. Yet, in the mid-1990s, the item suddenly turned up in a collection of documents that were returned to Germany in a gesture of goodwill by far-away Georgia in the Caucasus (formerly part of the Soviet Union). That's where some of the trophy valuables taken by the Red Army at war's end had ended up. The passport is now in the archives of the Berlin-Brandenburg Academy of Sciences.

As was his way, Humboldt expended his abundant energy in the effort to understand New Spain. He was in the mines; he climbed volcanoes and inspected craters; he was in the field. He was at the Royal Academy of Art; he investigated drainage systems; studied Aztec antiquities; visited the temple city and pyramids at Teotohuacán; dropped in on a cigar factory, observed people; and buried himself in archives and libraries. He measured, calculated, interviewed, watched, thought, wrote, and constructed profiles and maps. He corrected imprecise readings of longitude and latitude on various maps. He taught at Mexico City's School of Mines (founded in 1792) and participated in the social life of the clean and handsome capital. It was the largest urban center in the Americas. He called it "the city of palaces," but he also saw much poverty. Overall, the country was happy with him. It made him a citizen.

One result of Humboldt's work in Mexico was the *Essai Politique sur le Roaume de la Nouvelle-Espagne*, or the *Political Essay on the Kingdom of New Spain*, translated by John Black. The first English edition was published in 1811. Accompanying the essay was the atlas titled *Geographique et Physique du Royame de La Nouvelle-Espagne*, which contained important maps of the *provincias internas*, and thereby of Louisiana, Texas, California, and the northern frontier, New Mexico, which, at the time, included Arizona, parts of Utah, and southern Colorado. These maps—which showed Santa Fe—would play a substantial role in the future of New Mexico and the American Southwest.

The Political Essay on the Kingdom of New Spain was the first study of its kind written about a single country. It describes and analyzes political conditions, science, geography, history, population, the economy, labor, learning, infrastructure, social progress and also the paralysis of progress. It deals with racial issues and castes—with Spaniards, creoles (Spaniards born in the Americas), Indians, Negroes, mestizos, mulattos, chinos, zambos—and with further branchings of the human family tree as perceived in Mexico at the time. It is not timid and states unequivocally, "Mexico is the country of inequality" (von Humboldt, 1811, p. 137).

It investigates revenues and the economy—including agriculture, manufacturing, import-export, and mining. It contains data and statistics derived from official sources. With his background and training, Humboldt needed no additional persuasion on the importance of mining for the economies of various countries. New Spain (soon to be Mexico) was, without doubt, the world leader in silver production. Yet in the essay, the author emphasizes the disadvantages of the reliance on precious metals. He stresses the symbiosis of agriculture, extraction of mineral wealth, infrastructure, commerce and city growth, which he found and studied in central New Spain. He criticizes an exclusive focus on gold and silver production to the neglect of lead, iron, and copper mining, which would be essential for developing the country's economy in a far more balanced fashion.

Ironically, and to Humboldt's dismay, publication of the essay in several languages led to a renewed investment surge in the gold/silver extraction industry of New Spain, with capital coming especially from England. The appetite for gold and silver was fierce, like a primal urge. This, as Humboldt saw it, was not in the country's best public interest.

In the beginning, it had been somewhat different. As Carlos Prieto pointed out, the first actual smelting done by Spaniards from ores they themselves had mined in New Spain was tin (used with copper to make bronze), as mentioned by Cortés in his Fourth Letter of October 14, 1524 to Charles V where he says that "'five pieces [of artillery] in all have been finished up to the present: two of them medium-sized culverins, two somewhat smaller, and a serpentine cannon'" (Prieto, 1973, p. 78).

Humboldt did not arrive as an outsider when he did his research in New Spain. Interest in science and the ideas of the enlightenment had paved his way in Spain itself. Open to new methods, King Charles III had recruited German mining specialists and technicians. A college of mines for research and the education of local engineers was planned. In 1786, the king appointed the director for the soon-to-be Royal School of Mines, Don Fausto de Elhuyar y Zubice. Born and educated in Spain, Elhuyar later studied in Paris and under the prominent geologist Abraham Gottlieb Werner at the Freiberg School of Mines in Saxony, just like Humboldt. In 1783, at the age of 28, he discovered and isolated the element tungsten. Five years later, "Elhuyar set out for Mexico in August of 1788, accompanied by 11 German mining engineers" (Prieto, 1973, p. 127).

Another former Werner student at the Freiberg academy became a professor at the Mexico City School of Mines. He was Don Andrés Manuel del Rio, the discoverer of vanadium. He had met Humboldt at Freiberg—they were fellow students. All these contacts preceded Humboldt's travels in Spanish-America.

As for German miners, a documented one already worked in the Americas during the days of Charles V in the 16th century. His last name was Tetzel, and it amused me to read that he shared his name with the notorious papal indulgence salesman who raised Martin Luther's wrath during the same time period (Shäfer, 1936–1937, pp. 160–170). The stamp mill was also an import shipped from Germany to New Spain. Arriving in 1536, these mills represented a considerable advance in mechanization. They were widely used in large European mining operations. New Spain put them to work with water wheels if a stream was at the location, and if not they were powered by mules. Later, at the end of the 18th century, the metallurgist Friedrich Traugott Sonneschmid was employed in the country for about 10 years. He criticized the Europeans for adopting the "patio method" or "kettle and cooking" procedure of amalgamation far too slowly. It had been invented around 1590 in Upper Peru by Alvaro Alonso Barba (Prieto, 1973, p. 80). Humboldt dealt positively with this method in his Political Essay.

The most essential and well-known German mining expert in the Americas never set foot in the lands across the ocean sea. He was Georg Bauer or—Latinized, as it was still customary—Georgius Agricola, a scholar, physician, geologist, historian, part-time diplomat, and all around Renaissance man and scientist. He wrote the landmark book *De Re Metallica*. It was published a year after his death in 1556 by the famous printing house Froben at Basle.

The Humanist Erasmus of Rotterdam served as editor. The book was illustrated with 290 splendid woodcuts, many of them technical. A picture of the stamp mill was among them. In Spanish America, the book became the bible of mining, and precious copies of it were kept secured on chains in various churches near the altar. This enabled the priests to translate the Latin text to knowledge-hungry miners without losing it. The *De Re Metallica* remained the definite work on mining, metallurgy, minerals, the study of the earth, and much more for 200 years until the start of the industrial

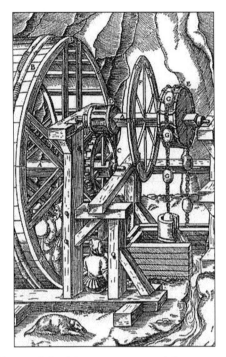

FIGURE 6. *Treadwheel for raising ore, one of many prints from the De Re Metallica by Gregorius Agricola, 1556.*

revolution. Actually, one could say that this revolution was really an evolution. Scientists know that they stand on the shoulders of those who worked before them, and without the fantastic ferment of the late Middle Ages and the Renaissance/Reformation, there would have been no sudden rise of invention and industrial production.

Herbert Hoover, mining engineer and a future president of the United States, was, of course, aware of this. Together with his wife, Lou, a geologist, he translated the *De Re Metallica* into English for the first time. Lou had come across the book in London and urged her husband to do the translation. Together, the couple worked for five years on the project, mostly during their spare time and on weekends. And since Agricola had to make up new words in common Latin to describe mining, geology, metallurgy and applied science accurately (this was similar to inventing the language of electronics and of cyberspace for today), the Hoovers had to understand exactly what he meant before they could translate him well. Published in 1912, the result was an excellent work of scholarship in its own right. The Hoovers understood the spirit of their Renaissance, yet already-modern colleague, perfectly well when they translated a paragraph from his preface as follows:

> I have omitted all those things which I have not myself seen, or have not read or heard of from persons upon whom I can rely. That which I have neither seen, nor carefully considered after reading or hearing of, I have not written about, ... for I have devoted much labor and care, and have even gone to some expense upon it; for with regard to the veins, tools, vessels, sluices, machines, furnaces, I have not only described them, but have also hired illustrators to delineate their forms, lest descriptions which are conveyed by words should either not be understood by men of our own times, or should cause difficulty to prosperity (Georgius Agricola, *De Re Metallica*, 1556, qtd. in Hoover, H.C. & L.H. Hoover, 1912).

—

So far, so good. But the trail leads even further back. I sometimes pause in amazement about the curious connectedness of things: The next stop is mining freedom, which grew, as Paige W. Christiansen (1974) put it in *The Story of Mining in New Mexico*, "from the great synthesis of Roman and Germanic elements [that] we call Medieval. The specialized form of law and social organization grew out of the Germanic codes of the 12th and 13th centuries and is commonly called Germanic mining freedom" (p. 85).

Germanic mining freedom? Oops—that looked a little off color to me: I am a graduate of postwar education. Yes, Germans exist, but the term *Germanic* has fallen into disfavor. The leadership during the infamous 12 years had shown an inordinate liking for things Germanic. Consequently, due to a conditioned reaction, which is likewise the result of postwar education, I even find it somewhat difficult to tolerate the word *leadership*—it translates as *Führerschaft*, and German students became definitely allergic about anything alluding to *Führers*.

Certain words became un-words, and even un-concepts, when I was a child. But perhaps the American geologist who wrote a scientifically accurate book on mining in New Mexico was not aware of the post-1945 re-education intricacies on the other side of the pond? Maybe he was interested in real, long-lasting history as contrasted to shorter-lived politics? I suspected that it must be so—in the U.S. scientific community, a phrasing like *Germanic mining freedom* had to be innocent and straightforward. Whatever the case would be, I was intrigued and decided to do more digging and mining of my own.

It turned out that the miner was a respected craftsman of the Middle Ages and during the Renaissance, Reformation, and the Age of Discovery. He stood at the starting gates of industrialization and capitalism. He was something like the prototype of an engineer. A professional division of labor produced several specialized sub-categories. In Old Europe, it had all started about 50,000 years ago with a bit of surface mining, so one can see that the activity had plenty of time to develop. The continent was rich in ores: iron, tin, copper, lead, silver, and even gold.

When the 12th and 13th centuries came along, mines started to be capital-intensive enterprises on a near industrial scale. Technical innovation, new forms of economic cooperation, and the writing of laws, evolved almost together. Unions (*Gewerkschaften*) were born: the Mining Law of Trient (1185) mentions organized groups of shareholders, bankers, entrepreneurs who lease mines, the mining law experts and judges, specialist miners who were paid according to their productivity and success, and wage-dependent laborers—all working together. The participants held an interest in the operation, the so-called *Kux*. These *Kuxen* were like early shares and before long, such shares could be bought or sold on Europe's developing bourses, or stock markets. Yet, as mining became a bigger and bigger business, large banking and merchant houses (the money men) acquired more and more Kuxen. The balance shifted in favor of capital.

According to legend, the law-giving Emperor Friedrich I, (the famous Barbarossa), sleeps in a Kyffhäuser cave in the Harz Mountains. One day, when the noisy ravens who circle the mountain fall silent, Barbarossa will wake up to bring peace and prosperity to his people. So much for the tale. The real Friedrich I solidified the law on the payment of royalty in the year 1158. The subsurface mining rights could be leased from the emperor, who was entitled to a share of the profits—in New Spain at the time of Charles V known as the royal fifth. Early on, in the 12th and 13th centuries, the lease would usually go to the regional nobility, to the dukes and princes of the realm. They, in turn, were tremendously interested in mining success.

The income tax hadn't been invented yet, so, to stimulate the economy, and to enhance their own revenue, the regional princes awarded privileges to those who prospected, filed claims, and worked the mines. Such persons were released from various duties. They often received permission to fish and hunt. They could bear arms, and they had the right to travel, roam, and establish mines wherever they wished. The medieval German law said: *Bergbaurecht bricht Eigentumsrecht* (mining right breaks property right), and with these social regulations and legal rules, we have the basic ingredients for the Germanic mining freedom: Everyone could look for minerals, start a small business if he found something, and acquire the subsoil property rights based on his discovery. Entrepreneurial men could prospect freely and work their claim, often with the help of their families, as long as the royalty was paid according to the law (Zimmerman, 1999). The beginnings of mining law in the United States were based on this "principle of free mining." It "emigrated with the German miners, and applied to all places their influence extended" (Christiansen, 1974, p. 85).

A downturn in the 14th and early 15th century was caused by the devastating European plague epidemic, a climatic change, a shortage of easily accessible timber, and the exhaustion of many mines. But in the midst of crisis, new ways of doing things were developed, and the miner's technical know-how was again in great demand. In some cases, he was now an employee, in others, a member of a *Gewerkschaft* or union which could include investors and management as well. (There you have a root tradition of German consensus building and the cooperation between management and labor!) He typically worked 44 hours per week, in shifts of four to six hours each. The miner's Saturday afternoon and Sunday were free. He received no vacation days, but there were many official holidays, so the year had about 270–280 working days. Occupational safety regulations were already in place. The law required that dangerous shafts had to have support structures in good repair for the protection of the miners.

We also know how miners dressed, both on the job and on holidays. The two practical items that caught my attention were the funny sounding triangular "*Arschleder*" (literally: butt-leather) which protected the seat, and the *Bergsack* which became the rucksack—which transmogrified itself into the contemporary back pack. The miner's "beautiful dress" for the holidays was colorful, with red and yellow as favorites. Vests were sometimes made from satin or silk. Silver buckles and berets completed the costume (Ludwig, 1987).

—

Now to the dollar and its birthplace in the Erzgebirge, or Ore Mountains. Some of the best silver mines of medieval Germany were located in this area but the yield wasn't enough to satisfy demand. Europe developed a silver coin shortage in an expanding economy. Just in time, new high-grade deposits were found in 1516. The town of St. Joachimthal experienced a boom and began minting the *Joachimsthaler*, a one-ounce silver coin.

The name was a bit long, so people abbreviated it to Thaler or Taler. Soon the handsome currency circulated throughout Europe and gained a reputation for quality and reliability. After the Spaniards discovered rich gold and silver deposits in the Americas, they built, in 1535, the first mint. They were amazingly quick with doing all these things, among them founding

FIGURE 7. *Joachimsthaler, dated 1525.*

universities and adorning cities with beautiful architecture. In addition, new technology spread with great speed. Four Germans set up Sevilla's first printing press as early as 1470. Reports from the voyages of exploration were rushed into print and found eager buyers in Sevilla, Rome, Florence, Nuremberg and Ausgburg. Even the Cortés reports from Mexico City were soon printed and publicly available. The first letter to Charles V was published by the German Johann Cronberger in 1522. Next, in 1538, he established a printing press in Mexico City.

⁓

The Mexico City mint didn't waste time either. As soon as it was finished, it began striking coins modeled after the prestigious Taler used back home. It became the *dólar* in Spanish. No problem: Charles V was Spain's king (as Charles I) and Germany's (which included St. Joachimthal) Holy Roman Emperor. Therefore, it was all an internal matter.

Spain's silver taler/dólar became a currency which spread even farther: It found acceptance in the British colonies of North America, and later, in the brand new United States. Alexander Hamilton, the first Secretary of the Treasury, recommended the dollar as the U.S. monetary unit. He also preferred the continental European decimal system to the much more complicated non-decimal British method of pound sterling = 20 shillings = 240 pence.

The origin of the dollar $ sign itself is not so clear. There are three different theories on the subject, but no one knows which one is correct (Bank of Canada Museum, 2016). Versions number one and number two are practical and prosaic, suggesting that the U was superimposed over the S, or a P (for peso) was written over the S. In both cases, this would construct something resembling the $ sign. Until 1961, the symbol had two vertical lines crossing the S. Theory number three, on the other hand, has an alluring pedigree that goes back to the Phoenicians, Greeks, Vikings, and Romans.

It is said that the Phoenicians erected two pillars on the Spanish and North African headlands flanking the Strait of Gibraltar around 1500 BCE. This was a warning sign to those who were tempted to venture out into the Atlantic, reminding them that they would fall off the rim of a flat earth and plunge into the underworld. The Greeks called the two columns the Pillars of Hercules or the gate to Hades. The Romans followed in the same footsteps and regarded the Strait of Gibraltar and the pillars as the border-line of the world—the *Non Plus Ultra*—from here go no farther (Davies, 2002). It was a barrier. Various "barbarians" and early explorers engaged in lively seafaring along the coasts of the Atlantic and the North Sea outside the forbidden gate, but they didn't know any better, worshipped weird and terrible deities, and upheld bizarre mythologies. Yet eventually, Columbus sailed across the ocean. Charles V was likewise bold when he changed the old Latin motto and ordered the design of a new Spanish coat of arms that is used to this day. It shows the two Pillars of Hercules, wrapped by S-shaped escrolls inscribed with *Plus Ultra:* farther away. The old barrier had fallen. The gate was open—not to Hades, but to the regions farther away—meaning the Americas and the world.

The Spanish coat of arms with its ribbon-wrapped pillars is depicted on the earliest Spanish-American dólar. The coin became an international standard currency from the 16th to the 19th century and was called the "pillar dollar."

It is easy to see how the columns with their scrolls can be simplified into the dollar $ sign, especially with daily use and over time (Bank of Canada, 2016).

FIGURE 8. *Pillar Dollar, Mexico: Carlis III—dated 1771.*

The unity of nature: Humboldt is seen as an early ecologist, and sometimes as the first one. I wonder how he would react to the environmental and economic muddle we've made of mining. He would probably agree with Wallace Stegner who once said about the U.S., "This country has never been settled, it's been raided, and whenever there is something to raid it for there will be new raiders" (Hepworth, 1998, p. 43).

The American Mining Law of 1872 is now completely out of date. It was signed by President Ulysses S. Grant, who was nicknamed "unconditional surrender Grant" during the Civil War. Under that law, hard rock minerals can still be mined on public lands for a ridiculously low price per acre. The days of the Germanic mining freedom are long gone. Lone prospectors no longer roam the forests and the mountains of the untamed West. Today, panning for gold in one-man-operations is a decorative tourist activity, and you pay for the privilege of pretending for a few hours. You may even end up with a few specks of overprized gold.

For concerned Americans, however, the give-away of public resources worth billions of dollars to big mining companies represents corporate welfare. Compared with it, the Middle Ages were rather advanced in their thinking: Mining paid a royalty to the government. Now, when Americans are supposed to have no kings, princes, or emperors, the "royal fifth" should go into the public kitty. It could pay for good and necessary things. It could even reduce the deficit. But what do we instead? We charge practically nothing and let corporations get a free ride on 270 million acres of America's public land. The government has the job of administering these huge parcels of earth for the benefit of the country's citizens, but it hardly gets a share from the billions made in mining profits. To the contrary, the

legacy of mining has been poor stewardship of public property. The West is littered with thousands of abandoned mines, polluting many rivers, lakes and groundwater with acidic runoff, lead, arsenic, cadmium and other toxins. Cleanup costs could range as high a $ 72 billion. In New Mexico alone, an estimated 3,000 abandoned mines are on Bureau of Land Management (BLM) Land (DiPeso, 2002).

～

Humboldt lived long enough to follow the mid-19th century California Gold Rush, which produced 3 million ounces of the yellow metal each year. What would he say about the fact that from 1983 to 1998, U.S. gold production rose from 1 million ounces to 11 million ounces per year? (Parsons, 2002).

"The wealth of the world will be found in New Mexico," the Prussian scientist had predicted and indeed, New Mexico derives a large part of her revenues from mining, oil, and gas production. Still, there are those 10,000 abandoned holes (both on public and private land) in the ground. Many of them were dug after the Mexican-American war and the U.S. annexation of the region in 1846/1848. Some of the mines boomed for a while and were later left behind as no longer profitable.

Prior to the annexation, mining was an ancient and limited activity within these arid areas. There was no infrastructure, and little water nearby to support economies of scale. The only commercial operation was open-pit copper mining at Santa Rita. It started around 1804 (during the time when Humboldt made his statement on New Mexico), but large operations did not begin until 1912— the year when New Mexico was finally admitted to U.S. statehood.

I have seen the Santa Rita mine. It is an enormous crater growing ever larger in concentric rings, with gigantic trucks crawling down in circles to pick up ore. From the observer's location on the rim, the monstrous trucks grow smaller and smaller until they are tiny moving specks in the recesses of the gargantuan pit. The evidence of human activity at this site is striking, yet the means of ferrying the ore in these seemingly minuscule toy trucks out of the deep hole looks almost futile.

7

Western Americana

Before being free, it is necessary to be just.
— *Alexander von Humboldt*

O h, dear. The French papers had already reported a year earlier that
the illustrious explorer found a miserable end caused by yellow fever
somewhere in the tropics. A Hamburg newspaper pronounced him as dead
and done for under the palm trees of Acapulco. But the Baron, as it turned
out, failed to do the favor of expiring to any of these sources. Instead, he
arrived in Philadelphia on the Spanish frigate *Conceptión* from Havana
(De Terra, 1955, pp. 172–173). Bursting with health and beaming at life,
he was perfectly happy to see that the multitude of boxes packed with the
expedition's botanical, geological, mineralogical, and zoological specimens
had survived all dangers, ranging from a nasty storm to confiscation by the
blockading British Navy.

It was late May 1804. France and Britain were at war. Later that year,
Napoleon would be crowned—or rather, crown himself—emperor. France
had lost all its North American holdings in 1763, when the Peace of Paris
was signed after the conclusion of the French and Indian War, also known
as the Seven Years' War in Europe. As far as conflicts go, this was a slippery
one. It was actually a world war taking place on three continents. In India,

France had also lost out to Britain. But now, a few decades later, an aggressive and energetic Bonaparte made plans to establish a New France on the North American continent. In October of 1802, the same Spanish king, Charles IV, who had given *carte blanche* to Humboldt for his explorations in Spanish America, concluded a secret deal and ceded Louisiana to Napoleon in trade for land holdings in Italy. Spain, with its large empire, had gradually grown weaker and could do little to stem the tide of American settlements and trade pushing ever closer against its boundaries. Policing Louisiana, "a wilderness so immense" (Kukla, 2003), drained Spain's manpower and its coffers.

At first, the Americans had no knowledge of this land swap, but when they found out, it caused much worry. Earlier, in 1795, the United States and Spain had signed a treaty that granted America the right to use the Mississippi and store goods in the port of New Orleans for subsequent ocean commerce. The big river was the artery that connected the westward expanding body of the U.S. with the world. Kentucky, Tennessee, and Ohio were just a few years old, and for them New Orleans was the gateway to the ocean and the markets. Without roads in these new territories, and prior to the coming of the railroads, economic life was centered on water transport. Civilizations usually developed first along the rivers.

So when Spanish authorities—who still administered the port city until France took possession—suddenly blocked access to the storage facilities for Americans, as ordered by Madrid, the outrage was intense. The Federalists called for war. Jefferson preferred diplomacy, and dispatched envoys to Paris with orders to buy New Orleans if possible. What the negotiators actually bought was far, far more. When all was signed, Napoleon invited the two Americans, James Monroe and Robert Livingstone, to dine with him at the Louvre. Not only was he satisfied with the deal, he also employed his long-range-vision with glee: America, he foresaw, would become a formidable maritime rival of Britain and would humiliate her sooner or later (Gerste, 2003).

Luck was on the president's side. (As I write this, I am mindful of the fact that one man's fortune can be another man's misfortune, and that all this has little to do with merit, or with the triumph of good over evil.) Before

Napoleon could turn his attention to the project of setting up a *Nouvelle France* in Louisiana, he had to deal with a slave revolt in the French colony of Haiti where the rebel leader Toussaint L'Ouverture fought for independence.

General Charles Leclerc and an expeditionary force of 20,000 men had been dispatched to crush the Haitian uprising. Afterwards, the general was to sail on to Louisiana. Unknown to the Americans, they had a tiny ally— temporarily, since it was disinterested in politics or economics, and would harm Yankees with perfect neutrality later on. Alas, juicy humans all taste the same to *aedes aegypti*, the mosquito that transmits the scourge of yellow fever (Gerste, 2003). Leclerc and many of his men perished from the fever during the campaign. Napoleon was furious and cursed these three: sugar, coffee, colonies. In the end, the rebel leader Toussaint L'Ouverture was taken prisoner and shipped to France. He died there in captivity.

After the demise of his forces in Haiti, Napoleon had few means to pursue the goal of establishing a new French dominion in North America. What he needed most urgently just then was cash for the war against England. This, in turn, helped Jefferson and his special envoy James Monroe to finalize the huge Louisiana Purchase on April 30, 1803, for the preposterously low price of 15 million dollars. The deal doubled the size of the United States instantly. The states of Louisiana, Arkansas, Missouri, Iowa, North Dakota, South Dakota, Nebraska, Kansas, Wyoming, Minnesota, Oklahoma, much of Colorado, and Montana would all be carved out from this gigantic real estate acquisition of 828,000 square miles. The U.S. government paid four cents per acre (Gerste, 2003). The president had to borrow the millions to pay for the acquisition, and he did so from Britain. The Brits preferred the young and still-weak United States to the fierce and fighting Napoleon as the new owner of all this land, so they were willing to assist at six percent interest. It was the British banking house of Baring that loaned the money to the U.S., which in turn used it to pay Napoleon for the Lousiana Purchase. Next comes Napoleon, who takes this British money to fight his war against Britain.

Who can doubt that history has a marvelous sense of humor? I feel a bit giddy. I need to take these events in. They make fiction look anorexic.

Today's U.S. real estate tycoons are midgets compared to the personages who divided up vast portions of the globe, traded or sold them back and forth among themselves, and decided the fate, future, or impaired future for millions of people who could become, by the stroke of a pen, Americans, subjects of the British crown, ex-French or Spanish colonials, or second-class citizens of whatever nation that purchased them. If you employ a morsel of malice, you can imagine the whole obsession as a mammoth slave market deal.

Even today, historians seem to have few qualms about the Louisiana Purchase or about buying huge tracts of colonial land—complete with various inhabitants—from a First Consul and soon-to-be self-appointed emperor of France for a young and freedom-loving republic. Curiously enough, the buyer was the U.S. model republic with the determination to behave differently from corrupt and decadent Old Europe. Actually, the big land deal can be seen as one of the early examples of U.S. nonexceptionalism. As the historian Walter A. McGougall pointed out, "Here we must ask, once and for all, after the significance of Jefferson's philosophical musings. One finds evidence of idealism throughout his writings and table talk. One seeks it in vain in his statecraft" (McDougall, 1997, p. 32). Thanks for the cold shower. I sometimes wish that I hadn't read so much about American history and instead had kept a few more sweet illusions.

This is not an attempt to be irreverent. In part, I think highly of Thomas Jefferson. Still, purchasing almost a third of a continent from a colonial power reminds me of buying goods with a doubtful provenance. It is perhaps not the best way of starting out with a clean slate, and of being more principled than bad Old Europe. At least over there if the lords didn't conquer new lands, they used to marry them. Take the Austrian Habsburgs, for example. Their saying was: Let others wage war; you, happy Austria, marry! (*Bella gerant alii, tu felix Austria nube!*) In any case, the old ruling class in Europe didn't buy territory and people outright.

It bothers me that the whole affair involved the acquisition of humans sight unseen. All those who happened to live on the land of the Louisiana Purchase had no voice in the matter, and did not receive the slightest democratic

consideration. To give him credit, Napoleon sold Louisiana with the understanding that the inhabitants would soon receive all the rights of U.S. citizens.

But do I make the mistake of projecting contemporary sensibilities back
to the early 1800s? That's doubtful. After all, the United States had been
an assembly of colonies and knew the ins and outs. It hated being colonial
property, and freed itself. Once independent, it became a shining example
for many liberty-seeking people elsewhere. As for Thomas Jefferson, savant
and elected president, he was well aware of the legal dilemma inherent in his
action: there was no provision in the Constitution for the buying of foreign
or colonial real estate. The president bypassed the Constitution not too long
after the ink was dry—for the good (as he saw it) of his country. Perhaps
Jefferson told himself, "It is the case of the guardian, investing money of his
ward in purchasing an important adjacent Territory; and saying to him when
of age, I did this for your own good" (Wilson, 2003, n.p).

In the meantime, William C. C. Claiborne, lawyer and former congressman from Tennessee, was appointed as territorial governor of Louisiana. He
arrived in New Orleans; he spoke no French. The first thing he did was to
declare that English would instantly be the language of local government—
despite an estimate that only one in fifty inhabitants could understand the
English language. The governor reported back to Washington that a state of
mental darkness prevailed in the city. First a widespread knowledge of the
American language, of U.S. laws, and of customs, had to be acquired. Until
then, Claiborne warned, representative government in Louisiana would
probably be a dangerous experiment.

Mental darkness shrouded Louisiana because the purchased population
spoke a different language. French. Or Spanish. In addition, there was also
the sudden conflict between two legal systems—that of the French civil
code, and the U.S. system based on English common law. A similar clash
occurred some forty years later when the U.S. annexed the entire Southwest
with California from Mexico.

Just a few years ago, a lot of people would have called the developments
after the Louisiana Purchase cultural imperialism. But we have progressed

since then. We don't use such unsophisticated lingo anymore. But no matter what we call it, I'm afraid that this became a recurrent refrain of American foreign policy: telling other countries and various peoples that we knew best and that we did things for their own good.

In any case, Thomas Jefferson had no authority to purchase a third of the North American Continent with the human inventory included. The president did not seek advice from Congress until the deal was done. Perhaps there had not been enough time for consultation. Napoleon was in a hurry, and communications across the Atlantic were still as slow as ships. Yet in the end, practical gain won out over the law of the land: The House voted 89 to 23, and the Senate 24 to 7, for the Louisiana Purchase (Gerste, 2003). What we have here is one of the continuous contradictions that run like a pattern through America's (and who knows of how many other countries) past, delineating the rift between the proclaimed ideal and political practicality.

Jefferson's risktaking had won the day. He had a grand vision to begin with, and promoted expansion. His interest focused not only on New Orleans and the Mississippi Valley, but also on the British Pacific coast of the Northwest. He thought big, and continentwide. That's why he dispatched Meriwether Lewis and William Clark with an expeditionary group called the Corps of Discovery on a mission. The explorers were charged with crossing the continent and with finding a commercially useful river route between the Mississippi and the Pacific Ocean. The party left during the spring of 1804, just before Humboldt's arrival in Philadelphia. Lewis and Clark didn't locate a connecting waterway, but this mattered little. Americans and immigrants became a river rushing westward right behind the pathfinders. Some 30 years after Lewis & Clark returned from the voyage, the Oregon territory had been settled for good.

Humboldt was an ardent admirer of Jefferson and the freshly-baked American republic, and he arrived at a strategic moment. He was just the person the president needed to see. So when the Prussian scientist wrote to Jefferson, expressing his desire for a meeting, the answer and an invitation followed quickly.

It is one of history's delights to look at special occasions when men with their motives and deeds group themselves together auspiciously. To me, the meeting and the developing lifelong relationship between the American president and the German scientist represents such an occasion. Geography was not the only element of their mutual interest. Actually, Humboldt was, among many other things, a maker of maps, while Jefferson was, at that point in time, a statesman in need of maps. The president didn't know what, precisely, he had bought from Bonaparte. The French left the borderland questions to be sorted out by the U.S. and Spain. This would later lead to the formation of Texas, to the Mexican War, and to the annexation of what is now the American Southwest.

So how many people lived in that huge area in 1804? What were the boundaries? On June 9, Jefferson wrote to Humboldt about the discrepancies between two nations. Spain said its land stretched from the Sabine River north to the headwaters of the Red River, while the U.S. claims reached

> to the North River from mouth to source either of its eastern or western branch, hence to the head of the Red River. Can the Baron inform me what population may be between these lines, of white, red, or black people? And whether any and what mines are within them? The information will be thankfully received (De Terra, 1955, p. 181).

There is an undated answer from Humboldt to Jefferson, written a few days later, originally in French:

> The president wishes to have information about the population, the area, and the mineral resources of the Spanish provinces ceded, assuming that the Rio Bravo del Norte [Rio Grande] should be the border of Louisiana? The king of Spain would cede in this case 2/3 of the immense administrative area of San Louis Potosi; he would lose a terrain of 11, 756 leagues . . ., he would lose the entire province of Texas, 7006 leagues; half of the province of Nuevo Santander, 1,900

leagues; two-thirds of the province of Cohahuila, 2,850 leagues; the entirety of this terrain equals 2/3 of the area of France. But the political value of this land, considering it before the joining of Louisiana to the United States, is almost nil (Humboldt Digital Library Project, 2016).

The note pointed out that the area in question was largely uninhabited, and that it had a harsh, hot climate.

Humboldt and his companions Bonpland and Montúfar (the latter an Ecuadorian revolutionary who was eventually executed by Spain) received a friendly welcome in the new and incomplete capital city of Washington, DC. They were taken on tours of the sights and invited to various lunches, dinners, and teas. Humboldt met Albert Gallatin, Secretary of the Treasury, and James Madison.

Dolly Madison, wife of the Secretary of State, gossiped in a little note to her sister: "We have lately had a great treat in the company of a charming Prussian Baron von Humboldt. All the ladies say they are in love with him, notwithstanding his personal charms. He is the most polite, modest,

FIGURE 9. *Alexander von Humboldt: pencil and ink drawing by Frédéric Christophe de Houndetot, Berlin 1807.*

well-informed and interesting traveler we have ever met, and is much pleased with America ... He had with him a train of philosophers who, though clever and entertaining, did not compare with the Baron" (Botting, 1973, p. 172).

It's my treat, too. It makes me chuckle. For Dolly Madison, I would dig to the bottom of my bag of odds and ends, bring up the curtsy we had to practice as children, and actually perform it for the gracious lady. Imagine. In June of 1804, pesky Prussia and the horrid Hun had not been invented yet! Those were the innocent times when a live Prussian could be perceived, in America, as a captivating human being. And since I was born in Berlin like the formidable Alexander, learning this made me merry. And never mind that later-born victorious Americans and nation-building persons decided to erase poor old Prussia from modern maps: it was not permitted to live any longer. Good grief, capital punishment for an entire region—my home turf was sentenced to be gone.

It certainly was different when Prussia was first among nations to ratify the pleasantly named "Treaty of Amity and Commerce Between His Majesty the King of Prussia, and the United States of America" as early as September 1785. The king was Old Fritz—Frederick the Great—who once held the hand of a young boy named Alexander von Humboldt. The American negotiators and signers were John Adams, Benjamin Franklin, and Thomas Jefferson. In the U.S., the agreement was ratified a year later. It called for "firm, inviolable, and universal peace, and sincere friendship." It also supported trade and "freedom of the seas for neutral vessels, even in time of war" (Jonas, 1984, p. 16).

A pleased George Washington wrote to the former commander of French troops in America: "It is perfectly original in many of its articles, and should its principles be considered hereafter as the basis of *connexions* between nations, it will operate more fully to produce a general pacification than any measure hitherto attempted by mankind" (Jonas, 1984, p.16).

About a week after his arrival in Washington, Humboldt was invited to have lunch with Jefferson at the Executive Mansion. The surroundings were simple, the food good, and the conversation stimulating. The two men shared views on politics and human rights and their lively interests in various branches of science. In fact, they got along so well that the 61-year-old president and the 35-year-old scientist spent much time together during the following weeks. Jefferson and Humboldt came to know and appreciate each other, and afterwards corresponded for years until Jefferson's death.

When the visitor sailed home to Europe in late June, he traveled with a letter of safe conduct from the U.S. government. James Madison instructed all American ships to help the scientists, and to assist in protecting their valuable cargo of thousands of specimens and samples.

Humboldt shared his research and information generously with the American government. He furnished data on mine production, demographics, the economy, and the geography of New Spain from his *Tablas Geográfico Politicas del Reyno de Nueva España* (1803). For Jefferson's convenience, he even translated the *Tablas* into French, adding "a two-page summary particularly on the Mexican border region of the Louisiana Territory" (Schwarz, n.d., p.3). Moreover, he allowed his manuscript maps to be copied. They were invaluable at the time. Information on mining was of great interest too. Humboldt told Gallatin that "Spanish America had produced gold and silver worth 5.6 billion dollars" since the beginning of the conquest (De Terra, 1955, p. 181). That was an enormous sum in yesteryear's money. Gallatin was later able to ascertain that the figure was correct.

A few years prior to Humboldt's visit with Jefferson and other members of the U.S. government, the 12-year-old son of a Hessian deserter turned farmer had discovered gold on the territory of the Cherokee Indians in North Carolina. He found a nice big lump of the yellow metal. Nobody lost sleep about it. Until 1802, the family used the piece as a door handle. A silversmith finally identified the knob as gold, and the farmer's son began prospecting in earnest. A year later he found a nugget weighing 28 pounds. He sold it for $8,000—a large sum in the early 1800s. It was this piece that became interesting to Humboldt, and he pursued accurate information for many years until it was finally forthcoming. It was his way to hunt down facts even if it required decades, and to pay attention to unanswered questions. Due to his early career experiences in the revitalization of German gold mines, he remained interested in the subject and studied gold production on a global scale, particularly in the U.S. and in Russia. The assembled statistics on gold mining, price developments, and economic data were published in 1838 in an essay titled "The Gold Fluctuations" (Humboldt, 1838, pp. 1–40).

Meanwhile, the young farmer with the nose for finding the yellow metal became a rich man and a successful entrepreneur. He took on partners and founded several mines. His name was John Reed. By 1830, there were 30,000 people digging for gold in North Carolina. Gold rushes, however, tended to be injurious to the well-being of the Native American populations in North America—and in this particular case, to the Cherokee. They became the subjects of removal policies and had to leave their homelands. The Louisiana Purchase made it possible to deport entire Indian Nations to the new western territories across the Mississippi.

As Jefferson's guest, Humboldt also discussed the feasibility of constructing a canal at the Isthmus of Panama, a project that continued to hold his attention and engage his passion throughout a long life. Did Humboldt have any doubts about sharing his research with the U.S. government? No. He planned to publish his work anyway, and saw no problem with giving it in advance to someone with the reputation and qualities of Thomas Jefferson. He strongly believed in the freedom of science. He even distributed his own riches, and did not hoard them for profit or narrow national considerations. In 1803 he had shipped big crates of fresh seeds from Mexico City to the Botanical Garden in Madrid, to the Garden in Paris, and, via Trinidad, to Sir Josef Banks in London. Next he assured his old friend the botanist Karl Ludwig Willdenow in Berlin that he too would receive a substantial delivery.

In thought and deed, Humboldt regarded the findings of science as a public good. Results should be accessible for the benefit of people everywhere and for the betterment of the human condition. He intended to hand over what he had, and he did.

It was the Director of the Royal School of Mines in Mexico City, M. d'Elhuyer, who encouraged Humboldt to do cartographic work in New Spain. There were no reliable maps of the country's 37 mining districts available, so the visiting scientist produced one. Once engaged in the project, it was difficult to stop. More maps were sketched, and in good time published (Paris, 1811) in the Atlas *Geographique et Physique de Royaume de la Nouvelle-Espagne* as a companion work to the *Essai Politique sur le Royaume de la Nouvelle-Espagne.* The atlas contained, among other beauties, an east-west hypsometric profile map of Mexico, the first one of its kind done for an entire country. But the key item in the volume was the *Carte Generale du Royaume de la Nouvelle Espagne.* It is a physical geographical map from 16° to 42° N latitude that covers both today's Mexico, the greater American Southwest, and even an obscure minor place like Los Angeles.

For the first time in almost a century, the *Carte Generale* offered information on Texas, the Southwest, and California. Only Humboldt had been given access to Mexican and Spanish archives and localities, and no other visiting scientist had been able to make astronomical measurements that helped to fix the accurate location of places like the port of Acapulco or the northern frontier capital of Santa Fe. To Americans at the time, this entire region was, for the most part, still unknown. But now it was suddenly put into a framework and relationship to the American states along the Atlantic coast and to the territory of the newly acquired Louisiana Purchase. In 1811, Humboldt's work was, as map bibliographer Carl Jackson put it, "a truly magnificent cartographic achievement" (Goodwin, 2000, p.1). There was no other map that was so accurate, and the U.S. government had received a copy of the manuscript map years earlier, in 1804.

Katherine Goodwin, cartographic archivist for the Special Collections Division at the University of Texas, wrote that Humboldt's essay on New Spain, which included maps,"is regarded as one of the seminal works of Western Americana" (Goodwin, 2000, p.1) When Humboldt shared his cartography with Jefferson, Madison, and Gallatin, Texas, the Southwest and California had long been, and still were, possessions of Spain. So how could a map of New Spain undergo a magical transformation that turned it into an item of Western Americana? It's simple: Just employ a characteristic tool of official American history and treat the whole thing as a United States story. It's habit. In the standard popular versions of the national narrative, the Native Americans and Spaniards of the Southwest are far too often relegated to playing the bit parts, or none at all.

Humboldt's map was certainly of strategic value. But it could become a landmark of Western Americana only later—with hindsight. First, the large territories in question had to be conquered and annexed-purchased by the United States. This happened some four decades after the baron's visit to the U.S.

Today, the Humboldt map is credited with opening the region to American trade and immigration. And south of the border, in Mexico itself and elsewhere in Latin America, "Alejandro de Humboldt" has been adopted as the scientific discoverer of the southern half of the hemisphere. He is recognized for breaking the so-called cognitive continental blockade between Europe and South America. "Humboldteanization" is a tongue-breaking keyword in Latin-American studies. Children know him as the man who named their flowers. There are commemorative plaques and monuments in many places throughout South America. Mexico considers the German scientist a benefactor of the nation who, apart from his other work, introduced the cultural achievements of the pre-Columbian societies to a wide range of readers (Humboldt, 1914).

Further south, while exploring the connection of the Orinoco and Amazon River systems, Humboldt found petroglyphs. He tried to decipher these ancient rock art images. He also collected various artifacts, jade objects, and small antiquities during his travels. He showed a high regard for the cultures he encountered, and had little patience for the superiority claims of Europeans.

Venezuela named two of its mountains the Humboldt (4942 meters) and the Pico Bolivar (5007 meters). They are the second highest and the highest mountain in the country. They stand together—only five kilometers distant from each other. They allude to the acquaintance of the two men, and to the influential role assigned to the German scientist in the process of Latin American emancipation.

Still, like all outstanding personalities Humboldt was not without critics. Some say he was far too open-handed with the results of his labors. The historian and Humboldt translator José Ortega y Medina, for example, asserts that Mexico provided a feast of resources and materials ready for Humboldt's appetite, and that the baron enjoyed New Spain's banquet, and then nonchalantly gave away the recipes to the U.S. government. As Ingo Schwarz wrote, "Thus he paved the way for the North American expansion into the South and for the economic conquest of the southern parts of America" (qtd. in Schwarz, n.d., para. 3). Recently, a Mexican newspaper even posed the rhetorical question: "Was Humboldt a U.S. spy?"

Humboldt was not a spy. He was a hunter for truth, an independent scientist, and an advocate for human rights—all human rights. He urged the Mexican government to change the fate of the few Apache raiders caught in what is now New Mexico and then imprisoned in the tropical lowlands of Veracruz. Due to climate and conditions, these unfortunates perished quickly. Humboldt had a sharp eye for the inequities inflicted upon the copper-colored race. In one case, he was asked by the leadership of the Franciscan missions along the Orinoco to furnish a reference letter that commented on the mild treatment of the *Indios*. Humboldt wouldn't do that, and later wrote an irony-laced passage about it. The worthy Franciscans undoubtedly held the view that people who pick up plants and poke around among rocks shouldn't stick their noses into affairs related to the well-being of the copper-colored race und associated issues.

This wish is very common in among colonists, mocks Humboldt, and one encounters it in all those places where force is frightened because she fears her footholds are not secure. The Humboldt-scholar Ottmar Ette put it this way: *"Humboldt war and blieb vorlaut,* meaning he was and remained forward, outspoken" (Ette, 2005, p.). Indeed, he would stick his neck out and speak his mind persistently, especially on matters of human rights. There was nothing ambiguous about Humboldt's anti-colonial attitude. To him, "The colony is a land in which one claims to be able to live in freedom because one can mistreat one's slaves without fear of punishment and can insult the Whites if they are poor" (Lynch, 2006, p. 35).

Humboldt the investigator was beholden to no one. He used his own funds for the travels and researches in Spanish America. That the king of Spain granted him free access to all archives and resources was amazing. That this king risked objectivity and often severe criticism from an outsider was even more remarkable. A partial explanation for this can be found in the fact that Humboldt had contacts with the Spanish branch of the European Enlightenment: ideas traveled and influenced reform-minded members of the elite both in the motherland and in Spain's American dominions. There was hope among these persons for political and social progress and for revitalization.

It was a period of shifting foundations. Napoleon, successor to the liberty-seeking French Revolution, was not bothered about putting Humboldt under constant surveillance. After his return to Europe, and starting in 1807, secret police intercepted and read his mail, broke repeatedly into his Paris apartment while he was traveling, searched through his papers, and copied (by hand, in those days) whatever was wanted. After all, the famous and celebrated German was classified as an enemy-due-to-his-birthplace: Napoleon's army had invaded and occupied much of Germany and all of Prussia, and held power until the tide turned.

Humboldt, however, loved Paris, and needed the many artistic, intellectual, scientific, and graphic resources it offered for the long-term project of publishing his multi-volume illustrated works. Nevertheless, in 1810, Bonaparte asked his minister of the interior, the chemist Jean Antoine Chaptal, to make arrangements for the deportation of Humboldt back to his native sandbox of Prussia. Chaptal managed to talk the emperor out of it. Humboldt was a leading scientist who had contributed to the worldwide esteem and glory of France.

It is perhaps understandable that Napoleon was a little irritated because the Prussian was certainly number two in public fame, right after the emperor himself. In addition, Humboldt had shown the gall of securing the supervisor position at the Malmaison gardens for his friend and fellow South American explorer, the botanist Aimé G. Bonpland. Napoleon's wife, the empress Josephine, was quite pleased with his expertise.

Bonpland returned to South America after the emperor's fall from power. That region was soon embroiled in political turmoil and revolutionary struggles for independence. The remaining years of Bonpland's life were difficult.

Humboldt took his lively interest in the United States with him as he returned to Europe. It never diminished, even if it changed and grew somewhat disillusioned in some aspects over time.

8

How to Make Destiny Manifest

"I am at present studying Humboldt's
History of Mexico, in Spanish."

—*T. J. (Stonewall) Jackson in a letter to his sister
written at the National Palace in Mexico City
on April 10, 1848, during the U.S. occupation. (Virginia Military Institute, Stonewall
Jackson Papers).*

Do we call this the land of the free?
What is it to be free from King
George and continue the slaves of
King Prejudice?

—*Henry David Thoreau,
"Life Without Principle"*

We don't talk much about the Mexican War. We don't hear, read, or see much about it either. That's why one public occasion roused my interest. It was a September 2003 Paul Espinosa Film Festival sponsored by the New Mexico Endowment for the Humanities and the Southwest Hispanic Research Institute at the University of New Mexico. One documentary was titled *The Mexican War: 1846–1848*, and another one *The Hunt for Pancho Villa*. The second film deals with the revolutionary leader's 1916 raid on the small border community of Columbus in New Mexico, and with the subsequent punitive military expedition led by General John "Black Jack" Pershing. He pursued Pancho Villa unsuccessfully across northern Mexico. This is the same general who would soon be appointed as commander of the entire World War I American Expeditionary Force in Europe—but more about this later.

In Mexico, the 1846–1848 war has a different name. It's called *Invasion Yanqui*. Our southern neighbors are less forgetful, although many Mexicans are probably reluctant to dwell on an event that cost them half of their country. Nevertheless, every year on September 13 they honor *Los Niños Héroes,* the heroic children, six fighting cadets who died by leaping from the ramparts in the doomed defense of Chapultepec castle. The youngest, Francisco Marquez, was 13 years old.

The Mexican War was not one of America's "good" wars. Yet it intrigued me for two reasons: Firstly, it was the means through which New Mexico became a U.S. territory and finally a state in 1912, and secondly, many of those who fought on the American side were German immigrants. Actually, there were some Germans who battled for Mexico, too. But these men were deserters who joined John Riley's rebellious *San Patricios,* a sort of foreign legion battalion formed from Irish soldiers and other Europeans who had gone 'over the hill' to fight with Mexico. There is a plaque with an inscription in the Plaza San Jacinto. It reads: "In Memory of the Heroic Battalion of St. Patrick, Martyrs Who Gave Their Lives for the Mexican Cause during the Unjust North American Invasion of 1847." Most of the names on the memorial are Irish. Thirteen are German.

Large-scale rearrangements of land ownership were in full swing during the 19th century, and the tempo increased as the second half progressed. The Western powers colonized big parts of Asia and nearly all of Africa. I recall a political cartoon showing a colossal Cecil Rhodes standing astride on the entire continent of Africa, one powerful leg placed firmly on Egypt, the other one on diamond-rich South Africa. Conquest, nation building, and introducing all those lesser peoples "sitting in darkness" (as Mark Twain satirized it bitterly) to the light of Western civilization was a widely accepted mode of operation. In some quarters, it even seems to be fashionable to this day.

In any case, back in the 1840s it was not too surprising that the United States was similarly infected with the happy fever of expansionism. Yet homegrown values and foreign-rooted imperialism were widely regarded as incompatible, at least by common folk. America, the populace had learned from the nation's venerable story of origin, was different. As a consequence, imperial undertakings were not terribly popular among the voting public. So if persons in high places nurtured unexceptional ideas of conquest, they had to package such notions skillfully in order to show that the behavior of the United States leadership must never be compared to those degenerate, land-grabbing, belligerent royal rulers of Old Europe.

Let's turn to the British Empire for a moment. Byron Farwell (1985) wrote a memorable foreword for his book *Queen Victoria's Little Wars*. Lacking a taste for puff pastry, he went straight for the beef in the very first paragraph:

> This is the story of what Kipling called "the savage wars of peace," and of the men who fought them. Scant attention is paid to the causes of the wars or the political maneuverings [that] preceded the hostilities. They are not of much importance. Reasons for going to war are continually being made available to great nations; the more far flung their interests, the more pretexts for war present themselves (p.1).

Marvelous, isn't it? Never forced to go begging for a pretext, the "savage wars of peace" were fought by Britain throughout the long Victorian century. There were dozens of them, far away and across the globe. All these actions were seen as necessary for the maintenance of the *Pax Britannica*. But in the end it was all for naught and Brexit.

Which reminds me: these days, we are living in the era of the *Pax Americana*.

Back in the mid-1800s, expansion-minded persons in the United States required a term that was potent, as well as euphemistic. And just when it was needed, such a new phrase made its appearance. In July of 1845, an editorial in *The United States Magazine and Democratic Review* declared that it was America's "manifest destiny to overspread and to possess the whole of the continent which providence has given us for the development of the great experiment of liberty and federated self-government entrusted to us" (Editorial, 1845).

Such high-flying bluster had opponents, among them Henry Clay and Daniel Webster, who regarded the looming Mexican War as a ploy for conquest. Abraham Lincoln, a freshman in Congress, called it immoral and a threat to the nation's republican values. And the cosmopolitan abolitionist Charles Sumner saw the annexation of Texas as "our original sin." In an 1847 speech, he thundered against the Mexican War as follows:

> A war of conquest is bad; but the present war has darker shadows. It is a war for the extension of slavery over a territory [that] has already been purged by Mexican authority from this stain and curse. Fresh markets of human beings are to be established; further opportunities for this hateful traffic are to be opened; the lash of the overseer is to be quickened in new regions; and the wretched slave is to be hurried to unaccustomed fields of toil. It can hardly be believed that now, more than 1800 years since the dawn of the Christian era, a government professing the law of charity and justice should be employed in war to extend an institution that exists in defiance of these sacred principles (Sumner, C., 1847, p.333).

John Quincy Adams didn't mince words either. He attacked anti-Mexican stereotypes and the conflict in Texas as early as 1836. He vehemently opposed the war and all efforts to drive the U.S. into a fight on the side of slavery. Indeed, the backward Mexicans had already abolished slavery in 1810, while the new Republic of Texas (and soon to be U.S. Texas) reestablished it in 1836. Two years later, during a filibuster in June and July of 1838, Adams spoke every morning against the annexation of Texas in the U.S. House of

Representatives. Still, Texas was finally taken into the Union in 1845—as a slave state. The war with Mexico was to follow soon.

Other U.S. dissenters denounced that war as aggression against a poor and weakened country. Gaining independence from one's colonial overlords and building a new society is a hard and exhausting job, and Mexico was not yet done with it. In the U.S., the Northern opposition argued against the Southern planters and their support for the military campaign. Yet, despite the voices raised against it, Manifest Destiny caught on. The slogan didn't have the detested imperial connotations. It sounded celestial. And what's more, putting it to use as a cosmetic make-up kit made the concept fairly unassailable. All of a sudden it was possible to paint a piously pretty face on covetous appetites. Such political masquerades were nothing new, but one must search far and wide to find one done with so much innocent panache. With the help of the new concept, all the annoying little blemishes on the skin of the republic could be covered up.

Why waste time? In August, only a month after Manifest Destiny was coined, the New York Herald had it on the highest authority that "the multitude cry aloud for war."

There was one especially demanding war-promoting segment: The secretive so-called Know Nothings (who always insisted they knew nothing when questioned), active since the 1830s, were associated with Protestant revivalism and turned their fury primarily against Catholic Irish immigrants but also against Germans, those G—d—Dutch. Deutsch was difficult, so it became 'Dutch.' In 1844, riots broke out in Philadelphia, and violent attacks occurred elsewhere. It was a major goal of this faction to deny naturalization and voting rights to newcomers for the first 21 years of residence. Considering the hardships many immigrants faced, that would have put the more unfortunate safely into their graves before they were eligible for citizenship.

Nativist movements seem to appear in cycles, again and again, and like flu viruses in ever- changing mutations. They are ugly, but perhaps comprehensible up to a point. In the 1840s, those who had come earlier now had to face a footloose multitude sweeping into America's fast-growing cities, or across the land. Earlier arrivals had also fled from religious, political, or economic trouble. They had coped with their own hardships and now felt that they had earned a bit of stability and peace, especially in the aftermath of the 1837 financial panic.

Boom times led to a speculative fever primarily in western land deals and on May 10 of that year, banks stopped payment in gold and silver coinage. Trust in banknotes (paper money) evaporated, unemployment soared, more than 40 percent of all U.S. banks failed, and six years of a deep recession followed. When it was finally over, the flood of starving and destitute Irish arriving in the so-called coffin ships was near its crest. But with the Naturalization Act of 1790 stipulating an open border policy and stating that "any alien, being a free white person, may be admitted to become a citizen of the United States," there was little Americans could do legally to stem the flood.

During the first decades of the 19th century, many of the German immigrants were Catholics. They came mostly from the southwestern and western regions of the country. Frederick Zeh didn't fit this profile: Born in 1823, he was a Protestant from the proud imperial city of Nürnberg which, so far, had yielded few persons leaving for the United States. Frederick's father was a minor administrator employed by the Bavarian government and his grandfather was a small publisher. Frederick grew up around books, received a good education, and was apprenticed to learn the bookseller's trade. Apparently his family was well established, so why did young Frederick leave? Especially since one of the numerous how-to-guidebooks published in Germany warned prospective immigrants that there was little American demand for people trained as book dealers? Was life too sedate at home? Was Zeh eager for adventure? No one knows, but judging from his activities after the Mexican War, the fellow had no *Sitzfleisch:* He couldn't sit still for long, or stay in the same place.

Things were rough for Frederick after his arrival. He soon ran out of money and took a job as a farmhand near Philadelphia. At the start of his skillfully translated memoir (the first book-length account of this conflict written by a German-American that was recently published in English), titled *An Immigrant Soldier in the Mexican War,* Zeh (1995) wrote in his characteristic satirical tone:

> "Love of my new homeland was definitely not the reason I became a
> soldier, because the bitter experiences of my six to seven months stay in
> the United States certainly instilled no patriotism in me. Homeopathy
> drove me to it!" (p. 4)

In fact, young Zeh had been terribly hungry. He sometimes fainted, subsisting on minute "homeopathic," meaning tiny food rations while doing chores and caring for the horses of a doctor of homeopathy who had helped him earlier during a bout with malaria acquired while working along the Delaware River. The good doctor, however, turned out to be "a homeopath in every way" and Zeh couldn't bear his empty, growling stomach any longer. He needed a job that could feed him. The only opportunities available at this time of a general economic downturn were with the military. So Frederick changed his mind. Hoping to get enough to eat, he enlisted with the regular army in a newly-formed Mountain Howitzer and Rocket Battalion bound for the Mexican War. He became a simple laborer in the service of the big guns. He would find himself often enough in the thick of combat. Signing up with this unit put him on the cutting edge of military technology at the time: artillery. It was artillery and the innovative mobile use of it in flying batteries that helped to win the war.

Already in his new uniform, Zeh was stopped on the street in Philadelphia by another German who said to him: "Aren't you ashamed to fight for these natives, who treat us worse than blacks?!" (Zeh, 1995, p. 5). Well, perhaps. But all this couldn't stop a young man from having a bit of fun along the way. Boarding a ship in Baltimore together with civilian travelers, Zeh was delighted two discover two young German female harpists among them. "Warriors of every epoch have been distinguished by their gallantry toward the fair sex," he explained, "so it was inevitable that we would promptly follow in our ancestors' footsteps" (Zeh, 1995, p. 6).

Later, when he began to wonder what would happen in the campaign, he talked to himself, calming his mind with a verse from *Fridericus Rex,* an old marching song:

So adieu, Louise, dry your tears;
Of bullets have no fears.
For if bullets strike your man,
Where would kings get their soldiers then? (Zeh, 1995, p. 6)

It was a strange army. It had a meager total of 8,613 men scattered across the already huge expanse of the United States, and of those only about 6,000 wore the uniform. It had experienced and hardened officers who had seen action as early as the war of 1812, then during some of the Indian wars, and after that in the long and bloody campaigns against the Seminoles (1816–1818; 1835–1842) and the runaway slaves who found refuge with them in the swamps of Florida. The younger officers, among them the first crop of West Pointers (or "Academy Turks"), served in the Mexican campaign and subsequently gained fame or high office during and after the Civil War. Some of these men would later fight on opposite sides and face each other as enemies. Two participants, 'Old Rough and Ready' General Zachary Taylor, Commander of the Army of the Rio Grande, and Ulysses S. Grant, future commander of the Union armies in the Civil War, would become presidents of the United States: Taylor in 1849, and Grant in 1869.

To fight against an estimated Mexican force of 30,000 to 50,000, the army had to grow fast. It did, before and during the war, until it peaked at about 104,000 men. They served either as regulars or as volunteers. The latter were a subclass of militia raised by individual states. Militia could only serve for 90 days. This was much too short a time for training and a campaign in a foreign country, so Congress authorized the creation of a volunteer force. It could be employed for one year, and this was ultimately adjusted to cover the duration of the war. Overall, more than 73,000 volunteers participated.

In this U.S. Army, there was little contact between officers and men. It was customary to know one's place, and to stay there—as if the military revived some remnants of feudalism from bad old Europe or was, at the very least, heavily class-conscious. The pay for privates was seven dollars per month, too low a remuneration to attract scores of Americans. As a consequence, many of the enlisted men and even some of the non-commissioned officers were foreigners. The same was true among the volunteers. Although they were recruited by the states, the composition was, as one sarcastic account put it, the greatest medley ever congregated in one regiment during the War ... New York, for example, enlisted rejected boys, men who were diseased and broken down, some lame and blind in one eye, others were 60-year-old boys ... among them were gentlemen from the Tombs, ragamuffins from Blackwell's Island, Alms House, and a sprinkling of "Five Pointers"; and a more rascally, lousy set was never thrown among decent men (Smith & Judah, 1968, p. 20). The regiment that was so described assembled about 800 volunteers. Of these 300 were Americans, and the rest were English, Dutch [German], Irish, Polish, Swedish, Chinese, and Indian.

Further south in North Carolina, recruits were tempted to join with enticements such as these:

> If you go, you will get to see the whole Southwest, with the expense incident to traveling. And you will doubtless, independent of your common wages as soldiers, receive a handsome bounty of the choicest lands. Why do I say so? Why, because Mexico will have the expense of the war. She has no money, but she has lands: hence California, New Mexico, &c., will have to pay the forfeit of Mexican madness and barbarity (Smith & Judah, 1968, p. 14).

At this point, I catch myself shaking my head: The sales talk of war repeats itself again and again. America always fights the good fight, exclusively against bad guys and barbarity. The U.S., the shining example of modernity, follows in the footsteps of very old Greeks and Romans who used to call all foreigners barbarians—meaning "babblers." Amazingly, an immigrant society like the U.S. entertains little regard for alien languages and can slip into such a hostile attitude without even trying. Anyway, for all the caterwauling about Mexican madness, let me just say that I have now lived here in New Mexico next to Hispanics, Mexicans, and Native Americans for many years, and I haven't detected any collective barbarity among them yet.

Back in 1845, recruitment methods were persuasive. A bonus of wages for three months and a set of new clothes lured unemployed men to sign up. Many did it for the sake of their families. This was a time without any social safety net for people in distress. The pauperized, also labeled the dangerous classes, were on their own. That's why the extra 21 bonus dollars represented the honey that attracted destitute men like flies. It could help their wives and children to survive. On the other hand, young men without family had nothing much to lose: They responded to the prospects of escape in their own fashion. They fell for the unabashed advertising of "roast beef...., and plenty of whiskey, golden Jesuses, [and] pretty Mexican gals" (Stevens, 1999, p. 32).

It wasn't easy to forge an instant army from an untamed bunch of recruits. One officer, Capt. John W. Lowe of Company C, Fifth Regiment of Ohio Volunteers, recorded his trials and tribulations while traveling on the steamer Trenton to the Gulf of Mexico. He explained that his "duties are very complicated ... I have 80 wild, thoughtless, careless boys to look after" (Smith & Judah, 1968, p. 44). Was it condescending to call the prospective canon fodder "boys," or was it simply a customary way of talking about young and old soldiers at the time?

Alexander Konze, a German volunteer from Wisconsin, wrote about conditions from an army private's point of view. He let off steam during the trip down the Mississippi, irritated about inconveniences such as extreme heat, bad crowding in steerage, and nothing for thirst but warm river water. To him, the conduct of the higher officers was appalling. "Our worthy superiors," Konze informed us, who but recently possessed a knowledge of military science as limited as could be expected from an honest Philistine, seemed at least have fixed the idea into their heads that the common soldier is a being far below those whose woe or weal does not merit any particular attention. These gentlemen enjoyed life in the saloon (qtd. in Smith & Judah, 1968, p. 45).

Yes, it was a bizarre army, containing an extremely mixed lot of men. It tried to keep hatreds, tensions, and rebellion against bigotry under control by the strictest and harshest discipline. Apart from raw recruits, it had many experienced and well-trained veterans in its ranks. Some of the Irishmen had served under the British in India, South Africa, and Afghanistan, while the Germans had fought against Napoleon. None of these skilled soldiers had ever seen human beings being branded like livestock.

It was an army that punished: In addition to hangings and execution by firing squad for serious offenses, it branded, flogged, and tortured its soldiers, sometimes for the slightest misdemeanors. In the British, French, and Prussian armies, drunkards were incarcerated or dishonorably discharged. In the U.S. Army, repeat offenders were branded like human cattle, with the letters "HD" for *habitual drunkard* burned onto the forehead, or with a "W" for *worthless* singed into the face. All this was done with the screaming wrongdoer bound on hands and feet, held down by soldiers, and in full view of his comrades, who were ordered to witness the procedure.

Among the other punishments inflicted was "riding the wooden horse," a verdict handed out for mere trifles like a stain on one's uniform, or a less than perfect step during drills. As Peter F. Stevens (1999) described it in his book *The Rogue's March,*

Officers routinely put men atop a high, sharp-backed saw horse. I saw a drawing of such an instrument of punishment as used by the British in 1760. Sadly, our progressive U.S. military, strengthened by an enlightened Constitution, had been unable to resist the importation of such archaic means of disciplining troops. The offenders sat on the narrow beam of the contraption for hours on end with their hands bound behind their backs and with iron weights chained to their feet. If they crashed to the ground, as many did, guards forced them to remount. Some, according to an immigrant, could not: the fall broke their necks (p. 49).

Also popular was the torment of bugging and gagging: The soldier had to sit on the ground with his knees drawn up to his chest, arms clasped around them. His wrists were bound, and wooden sticks were fastened under his knees and over his arms. Then he was gagged and left to suffer many hours of excruciating pain, rain or shine, and during the hot months under a merciless southern sun. Additional niceties included repeated near-drownings while being bound hand and foot, hanging by one's wrists or even from one's thumbs on a rope from a tree or pole, imprisonment in dark, dug-out holes underground without a blanket and with a daily ration of only three crackers and some water.

Isolated incidents? Apparently not. Many offenders in their various agonizing constrictions were placed all over the parade grounds and camps, with the rest of the troops doing their marching and their daily routines around them. There is no shortage of documents, letters, and reports about the appalling conditions within the U.S. Army during the Mexican campaign. An infantryman from Pennsylvania wrote home:

> We are under very strict discipline here. [Some of our] officers are very good men, but the balance of them are very tyrannical and brutal toward the men. They strike men with swords and abuse them in the most brutal manner for a human being to be treated ... Tonight on drill an officer laid a soldier's skull open with a sword (qtd. in Stevens, 1999, p. 51).

A Scotsman, George Ballantine, observed in his book *Autobiography of an English Soldier*, published in 1853, that

> The barbarous treatment [that] foreign soldiers ... received from ignorant and brutal officers and non-commissioned officers on that campaign, were I to relate it in minute detail, would seem almost incredible ... In fact, such a bad state of feeling seemed to exist between men and officers throughout the service that I was not surprised that it should lead to numerous desertions (qtd. in Stevens, 1999, pp. 285–286).

It was a period without photographic evidence. Mexican pamphlets and American punishment led to the highest rate of desertion ever experienced by the U.S. military. Soldiers went 'over the hill' in droves. Among regulars, nearly 13 percent deserted: about 1000 Irishmen, 445 Germans, and 457 other Europeans (Stevens, 1999, p. 3). Slaves working as servants also deserted their officer-masters and fled to Mexico, and freedom.

The Mexican government and its generals published various tracts to win the hearts and minds of immigrant soldiers serving in the U.S. Army. These broadsides stressed that the war was unjust and that Mexico had no quarrels with the nations of Europe, or the people of the United States. An early example, published on April 20, 1846, by General Mariano Arista at Matamoros, invited soldiers to come to Mexico, where they would be embraced as "true friends and Christians." This is an excerpt from this particular proclamation:

> Soldiers! You have been enlisted in time of peace to serve in that army for a specific term, but your obligation never implied that you were bound to violate the laws of God, and the most sacred rights of friends! The United States government, contrary to the wishes of a majority of all honest and honorable Americans, has ordered you to take forcible possession of the territory of a friendly neighbor ... The North Americans are ambitious, overbearing, and insolent, as a nation, and they will only make use of you as vile tools to carry out their abominable plans of pillage and rapine ... In the name of justice, honor, and your own interests and self-respect ... Abandon your desperate

and unholy cause, and become peaceful Mexican citizens (qtd. in Stevens, 1999. Pp. 106–107).

One story with a German angle comes from Puebla. During General Scott's occupation of the city, officers heard reports about a tall, blond, neatly dressed man who handed German-language leaflets to immigrant soldiers serving in the U.S. Army. The flyers were collected, and in June of 1847, the watchmaker Martin Tritschler, tradesman, Mexican citizen, and captain in the city's National Guard was arrested. His trial began a day later before the American Council of War. He was accused of spying and of instigating desertion by distributing leaflets. Both charges were punishable by death.

A crowd of Mexican civilians gathered at the gates of the hacienda where the trial was held. They waited for Tritschler's verdict. He was popular. He had fought valiantly at Cerro Gordo, where the Americans annihilated his unit. Seriously wounded, Tritschler had managed to drag himself back to the city. The watchmaker didn't deny the charges. He was sentenced to stand in front of a firing squad. The crowd went wild when it heard the verdict. U.S. soldiers armed with bayonets managed to disperse the shouting and cursing residents of Puebla.

Before he joined the military, General Scott studied law. The agitation of Puebla's 80,000 inhabitants and the creation of a martyr was not something he desired. Only a day after the sentencing, petitions came rolling in—neighbors and acquaintances pleaded for Tritschler. The city's bishop also visited Scott in person with the same purpose in mind. A week later, General Scott announced that the condemned man had shown "signs of partial insanity in jail, and the court, in all good conscience, could not stand an addled man in front of a firing squad" (Stevens, 1999, p. 227). The general had found a way out of an explosive situation: Tritschler was set free. He "recovered" very quickly from his sudden bout of "mental illness" and lived happily ever after in Puebla. The townspeople cherished him as a brave man. Two of his sons became Mexican archbishops.

Contributing factors to the desertions were not only the verbal abuse and the physical cruelty meted out to the foreign-born soldiers. In addition the men had to endure blatant legal discriminations, especially if they were Irish or German. Europeans, which, for example, furnished about 47 percent of the manpower in Taylor's army, received routinely far harsher sentences than native-born soldiers—for the same offense. An example of the two kinds of military justice is given in the cases of Irish-born sergeant James Bannon and U.S.-born private George Miller. Both men were court-martialed for drunkenness and verbal threats against officers. Miller, the American, was sentenced to 50 lashes, imprisonment until war's end, a fine, and dishonorable discharge. Bannon, the Irishman, was executed in front of a firing squad (Stevens, 1999, p. 53).

In stark contrast to the widespread mistreatment meted out by a youthful U.S. officer corps, Old Rough and Ready General Taylor, aged 62, was cut from a different cloth. Although he came from a slave-holding southern family, he prevented numerous floggings of soldiers and paid special attention to punishments given to immigrant soldiers. Perhaps the culprit acted not with unruliness, but simply had an insufficient knowledge of the English language. As told about one incident, a huge Irishman failed to obey an order given by Taylor. The general walked to the soldier and grabbed his ear—this was called "wooling." The private brayed, and angrily knocked Taylor down. After a shocked silence, several officers drew their swords. Many expected that this would be the end for the offender. But Taylor, guessing correctly that the man had not understood the order, staggered to his feet and shouted: "Let him alone! He'll make a good soldier" (Stevens, 1999, p.55).

Frederick Zeh (1995) wrote one of the surviving accounts on General Winfield Scott's amphibious landing with 12,000 men near Veracruz and his subsequent advance to the capital along the same route taken by the first conqueror of Mexico, Cortés. Bloody battles had to be fought before U.S. forces reached and occupied Mexico City.

Throughout his chronicle, Zeh (1995) managed to maintain a pleasant, and often ironic tone. He displayed no hatred. He takes his time to describe

FIGURE 10. *The Battle of Cerro Gordo.*

the beauty and fertility of the countryside, the appearance and manners of the Mexicans, and the architecture of cities and towns.

After the army's entry into the city of Jalapa, there was a long wait for quarters and provisions, and a pressing awareness that belts had been tightened down to "the last notch." The troops had gone through a stretch of deprivation. But when the commissary wagon finally arrived, there was nothing to be had except a pound of flour per soldier. There was no salt, no fat. Some of the men broke into a rage and flung their flour across the floor. A few soldiers tried to make gooey dumplings or pancakes. For want of anything else, they used the stumps of candles as cooking grease. Zeh mused about the lack of foresight and planning that condemned the men to go without food. This was not the only breakdown of supply lines during the campaign. Young Frederick was on homeopathic mini rations again and again. He was upset about the flour ration just like the others. He threw his away in disgust.

Enter Hermann Kessler, best buddy, and "an educated soldier from Germany" (Zeh, 1995, p. 39). Hermann had a plan. They had no money; plunder was prohibited (although it happened frequently enough, particularly as a sport of the disorderly volunteers); and the army couldn't feed its own—so the way out was to find a nice enemy family willing to invite two ravenous invaders for dinner.

The friends walked to the outskirts of town, chose a fine building, entered lovely gardens through a gate, admired stables housing spirited Andalusians, and then encountered the rapidly- speaking owner of the estate. He didn't look happy. Frederick and Hermann spoke no Spanish. What to do? Use universal language: Hermann pointed to his mouth and Frederick rubbed his stomach. The Mexican's frown disappeared like a cloud from the face of the sun. He bowed and guided them to an elegant room in the main house. They were shown to a table. It was soon decked with cold foods and bottles of wine. Seated next to his guests, the host tasted a morsel of every dish and sipped from the wine first, probably as a way of demonstrating that the delicacies were free of poison. The two friends feasted like gods in France. After the meal, cigars were presented. Finally, not wanting to impose any longer on the their gallant host, they took their leave in a sequence of mutual bowing maneuvers.

I have no idea if the narrator embroidered this incident. Perhaps he did, but if so, it doesn't diminish the quality of his description. Zeh was able to maintain a light touch throughout the story, even when he dealt with the severe and painful experiences of that war. The affair of Kessler's insubordination provides a good example. The droll undertone reminds me of Jaroslav Hasek's *The Good Soldier Schweik,* which was written later—in the 1920s. It was published in the U.S. during the Great Depression. On the other hand, the good soldier Zeh was no shirker (Schweik was), and neither was Kessler. The account tells us how Kessler's initiative rescued "the battery from certain annihilation" (Zeh, 1995, p. 63). And Zeh himself apparently had a similarly enterprising spirit in battle, which earned him the thankful shouts of his superior. Not much is made of it. The men were doing their jobs without fanfare. The inflationary use of the word "hero" was not one of Zeh's habits.

But back to events in Jalapa. After their return to the battery, Kessler was ordered to report for guard duty. He asked his pal Zeh to tell the non-commissioned officer that as of now, he, Hermann Kessler, regarded himself as "freed from all obligations toward the United States" (Zeh, 1995, p. 40). The good-natured NCO wants to know what he was talking about. Zeh was reluctant to translate. He tried to persuade his pal. But Kessler insisted. So Zeh related that his comrade refused to serve any longer. Higher ups were called to deal with the reasons for insubordination. Assisted by Zeh in the role of interpreter, Kessler listed them:

> First, inadequate provisioning without extenuating circumstances; second, breach of contract in the matter of remuneration, which was supposedly due every two months and was now four months in arrears. Finally, he pleaded to be brought before a military court to present his grievances (Zeh, 1995, p. 40).

The officers were nice about it, asked Kessler to drop the whole thing, and told him to report for duty. It didn't work. The captain in attendance asked who should be held responsible for these grievances, and the soldier on strike had the gall to answer that he thought that he, the captain, was responsible. So the officer gave the order to put Kessler in the buck for the night. "Kessler," Zeh (1995) indicated, "accepted this cruel punishment in the best possible humor" (Zeh, 1995, p. 41). He didn't budge. He was trussed like a chicken for roasting, but somehow managed to get rid of parts of the rope when no officer was around to watch him. He then spent time "drawing caricatures of his tormentors" (Zeh, 1995, p. 41).

After a few days, the captain returned to inquire again. Kessler remained as firm as before. The punishment increased: Now the German's thumbs were bound together and he was hoisted up on a tall pole. His hands turned dark blue after a few minutes. The captain was furious and leaves in a huff. The stubborn soldier was taken down and dumped back into the guardhouse. Additional days passed. Then the mother hen of an NCO came to Zeh and ordered him to tell Kessler that the battery would get its outstanding four months of pay today, and that all would be forgiven and forgotten if Kessler resumed his service. But the attempt to persuade failed again until, on a hunch, Zeh started "singing an aria from *Freischütz: Kartenspiel und Würfellust* [game of cards and lust for dice]", etc. As a result, Kessler tore on his ropes, jumped up, was freed and, as the tallest person, marched at the head of his company to the paymaster. Each soldier in the ranks received thirty-six dollars. As if by a stroke of magic, Zeh (1995) told us, "Our situation now assumed a different character. Nothing but joy reigned in our quarters" (p. 41).

FIGURE 11. *Plucked, or the Mexican eagle before the War! The Mexican Eagle after the War! Published in Yankee Doodle, May 15, 1847.*

It all was a profitable undertaking: Mexico lost 500,000 square miles of land while the victor conquered and annexed (oops, "bought") Nevada, New Mexico, Arizona, California, and parts of Colorado and Wyoming. Lt. William D. Wilkins put it as follows:

> We do not want Mexico. Its annexation to our country would be productive of far more evil than good, but if we want to close the war we must commence a new system. We must teach them, that if we are just, magnanimous and liberal, we know, also, how to be terrible. Impose crushing contributions, burn every town that offers resistance, blow up their churches and take no prisoners, and they will humbly sue for terms (qtd. in Smith & Judah, 1968, p. 442).

———

And indeed, under their banner of green silk, with its Mexican coat of arms on one side and the words *Erin go Bragh* (Ireland For Ever) embroidered under a harp on the other, the deserters who had formed the renegade San Patricios fought like devils, and to the last. No white flags for them. They knew what would happen to those taken prisoner, and it did. Fifty men were sentenced to death by hanging. Fifteen others, among them the leader of the San Patricios, John Riley, had deserted shortly before the war began. Therefore, according to the law, they could not be executed. They would receive fifty lashes with a rawhide whip, and a "D" branded on their cheeks.

Scott's officers were unhappy that Riley escaped the death penalty, and they hoped the rawhide tails would kill him. Being whipped by Americans was too good for him, so a Mexican muleteer was hired to do the job. The general in charge, Twiggs, offered a monetary bonus if the flogging of the deserter ended in death. And they didn't singe just one "D" on Riley's cheek, but two. The first one was upside down, so a second branding was administered. It was only then that the bloody lump that was Riley cried out and fainted.

General Scott pardoned five deserters, among them John Brooke, 16 years old, and David McElroy, 15 years old, because army recruiters had enlisted these underage youngsters without their parents' knowledge. One German immigrant, Henry Neuer, was also pardoned. He served as a stretcher-bearer for the San Patricios and had not fired a single shot.

The hangings were exemplary in vengefulness and cruelty. The convicted men were made to wait for death, standing on carts with their heads in nooses for hours, until another battle was won and an American flag was hoisted up on the tower of a castle. One deserter was missing among the condemned: the dying Francis O'Connor. When told that the man had just lost both legs through amputation, the commanding general gave orders to the surgeon to "bring the damned son of a bitch out!" The unconscious O'Connor was carried to the place of execution, dumped on the driver's bench of a wagon, and fitted with a lengthened noose to compensate for the missing legs.

—

It was the American republic's first war of conquest, and it concluded with the first occupation of a foreign country. In addition, it was acknowledged as a "total" war by Dr. Stetson Conn, Office of the Chief of Military History, Department of the Army. Conn prepared a staff support project for the White House liaison officer, which listed "Examples of Total War from 149 B.C. to 1945 A.D." For the more than 2000 years up to 1945, only 17 examples of total war are given. They started with the Third Punic War, which ended with the complete destruction of Carthage and the killing of 90 percent of its population (149–146 BCE); they concluded with World War II. The selected conflicts were broken down into wars of extermination, wars rendering the enemy incapable of self-defense, and knockout wars. The Mexican War is listed as a "knockout" total war, which led to a complete defeat for the Mexicans (Conn, 1968).

As far as wars go, it was a costly conflict even for the U.S. About 13% of U.S. forces, or nearly 14,000 servicemen, died during the campaign from combat and disease. Between 800 and 900 men had to be left behind in Texas field hospitals even before the fighting started. More troops perished from digestive and respiratory ailments, measles, mumps, typhoid, yellow fever, scurvy, and malaria than in battle. In the end, the U.S. Army suffered the highest mortality rate ever experienced in a war. Now, if I were cynical, perhaps I would say that many of the lowly fighting men were immigrants, and therefore believed to be expendable. But I think that's not the answer. The Army was simply unprepared and inexperienced.

I had not known a thing about the Mexican War except for a date. But dates have no story. I recall how my daughters would come home from school after social studies classes, flipping through their pasteurized textbooks, and groaning that this stuff was simply too boring. I looked at the books and agreed. But, oh, if you started to dig, how exciting and complex it would get!

To me, the most perplexing element of the 1846–1848 war is its excessive anachronistic religious intolerance interwoven with a ferocious racism. It is tiresome to present documented views from the time—there are so many to choose from. They become almost overwhelming, especially for someone who has been schooled, in postwar Germany, in accordance with the ideals of the American Enlightenment, the Bill of Rights, and the U.S. Constitution. We were educated to fear and despise racism, which seemed to be the particular vice and the terrible crime of our Teutonic fathers and grandfathers. We were sensitized to detecting and rejecting every sign of fanaticism and prejudice. If you absorb such things during your childhood, it is difficult to let go later. I could not, and did not, wish to get rid of them after I moved to the United States and became a citizen.

So what should I learn from a man like Edward D. Mansfield, an officer serving in the Mexican War, who portrayed the conflict as the struggle between two races? To him and assorted others, it was the 'mission' of the Anglo-Saxon race to conquer the savage and make the New World the home of democracy and economic progress. And what can you teach the inferior race of the Mexicans (who had already outlawed slavery) if you bring your own personal black slaves with you as servants during the war?

And how about these comments from the *Philadelphia Nativist*? "Providence intended the New World for the Anglo-Saxon. If Mexico should oppose the decree of Heaven—so much worse for Mexico!" (Slotkin, 1994, p. 176).

Compared with such hallowed humbug, sold as a direct decree from heaven, Brigadier General William Worth sounded almost refreshing, and for once free of bombast and baloney: "Why [does] Mexico matter? Have not our Anglo-Saxon race been land stealers from time immemorial and why shouldn't they? When their gaze is fixed upon other lands, the best way is to make out the deeds" (qtd. in Stevens, 1999, p. 28).

And let's ask: What do you teach to the foreign immigrant soldiers who are putting their lives on the line in an American war if you force them to attend Protestant services even though they happen to be Catholics?

9

Blümner's New Mexico

Between 1821 and 1848 this was Mexico, and in the late
1800s to early 1900s New Mexico was made up of *abuelitos*
who were born Spanish citizens, parents born Mexican
citizens, and children born American citizens.

—*Daniel Aragon Ulibarri, Santa Fe New
Mexican, February 27, 2000*

On March 24, 1836, just days before he joined a Santa Fe Trail wagon
train bound for New Mexico, Carl Blümner wrote to his mother in
Prussia from Warren County, Missouri. He tried to reassure her that his
continued wanderings were all in day's work:

I myself used to believe that having found a home here in a far corner
of this endless North America; that I would put down my walking
stick, saying 'this far and no further!'— But I am picking it up anew,
will try it again, ever onward in the good wide world; God's dear sun
shines everywhere; His hand guides us everywhere! ... Well! Anyhow!
The journey itself is actually a trading venture to a distant Spanish
province, Mexico; southwest of here ... This wagon train leaves here
every year in the month of April and returns in October or November.
Up until now no one has made the journey but Americans; last year

however a German went along for the first time; a Swiss fellow by the name of Sutter; now, after his return, several Germans are joining him, since he is a clever man of good character, one you can believe and trust, also because we have known him for a long time (qtd. in Kamphoefner et al., Helbich, & Sommer, 1991, pp. 99–100).

Blümner couldn't foresee that this man was the same Johann Sutter who would gain Gold Rush fame when the yellow metal was found on his California land at Sutter's Mill. In his long letter, Blümner told his mother that he had decided to become a merchant because he couldn't earn very much as a farmer in a sparsely populated region. Rural Missouri, in the mid- 1830s, was still a remote place. To survive, one had to have help and be married, but there were hardly any eligible young women in the county where he had purchased his land.

So finally Blümner decided to rent out his farm to a friend and appoint his brother, August, likewise a farm owner in Missouri, as his legal agent to keep an eye on things. Yes, more than half of the long haul on the trail would cross uninhabited land. But not to worry, it was no longer as dangerous as a few years ago. Some Indians would probably come to the caravan, but these days they usually approached to trade, not to fight. And later at the Spanish [Mexican] border, the caravan would be met by Spanish [Mexican] cavalry, which would guide it to Santa Fe. Some 150 or more men planned to take the trip, and with them would be 16 Germans,

all well acquainted, among them older experienced men; as well as two doctors ... Well!—My beloved mother! Perhaps, if I am lucky, I can make enough money to venture a trip to Germany; then I would be happy enough with my fate; then my deepest wish would be fulfilled! Farewell, dearest mother! Farewell, dearest sister and brother Fritz! Farewell, my loved ones! Give my best to mother Bismark ... Your true son forever/ Carl (qtd. in Kamphoefner et al. et al., 1991, p. 101).

Carl Blümner was 31 years old when he arrived in Santa Fe during the summer of 1836. Earlier, his group of immigrants, called the "Berlin Society," had sailed from Hamburg in 1832, the year Goethe died. The 14 travelers, all friends and relatives, arrived in Baltimore on September 10. Among them were the Baron von Martels with three sons, the brothers August and Carl Blümner, and Wilhelm von Bock, portrayed by those who knew him as a pleasant eccentric with a taste for utopian dreaming. Shortly after reaching Warren County, Missouri, an area highly praised in the widely read Duden immigration guide published in Germany, the group purchased "a very nice farm with a stone house, liquor distillery, mill, and the entire harvest for $1,600" (qtd. in Kamphoefner et al. et al., 1991, pp. 96–97). That's how they started out.

Two years later, the members had all acquired their own properties and some of them lived the good life as so-called "Latin Farmers," a nickname given to immigrants who knew more about the classics, ancient languages, arts, and music than they did about nitty-gritty farming on the prairies.

⁓

Daily life had never been easy in New Mexico, and it certainly wasn't undemanding when Carl Blümner arrived in Santa Fe. As his advance description in the letter to his mother notes, he traveled in an annual caravan of covered wagons along the trade route of the Santa Fe Trail across a 1000 miles of wild prairie and rugged mountains to the old capital city on the northern frontier of New Spain. Founded in 1609, it now had 3,000 residents and belonged to the newly independent country of Mexico.

Various descriptions of Santa Fe survive. Each one is based on subjective impressions and most didn't paint a glowing picture. Reporting back to Mexico City, exasperated Spanish colonial officials residing in their mud-palace in the city occasionally called the northern province "this miserable kingdom." One British gentleman and member of the Royal Geographical Society expressed his disdain in even stronger terms:

The appearance of the town defies description, and I can compare it to nothing but a dilapidated brick-kiln or a prairie dog town. The inhabitants are worthy of their city, and a more miserable, vicious-looking population it would be impossible to imagine. Neither was the town improved, at the time of my visit, by the addition of some three thousand Americans, the dirtiest, rowdiest crew I had ever seen collected together (qtd. in Twitchell, 1963, p. 275).

These Americans were the volunteers in General Kearny's Army of the West. We will meet them again a little later.

—

The earth-colored clay dwellings strewn about the high desert along a little stream at the foot of the Sangre de Cristo Mountains must have been a strange sight if you came from Missouri, or per chance even from northern Germany, like Blümner.

Recently, embedded journalists traveling with the U.S. Army in Afghanistan and Iraq described local dwellings in these countries as "mud houses" or "mud huts," just as their forebears did when they first came to New Mexico on the Santa Fe Trail. This trading route was opened in the early 1820s after Mexico gained its independence. And indeed, how could anyone anticipate that these simple and unpretentious adobe (from the Arabic *atop*) buildings of old Santa Fe would transmogrify themselves, toward the end of the 20th century, into the *Santa Fe Style* with its highly sought after multi-million-dollar trophy homes for the rich and famous? Today's updated mud-huts provide numerous photo opportunities for glossy magazines.

When Blümner came to town, everything was made from local earth, and in good time it would return to earth. I have seen various old adobe walls that slowly melt under the breath of sun and the touch of rain. Curiously enough, they don't look broken down or decaying; they look as if caressed and softened by the elements. So no matter what newcomers reported about Santa Fe, there must have been an air of gentle antiquity about this mud-made place. After all, the practice of using adobe construction goes back for 9,000 years. Wherever the climate is dry in Asia, Africa, or even in Europe (Rhone Valley), adobe architecture can be found. If kept in good repair, it lasts for a long time. And the process is environmentally practical: Adobe stays warm in winter and cool in summer. Sun-baked mud-bricks insulate well, resist fire, and walls made from it can be molded and sculpted like clay under the hands of an artist.

As it happened, when the Spaniards brought the technique with them to the American Southwest it had traveled full circle: The native peoples here knew it and had already used it for centuries. Despite its humble outside appearance, the interiors of aged adobe buildings can be comfortable, well appointed, and even elegant in an understated way. Anyone who inspects the oldest public building in the United States, the 17th century mud Palace of the Governors on the Santa Fe Plaza, can attest to that. It's gorgeous.

Apparently, Carl Blümner took to Santa Fe and Santa Fe took to him. He stayed on despite intermittent bouts of home sickness. In the beginning, he may have felt like someone who is stranded, didn't have the means to venture further, and couldn't return to Missouri either. But that changed. A letter written in April 1838, again to his mother, described his life and activities. Yes, he had written to her twice, but one letter was lost when one of his friends, a German, was robbed and killed by Indians on the trek back to the United States. The trail wasn't all that safe after all. The second letter had also disappeared. He had no clue what had happened to it. Mail could be sent or received only once per year, with the caravan. In the past, New Mexico's contact with the outside world depended on the wagon trains of goods coming north from Mexico City on the ancient *Camino Real*, the King's Road. Now, during its Mexican period, the increasingly important lifeline of the Santa Fe Trail stretched out in the other direction, to and from Missouri in the United States.

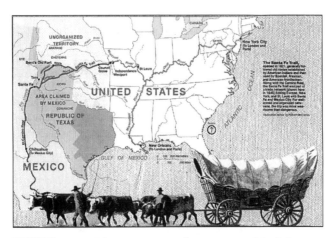

FIGURE 12. *Map of the Santa Fe Trail, US National Park Service.*

Blümner's early letters are fairly long. He takes advantage of the rare opportunity of communicating with his family. Each dispatch provides a window that lets us catch glimpses of New Mexico as it was in the 1830s. Conditions had grown unsettled and daily dangers faced the residents. Hardships were nothing new for this perpetual frontier province, but lately things had deteriorated badly. Nomadic Indians attacked incessantly.

His hopes for profitable trading dashed by economic turmoil, Blümner adapted himself quickly and tried to earn a living by gold mining. He and his partner produced some of the yellow metal by small-scale mining in the area, but then the other man fell ill and left. Unable to do the job alone, Blümner had to return to Santa Fe. Credit was given to him by some Americans who knew him. He opened a little store and a wine tavern. Now he did well, and soon added a billiard table. But just as things looked up, there came another bump in the road.

Northern New Mexico farmers rose in the Chimayó rebellion, protesting against taxes imposed by Mexico. The Governor, Don Albino Perez, tried to crush the uprising but lost. He was killed, together with various other officials. As Blümner put it in a letter: "They carried the mutilated bodies right past my door to the churchyard!" (qtd. In Kamphoefner et al., 1991, pp. 102–103). The rebels occupied Santa Fe briefly, and voted for their own governor, José Gonzales. He was the first elected, and the first Indian leader of the state. But the insurgents were soon defeated.

After the turmoil, the resourceful young Prussian entered the Chihuahua trade and traveled south into Mexico on the same old Royal Road that was first broken in by Juan de Oñate, his settlers, horses, and cattle in 1598. Although it followed the course of Indian foot paths (how else could one find a way through this wild, enormous land and survive?), the *Camino Real* became the first real European highway in America. It was something like a New World Silk Road. And, despite the fact that a caravan came only every three years to Santa Fe, the connection was all-important. Tools, seeds, the wheel, iron, writing, print, silks, and other contributions from Europe or even the Far East (goods from the Philippines arrived in Acapulco) traveled north on this thoroughfare. The round trip, with a rest period, required more than a year and a half.

The road remained a vital link even after Mexico gained independence. And very soon, with the addition of the Santa Fe Trail extending northward, one could travel 2,800 miles from south to north, and vice versa. Prior to the railroads, this was the longest highway on the entire continent. American traders took advantage of this new opportunity almost immediately, and Blümner was among them. After his return he continued to work on growing his business in Santa Fe. He now earned a sufficient income. He would stay for another year, he wrote to his mother. And then, if all went well, he wanted to return to his beloved family. He signed the latest letter with "your true son forever and ever" (qtd. In Kamphoefner et al. 1991, p. 103).

1841 still finds him in Santa Fe, still longing for home. He gets mail and letters from Prussia through his brother in Missouri. Sometimes he even receives newspapers—which are old papers by the time the caravan arrives. It doesn't matter: they feed his imagination. In a March 1841 letter to his sister he spins yarns about speed, knowing that this or that steamship has gone from England to *Neu* York in the unbelievable short time of 12 to 14 days. In my mind, I see myself transported to *Neu* York! I go on *bord* the mighty ship! Fly across the enormous ocean in 8 to 10 days! Land in Liverpool! In 2 or 3 days, I'm in Hamburg! From there—But halt! I'm traveling too fast! You laugh at me, dear Hannchen! You laugh at my somewhat overly swift fantasy!! (qtd. in Kamphoefner et al., 1991, p.105).

I also laugh—about the abundance of explanation marks in that letter. When Blümner was a boy, Germany found itself firmly embraced by Romanticism, although I don't recall the heavy use of such icons of emphasis among the poets and writers of the period. To me, it seems that the venturesome Blümner simply followed his heart, reaching out for his far-away home. Going out into the world doesn't mean that you will cease to love what you left behind, and that you won't miss it. Living in an era of high-speed communications, with emails and texting reaching their recipients instantly anywhere around the globe, it is difficult for us to slip into the shoes of earlier travelers, immigrants, and explorers who removed themselves completely from contact with the societies they knew.

We always hear about the millions of immigrants who came to the United States, but we know little about the emotional or intellectual price they paid. And how many of those who came decided to return to their countries of origin? Perhaps Blümner was only talking, but he was certainly tempted to go back to Prussia. When his sister Hannchen asked him why he had lived so long "in this country," he answered: "Circumstances and situations; business deals and wishing and hoping to earn next year that which was lost in the year before, or even more" (qtd. in Kamphoefner et al., 1991, p. 106). I don't know when Blümner started to call himself Carlos Blümner, but he did so sometime during these 'Mexican' years, and continued to do so until another change came to New Mexico, to its language, and to his name.

While Generals Zachary Taylor and Winfield Scott did battle in Mexico, a force called the Army of the West under the newly promoted General

Stephen Watts Kearny marched from Fort Leavenworth, Kansas, to Santa Fe, New Mexico. It had a company of dragoons, artillery and infantry units, and a regiment of 860 mounted volunteers commanded by Col. Alexander Doniphan. Traveling for nearly 1000 miles during the hottest months of the year across rough terrain soon made many of the troops feel sick and exhausted. Some wagons were used as ambulances, and they quickly filled up with incapacitated men. The degree of disease and suffering among U.S. troops stands in stark contrast to gung-ho Wild West imagery propagated by popular culture.

Fortunately, the tired troops didn't have to fight. Kearny took possession of Santa Fe on August 18, 1846, in a completely calm and peaceable manner. It was the first American conquest of a foreign regional capital, and up to this point not a shot had been fired during the invasion of New Mexico. The Army of the West had entered villages and towns, and an eyewitness account can serve as an example of how it was done. One of the general's soldiers recorded the conquest ceremony for the village of San Miguel on the Pecos River, not far from Santa Fe (Smith & Judah, 1968, pp. 115–117).

To initiate the proper formalities, the general required the presence of the *alcalde*, the administrator and judicial official of a community. The word comes from the Arabic *al-gadi*, meaning the judge. The *padre* was also invited. Once found, these local dignitaries showed little enthusiasm for Kearny's request: the new authority in the land wished to address the people from the flat roof of one of the mud houses. The *padre* was quicker and made the first speech to the villagers. The general interrupted him, saying that he had no time for useless remarks. Then the general stood on the roof and talked down to the people.

He told them about his superior force, and that he would take possession of the country, period. Resistance was futile and also unnecessary because the United States had come to offer friendship and protection. The same assurances couldn't be given to the government of Mexico, but they would be given to the people of New Mexico for the safety of their lives, property, religion, and their security against the cruel attacks by Indians.

After he finished his speech, General Kearny said: "Mr. Alcalde, are you willing to take the oath of allegiance to the United States" (qtd. in Smith & Judah, 1968, p. 116). The writer of the account put no question mark behind this sentence, so it comes across more like an ultimatum and less than a question. The alcalde, quite reasonably, replied that he wanted to wait a little longer, or at least until the capital city of Santa Fe was in the possession of the Army of the West. The general wouldn't hear of it. Perhaps he had indeed something of an ultimatum in mind because he told the alcalde that it was sufficient for him to know that the U.S. Army had taken possession of his village. The alcalde asked if he would be protected in his Catholic faith, and the general confirmed his freedom of religion.

The alcalde then swore allegiance to the government of the United States of America. Next, General Kearny informed him that he could continue in his office and that the inhabitants of the village should obey him as before. For the moment, the old laws would remain in effect. Any changes needed would be made for the benefit of the population. This happened some time later: the new version of the law became known as the Kearny Code.

Somehow, all of this reminds me of an affair that occurred 60 years earlier, in 1786. The main characters were the Spanish governor of New Mexico, Juan Bautista Anza, the Comanche leader Ecueracapa, and a cast of about 200 Comanche warriors. Anza, an uncommonly capable military strategist and administrator, managed to do what no one had done before him: he made a lasting peace with the fierce Comanche. It released New Mexico from years of bitter and relentless hostility. One of the most important ingredients in laying the foundation for that peace was Anza's readiness to respect the Comanche, their customs and rituals, and their sense of honor.

In her essay "Historical Lessons on Anza Day," Patricia N. Limerick beautifully sketches the scene: Anza lends his own ceremonial cane or staff of office to the Comanche leader; he participates "comfortably and wholeheartedly" in rituals and ceremonies of both Indian and Spanish origin; during the peace treaty accord Anza gave Ecueracapa "a banner and a saber," and the governor watched "graciously while the Comanches engage[d] in their ritual of peace, digging a hole and then ceremoniously filling up the hole, thus burying the war" (Limerick, 2000, pp. 122–123).

"Perhaps most strikingly," Limerick continues,

> Anza was a hugger. Anza embraced Ecueracapa; and on one remarkable occasion, in the midst of peace negotiations, Anza hugged and was hugged by 200 Comanche men in succession. Think about this. It is fairly time-consuming to shake hands with 200 people, but picture about 200 men hugging, in a row, and men representing quite a different culture from your own (Limerick, 2000, p. 123).

That's the point. Anza didn't waste his energies on hateful rhetoric and condescension. He didn't blast the Comanche as evil, nor did he call them savages and barbarians. He understood the simple gesture of acknowledging the dignity of the "other" as a man, however much the cultures differed. Humboldt would have liked that. I don't think he had heard about Anza, but he would've appreciated the individual and his deeds.

This brings to mind the fabulous habit of our television media to shun foreign heads of state during their visits to the White House. As one might expect, the American and the foreign leader make an appearance for the press. The cameras dwell for split seconds on the image of the foreign guest, leave quickly, and then focus almost exclusively on the American president. The photo opportunity has been arranged for the visitor in the first place—but he is cut off and out. (Even if that's not the cameraman's doing but is decided by the editors at the networks, the effect is detrimental). The reporters have the chance to ask a few questions. But what is later shown on the news is barely related to U.S. foreign affairs or to the visitor's country. Instead, it will usually zero in on the latest domestic scandal in the U.S.

The same ill-bred approach is used if the press corps travels abroad with the president. Compared with the diplomatic skill and polish of the lowly governor of a Spanish frontier province, Juan Bautista Anza, today's methods fail the test. What are the costs of such "coverages" to the American taxpayer?

Foreign embassies, diplomats, and their staffs will certainly watch and analyze what happens during a U.S. presidential meeting with one of their political leaders. And if this cavalier treatment of foreign dignitaries by the American broadcast media has been going on for years, what will be the result? Will it increase respect and goodwill for the United States?

Staff Officer Lt. Richard S. Elliott described the August 18 capture of Santa Fe to *The St. Louis Reveille*: "Our poor horses, tired beyond measure, had no hope of a single blade of grass to stand between them and starvation. Well—supper or not—here we are in Santa Fe—AND NEW MEXICO IS OURS!" (Smith & Judah, 1968, p. 123).

The good soldier Elliott reported that the army marched into the city "extremely warlike, with drawn sabers, and daggers in every look." Compared to some other observers from the far north, this officer had imagination and a certain sensitivity. "Strange, indeed," he wrote,

> must have been the feelings of the citizens when an invading army was thus entering their home—themselves used only to look upon soldiers as plagues sent to eat out their substance, burn, ravage, and destroy—all the future of their destiny vague and uncertain—their new rulers strangers to their manners, language, and habits, and, as they had been taught to believe, enemies to the only religion they have ever known. He seemed to detect a "wail of grief" rising from the city's 'gloomy-looking buildings' " (Smith & Judah, 1968, p. 123).

Fortunately, Lt. Elliott didn't have to witness the brutal treatment given to the Catholic immigrant soldiers who served in the other two campaigns of the U.S. Army down in Mexico.

~

On September 22, 1846, General Kearny announced the "Organic Law for the Territory of New Mexico." It was a nine-page document, commonly called the Kearny Code. The first paragraph stated: "The government of the United States of America ordains and establishes the following organic law for the territory of New Mexico, which has become a territory of said government" (Avalon, 2007).

It was that simple. Kearny, who was authorized by the president of the U.S. to arrange matters for the government of New Mexico, appointed officers to serve in the new territory. The signing of a peace treaty was to follow later, in 1948. In the meantime, also on September 22, 1846, Charles Bent was appointed governor, and Charles Blümner treasurer. Seven additional officers were selected, and of those only two had Hispanic names. The salaries each of the officers would receive were specified in the Kearny Code. The treasurer's remuneration was $500 a year, half of which was to be paid by the U.S. Treasury, and half by the territorial treasury. Blümner was one of a small circle of foreigners living in Santa Fe at the time of the invasion and takeover.

With New Mexico quiet and in possession of a new legal/political code, General Kearny prepared to rejoin the war. With new orders from the Secretary of War, William L. Marcy, he departed Santa Fe in late September, bound for California. A difficult desert trek lay ahead before the general was in a position to help the U.S. Navy with the conquest of that state.

—

An almost unnatural tranquility pervaded New Mexico at the time of the conquest. People had driven their livestock into the mountains, hidden their belongings, and kept quiet. After all, being on alert and without comfortable security had long been their way of life. It kept the inhabitants of this remote frontier province on their toes, and it helped them to outlast numerous crises. Yet the smooth surface during the take-over was misleading. Within a few weeks and months, troubles began to congeal. Perhaps one can't expect anything else during an occupation. Even President George W. Bush, a man without many doubts, remarked at one occasion in 2004 that he wouldn't like it either if his country were occupied.

It didn't help that harvests and food supplies were insufficient to satisfy the tremendous demands made by the Army of the West. New Mexico had always experienced years of partial crop failure due to the climate. Sometimes the monsoon rains came, sometimes they did not.

Things began to deteriorate steadily. A young member of the Corps of Engineers, Lt. Jeremy F. Gilmer, had sharp words to say about troop behavior in Santa Fe. He reported in early November of 1846:

> All the boys here are volunteers, numbering more than 1,700 men— and a sweet set of boys are they. All do as they please, and demonstrate to the Spaniards daily, that they belong to the freest and 'smartest people in creation.' The men are about as good as their officers—none have learned enough of military matters to know that they are ignorant (qtd. in Smith & Judah, 1968, p. 127).

Gilmer acknowledged that some improvements had been made: More guards were posted, and a gunshot announced the daily 10 p.m. curfew. Throughout the night no one was allowed on the streets without a special permission. It was hoped that these restrictions could reduce the rabble rousing, street fighting, gambling, and drinking that had plagued the old city since the arrival of the invasion army. But apparently it didn't work. A reporter from the *St. Louis Era* wrote: "When [Col. Price was] in command here the place was a perfect bedlam; no order in the streets and public places—no discipline among the troops—everything at loose ends" (qtd. in Smith & Judah, 1968, p. 133).

And if that wasn't enough, the men who arrived after Kearny and Doniphan departed were often sick. Some had malaria; others came down with tonsillitis, measles, fevers, or dysentery. By late October 1846, up to eight men died per day. Homes were turned into hospitals. They were soon full. There were now 2,700 volunteers in Santa Fe, with more arriving during the late fall. Supply shortages plagued the few medical officers on duty. They were unable to control the surge of illnesses, especially since some of the men didn't even have shelter. Located at an elevation of 7000 feet, the city grows cold during the winter. One soldier wrote in his journal: "A great mortality prevails among the troops who are dying from exposure and disease" (qtd. in Gibson, 1974/1935, p. 125).

~

The quick and decisive replacement of age-old laws by the Kearny Code was impressive. It took only a month to discard much of New Mexico's customary way of handling things into the dustbin of history. In due course, the Treaty of Guadalupe Hidalgo between the United States and Mexico was to follow. Both countries signed it in February 1848. It put an end to the war and included various protections for the inhabitants of New Mexico who had, through no initiatives of their own, been transformed from inhabitants of New Spain to citizens of Mexico and then to residents of a territory annexed by the United States. All this happened within a timespan of little more than a generation. It must have been a bewildering experience. Two views of the world met, represented by different traditions of law. One view had coexisted for centuries with the Civil Law Tradition (also known as the Roman-Germanic legal system), the other evolved from the Common Law system of England that provided the foundation for American law.

Roman law was based on the *Corpus Juris Civilis*. It was codified from the widely scattered rules of ancient Rome during the reign of the Emperor Justinian in the sixth century CE. The code honored three principles: living honestly, injuring no one, and giving every man his due. Sounds ideal. As societies changed, scholars, reformers, and jurists tinkered with the details of the code, adapting it to new conditions. The *Corpus* served as the basis for the legal systems of Continental Europe and its former colonies. It is also found in Quebec, and, partly, in Louisiana.

English Common Law began to evolve in the eleventh century and was not based on a written code, but instead on decisions made by judges in the royal courts. It is a system based on "precedent" or judge-made law. If a judge set a precedent with a case, then all the similar cases that followed stood on the shoulders of the first case, and so on. Experts say this way of proceeding permits a fair amount of flexibility when a society is faced with changing situations.

Common Law became the bedrock for the legal systems of England, Wales, Ireland, the colonies of the British Empire, and for the United States. In addition to the Panama Canal Zone and Guyana, the legal systems of all the former Spanish possessions annexed by the United States experienced the sudden conversion from Roman Law to Common Law: this happened in Florida, Texas, California, and also in New Mexico—which initially still included Arizona and other parcels of the West.

~

The problem was that New Mexicans didn't comprehend the strange system of law that was imposed upon them. In 1847, Fernando Aragon of Taos wrote to Acting Governor Donaciano Vigil: "It is my bad luck to have been appointed sheriff because I do not understand these laws. Please teach me to understand this new code" (qtd. in Sunseri, 1979, p. 43).

Far from New Spain's center of royal power in Mexico City, New Mexicans had truly lived on the Frontier—and not just during short periods of settlement activity, but for centuries. They had long shown a large degree of independence and self-reliance. Surrounded by often hostile nomadic Indians and an untamed, mountainous, and by and large arid land, they had no other way of surviving. Their sense of self-worth and honor was highly developed, and never mind that American rhetoric presented the invasion as an encounter between "barbarism and civilization," and the Hispanic population as an "alien and inferior people" (Sunseri, 1979, p. xvi).

For example, one well-regarded justice of the peace, Desiderio Baca, preferred to resign rather than live with the loss of face. He had made a decision as a judge. It was reviewed and invalidated. As he was accustomed "to the dictates of an independent mind"—his own, he decided to leave his office. The office should not be made a "laughingstock" (Sunseri, 1979, p. 43).

Among a number of incidents, another one stands out. There was a little military chapel in Santa Fe that had served as a place of worship for troops when New Mexico was a province of New Spain and then of Mexico. However, at the onset of the American occupation it was confiscated and used as a depot to store arms. In 1851, the American commander at that time, Colonel E. V. Sumner, removed the military hardware and turned the little church over to Judge Grafton Baker for use as a courtroom.

People gathered and protested "the desecration of their sacred edifice. Tearful women kneeled and kissed the floor of the holy place, and when the grand jury was summoned, many refused to take the oath in the converted courtroom" (Sunseri, 1979, p. 44). One very old man in Santa Fe said to an interviewer on August 10, 1968, in Santa Fe: "If they had but given us twenty years to learn their customs before forcing them on us we would have been better prepared to protect ourselves" (Sunseri, 1979, p. 44).

But this was not the American way. We know for certain that our system, our law, and our democracy are best.

—

The conquest of New Mexico had been easy, but the occupation was difficult. Discontent spread. The first uprising was being planned in December of 1846, but it failed. Secrecy was not tight enough: Col. Price received word of the conspiracy. Most of the rebels were apprehended, yet the leaders, Diégo Archuléta and Domingo C. de Baca, were able to escape. A month later, northern New Mexico rose up in open rebellion. At dawn on January 19, 1847, insurgents came silently into the town of Taos, combined forces with locals, and attacked. It was a cold winter day; snow covered the ground. People woke up from the noise of gun battles.

Charles Bent, appointed as the first civil governor in 1846, had not listened to warnings suggesting that he remove himself and his family to safety in Santa Fe. He firmly believed that no peril would touch him because he was a friend of the people and was firmly rooted in northern New Mexico. In the detailed report written by Army Headquarters in Santa Fe by Colonel Price on February 15, 1847, he stated that Bent,

> this valuable officer, together with five other persons, were seized ... by the Pueblos and Mexicans and were murdered in the most inhuman manner the savages could devise. On the same day, seven Americans were murdered at *Arróyo Hondo,* and two others on the Rio Colorado ... It appeared to be the object of the insurrectionists to put to death every American and every Mexican who had accepted office under the American government (qtd. in Twitchell, 1963, pp. 291–292).

One of those killed was Simeon Turley, brewer of a notorious beverage called "Taos Lightning." Highly prized by mountain men, trappers, and other males of the species, the fierce brew was once used in a performance called "shooting the cup." One trapper wanted to demonstrate his loyalty to a friend, so he put a cup of the drink on his head and told the other to shoot it down. It is unlikely that this stunt was copied from Friedrich Schiller's play *Wilhelm Tell,* which features the shooting of an apple from a boy's head.

During the next two days, the revolt spread to almost all of northern New Mexico. The U.S. Army used heavy artillery to put the rebellion down. On February 1, the town of Mora was leveled to the ground. A few days later it was the turn of Taos Pueblo, where 150–200 rebels were killed, both Hispanics and their Indian allies. Many of them had fled into the pueblo church to find protection behind its massive adobe walls. New Mexico's mission churches were built like fortresses, and had long served as the last places of refuge in times of trouble.

What followed was swift and rigorous punishment. In Taos, the leader of the rebels, Pablo Montoya, was sentenced quickly by drumhead court martial and hanged on the day after the battle. Judges Houghton and Beaubien then came from Santa Fe to Taos and indicted various captured revolutionists for murder and treason. An eyewitness recorded his impressions of the court sessions, the sentencing, and the executions.

It certainly did appear to be a great assumption on the part of the Americans to conquer a country, then arraign the revolting inhabitants … After an absence of a few minutes, the jury returned with a verdict of 'guilty in the first degree'—five for murder, one for treason. Treason, indeed! But so it was; it was deemed expedient to hasten the execution, and the culprits were sentenced to be hung on the following Friday—hangman's day. When the concluding words—*muerto, muerto, muerto*—dead, dead, dead—were pronounced by Judge Beaubien, in his solemn and impressive manner, the painful stillness that reigned in the court-room, and the subdued grief manifested by a few bystanders, were noticed not without an inward sympathy (qtd. in Twitchell, 1963, p. 306).

On the day of execution, soldiers and clergy in long black gowns gathered on the edge of town where a scaffold had been set up. Escorted by soldiers, "The miserable victims marched slowly, with down cast eyes—arms tied behind, their heads bare, with the exception of white cotton caps, fastened on behind, to be pulled over the face at the last ceremony" (Twitchell, 1963, p. 307). There was an absence of men. But many women and children stood silently, waiting to witness the proceedings. There had been no Taos hangings in living memory. Only Pablo Montoya, the rebel leader, had been executed a short while earlier. The prisoners were marched up to the scaffold. A wagon with two mules stood under it. The prisoners had to climb up. They were placed closely together, almost touching each other. The ropes had been soaped but were still stiff. They were put around the men's necks. The crowd was silent. Then the doomed men said a few last words.

Only one said [that] he had committed murder and [therefore] deserved death … The one who had been convicted of treason showed a spirit of martyrdom worthy of the cause for which he died—the liberty of his country … His speech was a firm asseveration of his innocence, the injustice of his trial, and the arbitrary conduct of his murderers … The last words he uttered between his gritting teeth were *"Carâjos, los Americanos"* (Twitchell, 1963, p. 309).

There were 21 public hangings. The last execution occurred on August 3, 1847. A number of other revolutionists were apparently harshly flogged and then released. As he pronounced the sentence in one of the trials, this one held in Santa Fe against Antonio Maria Trujillo, Judge Houghton said to the defendant:

> It would appear that old age has not brought you wisdom, nor purity, nor honesty of heart. While holding out the hand of friendship to those whom circumstances have brought to rule over you, you have nourished bitterness and hatred in your heart. You have been found seconding the acts of a band of the most traitorous murderers that ever blackened with the recital of their deeds the annals of history ... You gave your name and influence to measures intended to affect universal murder and pillage, the overthrow of the government and one widespread scene of bloodshed in the land (qtd. in Twitchell, 1963, p. 303).

The prisoner, 75 years old and head of a prominent family, was sentenced to death by hanging. Petitions were send to Washington, pleading for clemency. Congress asked President Polk for clarification. Had anyone been put on trial for treason against the United States while New Mexico was occupied by the U.S. Army? And if so, "by what authority of law was such a tribunal established?" (Twitchell, 1963, p. 303). The president replied that civil and criminal jurisdiction had been established by the military officer in command, and that the offenders deserved their punishment. The error consisted in naming their crimes "treason against the United States" (Twitchell, 1963, p. 303). The president didn't grant a pardon, but did ask the acting governor of New Mexico, Donaciáno Vigil, to do so. Trujillo's life was spared.

During the trials, New Mexico was occupied. It was not yet a Territory of the United States. The condemned men fought against a foreign power that had invaded their country. So how could the U.S. indict some of them as traitors? Later, on February 2 of 1848, Mexico and the United States signed the Treaty of Guadalupe Hidalgo. It ended hostilities and made New Mexicans, due to no action of their own, subjects of the United States. Or, as a familiar local saying has it, they suddenly became strangers in their own land.

—

So there was Blümner, another stranger and a voluntary New Mexico resident, one among a small group of men that had drifted south on the Santa Fe Trail and took root in Santa Fe. After General Kearny completed his conquest of New Mexico, he appointed Blümner to the office of treasurer. The Prussian was a product of the Vormärz, of the German pre-revolutionary period after the defeat of Napoleon at Waterloo and the ordering of affairs at the Congress of Vienna. Europe's monarchies managed to survive the threats of both the French Revolution and Napoleon. It is understandable that they did everything possible to arrange for their own continued existence. But this restoration of the old order drove many freedom-seeking young men from the Continent. Blümner was probably one of them. He came to America because he had a positive view of the United States, its form of government, and its promise for the future.

I wonder how Blümner coped with the sudden tremors triggered by General Kearny's occupation of New Mexico. Caught in the turbulence of events, perhaps the newly appointed treasurer didn't have the time or the opportunity to think much about such weighty matters.

Despite the fact that Secretary of State James Buchanan called the draft "a carefully considered ultimatum" (Ebright, 1994, p. 29) in 1848, the Treaty of Guadalupe Hidalgo finally was signed, and New Mexico was formally annexed by the United States. Blümner may have felt reassured and hopeful. The agreement was supposed to protect the rights—and among them especially the "property of every kind" of New Mexico's Hispanic population. Article 10 stipulated that land grants were to be regarded as legally binding if they had been valid under Mexican law. However, the U.S. Senate deleted this important Article 10 high-handedly from the Treaty before it was ratified. As a consequence, things didn't work out as planned for New Mexico's people. Blümner must have been aware of this.

⁓

In the summer of 2004, I saw the Smithsonian Institution's traveling exhibit *Corridos sin Fronteras* [*Ballads without Borders*] at the National Hispanic Cultural Center in Albuquerque. These Spanish ballads evolved into a vibrant form of folk poetry, social commentary, and storytelling. Mexican and New Mexican oral historians-musicians created the *corridos* to tell the tales of their people's honor and triumph, defeat and sorrow, bravery, betrayal, compassion, and determination. There was one called "New Mexico, How Much Longer?" performed by Robert Mondragón and recorded in the field by Enrique Lamadrid, Santa Fe, in 2000. It is long, has 22 stanzas, and tells what happened in New Mexico after the U.S. annexation. These are a few samples in the English translation:

> Now the years have passed
> and with generous hearts,
> we have opened our doors,
> and thieves have entered.
> We granted them shelter
> and they stole the mattresses.
> They broke the treaty
> and kept the lands for themselves.
> When we gave them a hand
> they ripped off our arm,
> they ripped off our arm,
> and kept the land for themselves.
> *Chorus*:

New Mexico, how much longer

will your misfortune endure?

The foreigner riding high

and our children in the dust,

and our children in the dust,

New Mexico, how long? (Smithsonian, 2002, pp. 54–56)

⌒

The Anglo-American or Common Law Tradition and the Spanish/Mexican or Roman-Germanic Civil Law Tradition clashed when New Mexico came under U.S. rule. Both were based on differing philosophies and visions of social organization and community life. As we have seen, Common Law evolved after the Norman Conquest in medieval England and was based on the decisions reached by the King's judges. These judgments acquired the cumulative force of precedent, of setting examples that the course of the law followed thereafter. And as the American eagle extended its wingspan from sea to shining sea, former areas of the Spanish Empire were also converted to the Anglo-American tradition of doing law.

In contrast with the English Common Law, the laws of the Spain came from the Civil Law practices of Roman law. Codified in the sixth century during the reign of Emperor Justinian, the *Corpus Juris Civilis* (or: *The Digest of Justinian*) became the foundation for most of continental Europe's legal systems. It has three parts: The Digest, the *Institutes,* and a textbook. As the *Corpus* explained,

> The study of law consists of two branches, law public and law private.
> Of private law, then, we may say that it is of threefold origin, being
> collected from the precepts of nature, from those of the law of nations,
> and from those of the civil law of Rome (Moyle, 1896, p. 3).

There seems to be an international tinge in the paragraph. It referred to "law of nations," not just one nation. It also referenced the laws of nature, which gave much work to do for generations of scholars. In the 14ᵗʰ century, reformers began to pay attention to the evolving principles of science; they asked questions about the "natural rights of man" and attempted to define the just society in which humans would prosper.

The legal system of New Spain and Mexico was also based on the *Digest of Justinian* and was aimed to support the community, while the Anglo-American common law was more oriented towards individualism and personal initiative. To indicate how this worked we have to go back to the Reconquest, when Spain struggled to retake the peninsula from the Moors. During this period the kings of Castile tended to reward soldiers with parcels of land for their service. But such grants were also made to towns and communities. These *tierras concegiles* became the private property of a community and would be used for the good of a particular village or town. The community could grant land plots to residents for their private use: to build a house, establish a garden, or plant an orchard. These lots were held in simple fee, and could eventually be sold, bought, or inherited.

In addition to these settlement plots, the community also reserved land as common property. It was used for recreation, as pasture for livestock, as hunting, fishing, and gathering terrain, and for the cutting of wood. Everyone in the community had access to these lands, and it didn't matter if the individual was poor or rich. The theory behind these arrangements held that the bounty of the common land was created by nature, and men had no hand in it. Such a view was, incidentally, relatively closer to Native American beliefs. The common land couldn't be sold or bought, nor could the benefits derived from it be burdened by taxes.

What we have here is Roman law directly from the *Institutes* of Justinian: It's called *usufruct* and means that the citizens of a community hold a share in the common lands, can profit from them, but individually they are unable to sell their share—for example in the form of watering rights, grazing rights, wood harvesting rights, and so on. It is important that the Treaty of Guadalupe Hidalgo was supposed to protect all types of property rights in New Mexico, and this included such community land grants as well as water rights. Here in

New Mexico the common lands were known as *ejidos*, or *montes*. King Philip II of Spain, son of Charles V, had very specific ideas about the founding of new towns in the Americas. He decreed:

> "A commons shall be assigned to the town of such a size that although the town continues to grow greatly, there will always be sufficient space for the people to go for recreation and for the cattle to be pastured without causing damage" (qtd. in Meyer & Brescia, 1998).

In addition, the care and handling of water in an arid land received meticulous consideration. When the Spaniards arrived, they found that Native Americans living in the pueblos along the Rio Grande were already old hands at irrigating their fields and garden plots. The Spanish, on the other hand, had learned much from the Moors who turned parts of Andalusia into a garden. Then, in 1513, came Gabriel Alonso de Herrera, often called the father of modern agriculture, with his book *Obra de Agricultura*. Familiar with his teachings, the first Spanish settlers in New Mexico were so concerned about proper irrigation that they tended to dig a community mother ditch before they worried about shelter or the construction of a church.

Out of the fusion of Arab, Spanish, and Native American knowhow grew an elaborate and practical system of water management. The elected position of *mayordomo*, or ditch boss, was proudly respected. This man acted as the keeper of the *acequia madre*, the mother ditch that controlled the delivery of water through sluice gates to individual farmers. Each spring, as they had done it for centuries, communities continued to band together to clean the ditches for another year's service. This well-functioning system of local self-government practiced by the *acequia* society was possibly the oldest type of democracy practiced by Europeans in the United States. Everyone had a stake in it, for without water and the fair distribution of it there could be no settled life.

If one looks closer at these realities, it becomes quite clear that the clash between two ways of life and two conflicting legal systems was not a minor matter. And who had the upper hand after the annexation of New Mexico?

Certainly not the local population. Hispanics were discriminated against. They also suffered massive losses of land.

The racist attitude of American opinion makers was widely shared. Hispanics were regarded as lazy, devious, spineless, good-for-nothing, superstitious, backward, and immoral members of a mongrel race. From such a charming estimation it was but a short step to contempt. As so often in American history, this was sold as a contest between "barbarism and civilization" (Sunseri, 1979, p. 93). Debates were held in Congress on the future of the acquired territory. Senator John C. Calhoun declared that

> Ours is the government of the white man ... The great misfortune of what was formerly Spanish America, is to be traced to the fatal error of placing the colored race on an equality with the white. This error destroyed the social arrangement that formed the basis of their society ... Are we to associate with ourselves as equals, companions, and fellow citizens, the Indians and mixed races of Mexico? I would consider such an association as degrading to ourselves and fatal to our institutions (qtd. in Sunseri, 1979, p. 99).

Senator Lewis Cass of Michigan voiced similar opinions. To him, the union of Mexicans and Americans "would be a deplorable amalgamation. No such evil will happen to us in our day. We do not want the people of Mexico, either as citizens or subjects. All we want is a portion of territory ... with a population [that] would recede or identify itself with ours" (Cass, 1848).

What mattered most was a real estate deal almost as big as half of Mexico.

～

As noted before, General Kearny appointed Carl (or Carlos or Charles) Blümner as the first U.S. treasurer in occupied New Mexico on September 22, 1846. At the time, only a few Germans had come so far south and west, and even fewer settled in New Mexico. Their numbers increased gradually, especially through the influx of Jewish-Germans who became prominent merchants. Among them were the Spiegelbergs, the Zeckendorfs, Bierbaums, Staabs, Ilfelds, and Seligmans.

Blümner became a Santa Fe resident when the province was still under Mexican rule, and the U.S. then recruited him for government service. That seems to be unusual, especially if one considers that this was a period of intense anti-immigrant agitation, Know-Nothing activity, and discrimination against Irish and German immigrant soldiers fighting for the U.S. Army during the Mexican War. Blümner's letters indicate that he held somewhat idealistic convictions about the United States. Perhaps this was known to Kearny, or perhaps the general simply made use of the talent at hand.

Apparently, Blümner had no racial obsessions. I didn't find any of the then-customary derogatory remarks about Hispanics and Native Americans in his letters. When the Americans came, he had already lived for a decade among the Indo-Hispanic population along the Rio Grande. He had an affinity with the locals and started a family. In a letter from Santa Fe dated October 31, 1852, he wrote to his mother:

> I've been married for about 4 years; my wife is a Mexican, the youngest daughter of a good but poor family; she is named Felisiana Quintana y Alarid. She is short on money, but she has a good heart and a noble character. She is pretty and about 26 years old. She presented me with a daughter as the first-born child, whom we baptized Carlota, (Charlotte). The little one grew to be a pretty, intelligent child until she was just 1 year old; then—she died! Oh mother, I can and will never forget my little Charlotte! She was my soul! (qtd. in Kamphoefner et al. et al., 1991, p. 113).

In the same letter, Blümner wrote that the couple now had a second child, a boy, "named Carlos, (Karl or Charles)." He was 15 months old, "a beautiful, lively, and intelligent boy" (qtd. in Kamphoefner et al. et al., 1991, p. 113).

It's a long, content-rich account, and in it Blümner tells his family that his brother August came to visit him in Santa Fe during the spring of 1849 en route to the gold mines of California. The Gold Rush was on. August stayed for only a few months, reached the West Coast, dug for gold along the Yuba River, fell ill with dysentery, and died four weeks later. Another German who worked with him sent word about his burial.

Charles was distressed about his brother's death, and worried about August's wife and children back in Missouri. He assured his mother that it would be his "sacred duty" to look after them. For the moment, Charles' wealthy brother-in-law had no family of his own, so he would most certainly take immediate care of his sister and her little ones. In a later letter, Blümner reported that this was indeed what happened: the young family without a father lived well protected with the brother-in-law. As for poor August, he had fallen on hard times even before he left for California and had soon lost his life in the pursuit of gold.

> "I myself, my dear mother," wrote Blümner in 1852,
>
> > have almost always been well in this country, since 1836; the climate here is one of the nicest, at least the healthiest, on earth ... My business here has almost always been as a merchant, about a year ago I gave up my trading company and am mostly employed in the service of the government. Since the United States of America took possession of this country, as a result of the war, as you all should know, since the year 1846, I have always had one or the other government post; Treasurer (Schatzmeister), Collector (Erster Steuereinnehmer), Vice Secretair (the second post next to the governor). The last two posts I had only for a time; the first one though, Treasurer, I have since 1846 and still have (qtd. in Kamphoefner et al. et al., 1991, p. 113).

He concluded the letter with urgent requests for political news about Prussia, Germany, and Europe. He wanted to know how things are after the recent uprisings and revolutions. He begged his mother to ask Rudolph to mail reports, which would certainly be much more accurate than those he sees in U.S. newspapers. I had to grin when I read this remark written a century and a half ago: the more things change, the more they stay the same. But fortunately, we creatures of the beginning 21ˢᵗ century have the Internet. We can travel in seconds around the globe and sample the world's news from credible (or so we hope) sources. Then we can compare.

⁓

Blümner was a census participant too: The 1850 Census for New Mexico has an entry for Charles Blümner in his own handwriting. And not long after the 1852 letter, on December 10, 1853, he took the oath of office as U.S. marshal of the territory. Funny: *Marshal* is a word from the Old High German. It means keeper of the horse. This position evolved under the Frankish kings to Marshal of the Cavalry, with the rank of knight and membership in the nobility. In its original meaning the word survived to the end of the Holy Roman Empire in the early 19ᵗʰ century. More recent times also produced the title of field marshal. Eventually, hereabouts a marshal became responsible for maintaining law and order at the court, and he could appoint deputies.

Due to the New Mexican resistance and the bloody uprising, civilian government had been replaced by military government for several years, until 1851. One can only imagine how difficult the life of the federal law enforcer was during the early American era. People didn't understand the new rules. Lawyers had been a rare commodity on the northern frontier during the Mexican period. To compensate for the lack of legal finesse, each party used to select an "*hombre bueno,* a good man, who acted as a lay representative and whose job it was to recommend a fair settlement to the *alcalde* hearing the case" (Ebright, 1994, p. 62).

Under American rule, such quaint practicalities were no longer acceptable. However, when Blümner, a man with a conciliatory disposition became a marshal, he lost no time in finding an Anglo deputy who was truly fluent in Spanish and knew the country customs and mores even better than Blümner himself. The deputy's name was Simeon H. Smith, and he was a frontier original who used to earn his keep as a quack healer and horse doctor.

Apart from the mental trials and tribulations, the job of U.S. marshal was physically demanding. It has been estimated that the lawman traveled at least a thousand miles on horseback, and that twice per year. He opened the spring and fall sessions of the federal court in person. It was a traveling court, with no fixed offices at various locations. From the start of the circuit, Blümner and members of the bar rode from Santa Fe to Taos to open the court in early March. At that time of year, it could still be bitter cold in the northern mountains, and the snow packs were often persistent. From Taos, Blümner rode to Chamita, and from there back to Santa Fe, then on to Albuquerque, Socorro, and finally down to Las Cruces. In the fall, he repeated the same itinerary. The *Santa Fe Weekly Gazette* announced each departure of the lawmen and that was a good, habit-forming practice since the federal officer and his deputies were by and large the only representatives of the new U.S. authority that were seen by the Hispanics and Pueblo Indians of the hinterland.

On May 15, 1857, Blümner, still serving as the U.S. marshal of the territory, wrote to his mother that he had no time to compose letters because "my duties are so extensive that I must travel 8 to 9 months a year and I am only home for 3 months" (qtd. in Kamphoefner et al. et al., 1991, p. 116). He was still dreaming of a visit with his family back in Germany, but as the years go by, the possibility seems to retreat ever more.

> I can not tell when I can come to see you; as long as I keep my present post it is not possible. My position here as Marshal carries great responsibility; I had to put up 20,000 dollars for the honest and exact administration and payment of the public funds of which I am in charge (qtd. in Kamphoefner et al. et al., 1991, p. 116).

By the fall of 1858, Blümner had resigned from his position as marshal. Being always on the road had taken its toll. He was no longer a young man. His fellow law enforcement colleagues honored him with the gift of a silver pipe in appreciation for a job well done. The governor could apparently not do without him and reappointed him as treasurer. His brother August's family in Missouri did well; the two eldest children were now married and lived on farms, the two youngest were still with their widowed mother. In Germany, however, there were losses. Three members of his family had died: his sister, Hannchen; his brother-in-law, Bismark; and his brother, Rudolph.

Blümner confessed to his mother that he often felt alone in New Mexico. He had always been too busy to give in to such thoughts, but now, with approaching age, they came to visit him. He missed his brother August. And who knows, perhaps he was aware of the ironies that governed his life: As a young man smitten with the zeal for freedom, he lost patience with the reactionary backlash that engulfed Europe after the defeat of Napoleon. He left and came to the republic of liberty, the United States. After a start in Missouri he moved to Santa Fe and witnessed soon enough the annexation of nearly half of Mexico by the United States. He also became an official in its service.

I wonder if he had any thoughts about these developments. Perhaps he now subscribed to a view similar to that of Whitelaw Reid, publisher of the *New York Tribune*, who regarded U.S. colonial policy as "the extension of ordered liberty in the dark places of the earth" (Crawford, 1992, p. 49). Some of the most amusing and instructive elements of our histories are woven from rationalizations. Governments fashion them into garments of camouflage. These can be worn on different occasions. In his essay *To the Person Sitting in Darkness*, Mark Twain sharply satirized our methods of bringing liberty and civilization to China and the Philippines. These days we call such efforts the spreading of democracy—if need be with the help of "shock and awe"— as prior to the invasion of Iraq in 2003.

In any case, around 1850, there were only 229 Germans in the entire vast Territory of New Mexico, which included parts of Colorado and Utah, as well as all of Arizona. The Territory stretched to the borders of California. If Blümner felt alone at times, he found solace in the company of his beloved surviving child, six-year-old Charles, whom he described as intelligent and innocent, with a good heart and an open mind. He promised to teach him German. English and Spanish he would learn in school.

This never happened. Little Karl didn't learn to speak German. He grew up to be the poor son of a well-off father. Why? It is interesting to speculate about the social decline of a New Mexico family, that of the German immigrant Charles Blümner and his Hispanic wife. Blümner died in 1876 at the age of 73. In 1860, liquid assets of $10,000 were recorded. In addition, his real estate holdings were valued at $ 12,000, although this fluctuated a bit. In any case, these were considerable sums of money at the time.

Yet when German relatives contacted Blümner's son Karl in 1904, he wrote to them: "I am not in good circumstances. I will tell you the true, I am poor" (qtd. in Kamphoefner et al. et al., 1991, p. 121). He requested that they please do not write in German to him again since he could not understand the language. He also apologized for his flawed English and explained that he generally spoke and wrote only in Spanish. The Census of the year 1900 listed him as a laborer. He was married to a Hispanic woman and apparently became, through his mother and his wife, a full member of Santa Fe's Hispanic community.

I have no idea what happened to Father Blümner's money. One of the bizarre shifts that can befall groups of people in the United States is briefly spotlighted in the story of the Blümner family. When the young Prussian came to Santa Fe in the late 1830s, he obviously adapted well to the Spanish life and culture of the province. He treasured his Hispanic wife. Then, not long after the U.S. acquisition of the territory, a reporter for the *Missouri Republican* stated in January of 1847 that Hispanics occupied "a station far beneath that of a Negro slave" (Sunseri, 1979, p. 102).

Many Americans had appalling attitudes towards "inferior" breeds. The Spanish had been more relaxed and less racially prejudiced. They gave a New Mexico land grant to a black man—as early as 1751. It became the mountain settlement of Las Trampas, and today it is home to one the most perfectly preserved Spanish colonial churches in the country.

The mood, the tone, and the economics changed during the territorial period. Even if Blümner, treasurer, U.S. marshal, and merchant, had once described his six-year old son as intelligent and innocent, with a good heart and an open mind," it meant little after the new American dynamics took hold. The newly acquired population had the chance to become American citizens within one year, and Blümner's little son probably became one.. And as Walter D. Kamphoefner et al. put it, "Although he was born an American citizen, the Spanish-speaking Karl Blümner had become a de facto member of an ethnic minority that experienced more discrimination than his immigrant father ever had" (Kamphoefner et al. et al., 1991, p. 121).

Still, Blümner the father had been lucky. If fate had made him an immigrant warrior in the U.S. Army further south in the Mexican War, his experiences could have been quite different. We have already looked at a few adventures of Frederick Zeh and his efforts to advance the cause of Manifest Destiny.

FIGURE 13. *Manifest Destiny—Spirit of the Frontier: Columbia, representing America, light from the East. Painting by John Gast, 1872.*

10
Scientific Gentlemen

Humboldt's ideas on the tectonics of the western U.S. influenced those who went to the field to inspect the geology in the SW United States until, and including, the Pacific Railroad Surveys in the 1850s. The Americans paid their debt to Humboldt by naming many physical features of the western U.S. after him.

—*Anke M. Friedrich (2002)*

Consider: the Spaniards held idyllic California for centuries, built missions, 'civilized' Indians, and let the world go by. Following his South-American explorations, Humboldt extrapolated and calculated where gold may be located in North America, but it wasn't found until the Mexican War was over and California, with all the rest of the Southwest, was annexed as a territory of the United States. The Peace Treaty ending the Mexican War, the European revolutions, and the California Gold Rush all happened during the same year of 1848. Humboldt was still alive.

Many people from Europe came to the United States, and by 1849, mobs of gold seekers were descending on California like a plague of locusts: "Westward the course of empire takes its way," wrote the good Bishop Berkeley in his verse on the *Prospect of Planting Arts and Learning in America*. That was back in 1726, and, indeed, the English expanded along the eastern shores of North America, while soon after gaining their freedom from their colonial masters, the Americans stretched themselves out to the Far West, to the Rio Grande and the Pacific.

They behaved, I can't help but thinking, much like their former colonial masters themselves. Suddenly the country expanded accross the entire continent. But this didn't do much good because it was dreadfully inconvenient to travel from the Atlantic coast to the Pacific coast either by ship around South America, or across an ocean of land from east to west. Something had to be done about it. Taking the land route, settlers and fortune seekers were forced to endure hardships with every step they made during their long, rough journey across prairie, mountains, and deserts to California. Today we call the vast interior the fly-over country.

I have found out quite a bit about the toil and trouble expended in developing America. It was a hard and mostly brutal job. Was it suitable for tales of purple prose? Mainly in hindsight. The pleasant gloss was applied much later, after the event. One marvels: How could the development be done at all? The obstacles, distances and setbacks were enormous. The climate was harsh. Bad weather could paralyze everything. Human life was cheap.

Under Stalin and his successors, Russia also struggled through a period of rapid development and massive industrialization; celebrating its heroes of labor and driving its workers (and prisoners) to slog on at breakneck speed; opening up the East and parts of the frozen North; building dams, railroads, factories, and infrastructure. Perhaps there are certain similarities between the early American and later Russian efforts to develop a continent-sized landmass.

In Russia, the rush and push forward was powered by governmental coercion, while in America most of the action was voluntary. Here, people were hungry for any opportunity. They took risks, setting out and spreading westwards, often outrunning their government. Topographical engineers serving with the military during the Mexican War had produced the initial written reports about parts of the unknown West. Among them was William

Hemsley Emory, chief engineer in the Army of the West under General Stephen W. Kearny. His accurate maps and descriptions of the Southwest were helpful tools for immigrants trying to make their way westward.

~

Congress began debates about the construction of a transcontinental railroad as early as the summer of 1848. For the mid-19th century, it was probably a project as ambitious and technologically challenging as going to the moon was a century later. Committees wrote reports and senators lobbied for the inclusion of their states and their cities in the grand railroad plans. Where would the line start? Memphis? Little Rock? St. Louis? Senator Thomas H. Benton of Missouri persuaded three St. Louis businessmen that the railroad should be built along the 38th parallel from St. Louis to San Francisco. A search for the best pass across the Rocky Mountains was led by his son-in-law, John C. Fremont. But that expedition ended badly. Ten of Fremont's men died from hunger and winter exposure at high altitudes in the San Juan Mountains.

As usual, interests clashed, and every town wanted to be a stop on the railroad in anticipation of the boom times to come. In the end, however, it was decided that the best route should be found through impartial scientific investigation. Congress passed the Pacific Railroad Survey Bill in 1853. It was funded with $150,000. The Great Reconnaissance was about to begin. The surveys would be done by the United States Army Corps of Topographical Engineers under the direction of Jefferson Davis, the Secretary of War. (During those good old days, we had a Secretary of War put in charge of peaceful scientific exploration. Today we have a Secretary of Defense who oversees preemptive war).

Four different survey teams were selected to study the four proposed routes, and each team had ten months to complete its work. The first envisioned route started in St. Paul and ended in Seattle; the second one would originate in Council Bluffs or Kansas City and reach the Pacific at San Francisco; route three stretched from eastern Texas to southern Arizona and from there to southern California; and route four, the Santa Fe route, is of special interest in the context of this book. It ran along the 35th parallel from Fort Smith, Arkansas, through New Mexico and into Southern California. It eventually evolved into Route 66, the legendary mother road for continent-crossing car travel.

—

Lieutenant Amiel Weeks Whipple was appointed to lead the survey along the 35th parallel. He was an 1841 graduate of the Military Academy at West Point, finishing fifth in his class. Soon afterwards he joined the Topographical Engineers, gained experience in hydrographic work, and was then assigned to the team that completed the postwar boundary survey with Mexico—extending from El Paso, Texas, along the Gila River, and to the Pacific. Whipple was promoted to first lieutenant in 1851 and completed the boundary survey report in early 1853.

Lt. Whipple's experience in the Southwest persuaded the War Department to appoint him as the leader of the railroad survey expedition from Fort Smith, Arkansas, to Los Angeles. The wagon train bound for the Pacific departed Fort Smith on July 14, 1853. It had several large freight wagons, 240 mules, a sizable flock of sheep, and about seventy men: soldiers, teamsters, herders, servants, plus eleven civilian scientists. Among the professionals were Dr. J. M. Bigelow, physician-surgeon and botanist; Jules Marcou, French geologist and mining engineer; Dr. C. B. R. Kennerly, physician and naturalist; and surveyors, meteorologists, and astronomers. Also included was one German topographer and artist, Heinrich Balduin Möllhausen. He had arrived from Berlin just at the right time to secure a position with the Whipple Expedition. Not only did he have a useful set of skills, but he was already an old hand in Western travel who had earlier joined the explorer Duke Paul of Württemberg during one of his American journeys.

In addition, he carried a letter of recommendation from Alexander von Humboldt in his pocket. This is an excerpt:

Instructed by the intimate relations which he enjoys with the learned naturalists of my country, acquainted with the deficiencies of the Museums, by his intelligent zeal and his courageous and enduring activity, he will be very useful as a Collector of the natural history … of animals and the study of minerals and rocks. A very remarkable talent for drawing, as applied to picturesque sites and scenes of Indian life, will add to the fruits of his distant voyages (qtd. in Miller, 1970, pp. 84–85).

Once in Washington, Möllhausen visited the Prussian ambassador to the United States, Leo von Gerolt, who was glad to assist him with his application to the war department for a position on one of the upcoming surveys. Planning time for these expeditions was limited and qualified professionals were in short supply. Therefore, Möllhausen didn't have to wait long: He had disembarked on May 3 in New York, and only a week later, on May 10, a job offer arrived from Lieutenant Whipple. The young Prussian was to join the 35th parallel survey as topographer and artist. The American Southwest beckoned.

—

Heinrich Balduin Möllhausen was born near Bonn in the Rhineland on January 25, 1825. He died at the age of 80 in 1905. Balduin was bitten by *Wanderlust* and *Fernweh* (longing to see and explore faraway places) just like his father, a Prussian artillery officer and civil engineer who had traveled wide and far. He died while working on a railroad project in Greece, and was buried in Odessa on the Black Sea. Balduin's mother was the Baronesse Elisabeth von Falkenstein. Her husband had shown little liking for a settled life. He also had an expensive passion for collecting costly copper engravings, which caused perpetual financial problems for the family. Elizabeth found herself alone with her children for much of the time. She too died prematurely.

Möllhausen, his brother, and his sister became orphans at a young age and were taken in to live with relatives. Balduin was to stay with his aunt,

Adelheid von Falkenstein, in Mecklenburg. But he continued his education at the gymnasium in Bonn until he was 14. Since he was without funds, he could not afford to attend the university. His relatives did not offer to finance his studies. Instead, they send him to Pomerania to learn farming so that he could later earn a living in agriculture, perhaps as a farm manager.

Young Möllhausen was not thrilled about these prospects. He had his head filled with adventure tales and spent every free minute buried in the stories of James Fenimore Cooper and Washington Irving. At age 21, he enrolled for a year of military service in Stralsund on the Baltic. Plans to enter the Austrian Army in Vienna as an officer candidate came to nothing because, once again, he lacked the financial means. Life as an officer, especially among young noblemen, was not inexpensive. During the revolutionary year 1848 he was called into service in Berlin but left the army soon after the upheavals died down. With various doors closed to him, and with no desire for the farming life in Pomerania, Möllhausen decided to ship out for America. There he would test his mettle and show what he was made of.

He arrived in the fall of 1849, had 600 Thalers in his possession, made it through the winter by doing routine jobs and hunting, and was in Belleville, Illinois, when another attack of Wanderlust struck. He wanted to meet real American Indians and explore the western frontier, and by the summer of 1851 luck came to the prepared: Möllhausen met Paul Wilhelm, Duke of Württemberg (1797–1860), a traveler-explorer extraordinaire. Like Humboldt's, Paul's name was practically a household word at the time. He was widely known in both the United States and in Europe.

—

When Paul was a child his uncle, King Friedrich I of Württemberg, took a liking to the bright boy and asked for permission to raise him. It was given by Paul's father. The prince was subsequently educated at the Karl Academy, an institution that began as a military school for boys and later received the university charter from the emperor Joseph II in 1792. Young Paul's uncle was a true mentor. Although the boy's training was to be military, in accordance with the traditions of the high nobility, the king called leading scholars to the court. With them, Paul studied the natural and physical sciences, ancient and modern languages, law, philosophy, diplomacy, and ethics. He read Latin and Greek, became fluent in Italian, French, Spanish, and English, in addition to his German. Which leaves me wondering how it was possible to learn so many languages: maybe brains at that time were uncluttered with trivia.

Eventually, Paul earned the degrees of Doctor of Philosophy, Medicine, and Anatomy, and was made a major general by a relative, Frederick II of Prussia, son of Frederick the Great. This was all well and good, but Paul's disinterest in a military career or in the formal life at court only increased with his level of education. It was true that that he was the descendant of an ancient family that could trace its male lineage back to the year 1060, but that didn't change the fact that he wanted to travel the world and devote his time to the study of nature, and of life. So he wrote to the American government and asked for permission to roam far and wide through the republic with the purpose of adding as much as he could to scientific knowledge. He planned to travel incognito.

The U.S. welcomed the prince, but was hesitant to grant his wish for anonymity. What if something happened? Finally, it agreed, but secretly told the authorities out West to look after the illustrious explorer in the most discreet manner.

Paul's first American journey began in New Orleans, which would become his home away from home. He visited Cuba, returned to Louisiana, and then traveled up the Mississippi to the little town of St. Louis, and from there continued on the Missouri. This trip was undertaken very early in the existence of the United States, from 1822–1824. Paul had many interesting things to say about life along the two great rivers. In 1823, he met Jean Baptiste Charbonneau, born during the famed 5,000 mile Lewis and Clark Expedition to the mouth of Oregon's Columbia River and the Pacific Ocean of the Northwest. Jean Baptiste's mother was the Indian Sacagawea who served as an able guide, and his father was the French-Canadian fur trapper and interpreter Toussaint Charbonneau. The child was nicknamed Pomp, and he was a young man of 18 when the duke, likewise a young 26 at the time, invited him to travel to Europe with him.

Permission was given and Jean Baptiste left to live at a German castle, with a social life among the European nobility and travels, with Duke Paul, across the continent. Six years later, in December of 1829, he returned, with the duke, to St. Louis. Pomp was now fluent in French, German, Spanish, and English, (another language wiz!) and he had especially liked the German forests. But in the end he missed the American wild places. Now back home, he and the duke parted their ways. Jean Baptiste signed up as a fur trapper with John Jacob Astor's American Fur Company.

The duke's second America journey lasted from 1829–1831 and led him to research the northern provinces of Mexico, Texas, western Kansas and Nebraska, the flora and fauna of the Rocky Mountains in Colorado, and the Missouri River up to its sources. Meanwhile, Paul's geological, botanical, and zoological collections had grown enormously. This mass of material needed to be properly processed: It had to be classified, and it needed a home. Eventually, a fine museum near the castle of his ancestors in Bad Mergentheim would house the treasures.

While busy with this organizing work, Mehmed Ali, Khedive of Egypt, urged the duke to participate in an expedition that would explore the regions around the upper Nile. He couldn't resist and mapped, in the course of the explorations, an area of over half a million square miles. It was inhabited by an estimated 25 million unknown people, which Paul described "with the exact portraiture of a trained ethnologist" (Butscher, 1942, p. 185).

The third and longest America trip began in 1849 and lasted until 1856. Using every available means of transportation from his own legs to horse-back to railway to boat, Paul explored virtually all the regions west of the Mississippi, including California during the Gold rush. He spent a month at the ranch of Johann Augustus Sutter. His travels also took him into Mexico, into Canada, and in 1853 he was in South America's Patagonia and the Tierra del Fuego. He reached the headwaters of the Amazon, explored the

Orinoco like Humboldt had half a century earlier, and investigated along the Magdalena and the Rio de la Plata. By 1858, one found him in Australia, trekking into the outback and studying the aborigines.

—

For Balduin Möllhausen, the encounter with the royal explorer from Württemberg was one of great good fortune, despite the fact that traveling with the duke would almost cost him his life. But in the summer of 1851, he wanted nothing more than to join Paul's westward expedition from St. Louis to the Rocky Mountains and Fort Laramie over the Oregon Trail. He had little money; he was driven by his longing to see the wilderness of the West; and he knew that he had much to learn.

The duke usually traveled with only one, or at most two, experienced valets and helpers. He preferred the company of Creole trappers or tough frontiersmen. The young German was still green behind his ears, yet he succeeded in persuading the duke that he could do the job and that he was also an artist who would produce a pictorial record of their expedition. This was tempting. Möllhausen was hired and warned: This trip wouldn't be a cakewalk. And indeed, it wasn't.

They reached their destinations without major mishaps, although the duke's companion fell repeatedly ill with a fever. This slowed them down. During these attacks, Möllhausen was of no help to the duke. Unfortunately, the return trip was much worse. It was plagued by serial misfortunes: They had run-ins with various unfriendly Indian bands; the duke's wagon with all their supplies and specimen collections got stuck in a patch of quicksand in the middle of the swollen Platte River; the fierce winter of the northern prairies overtook them early; they experienced a fire racing across the grasslands; they were frequently wet, cold, and hungry; and finally, more than a hundred miles from the first settlements in Missouri, a blizzard pinned them down.

They were snowed in. Their horses died from hunger, exhaustion, a tomahawk wound, and finally extreme cold. After surviving the storm, one of the stranded Germans had the chance to leave on a stagecoach (apparently the last) that miraculously passed by. They flipped coins. The duke won and left, eager to organize a rescue team at the first opportunity. It would find Möllhausen and the wagon packed with all their valuables, and bring them to safety.

It didn't turn out that way. It was an extremely harsh winter. Möllhausen cowered in his little leather tent, besieged by howling wolves, icy winds, and drifting snow. Between storms, he collected wood along the river for the small fire he maintained in a hole in the middle of the tent. He hauled water. He divided his remaining food consisting of pieces of buffalo meat, rice, horse fodder, and coffee into 14 tiny rations. It would take that long before, with luck, the rescuers could reach him. The wolves circled closer and closer. On one occasion he shot through the tent's skin to drive them off. It worked for a few hours. Then they came back.

Nine days passed slowly. He grew stiff from the cold, feeling almost paralyzed. In between, the fever shook him again. Then came the day when he shot two Pawnee attackers in self-defense. The next morning, he buried the frozen warriors in the still-flowing water in the middle of the nearby creek, horrified that the wolves had feasted on one of the fallen men during the night, right in front of the tent.

Möllhausen had now reached a trancelike state. He was barely awake when a sudden human voice hit him like lightning. First it greeted him with an Indian phrase, then in English. As it turned out, the visitor's father had been white, the mother was an Oto woman, and that's what the half-white man came to prefer: living with the Oto tribe.

The visitor's name was Louis Farfar. He and his band of hunters saved Möllhausen's life. They fed him, cared for him, fitted him with moccasins, and invited the half frozen and starving man to travel under their protection to the place they called home. There they took him in as an honored guest, and there he regained his health and his strength. Something else happened, too: He was able to repair his affection for and his interest in Native Americans. They were one of the reasons that drove him to explore North America. That he had encountered thieving, begging, and even murderous natives had been a blow to his expectations and his understanding. Even worse was the fact that he had shot two men when they attempted to kill him. The memory of these deaths never left him. He remembered a heated exchange with the duke. They had argued on how to proceed when faced with hostile Indians. "Who gives you the right to kill humans when your weapons are far superior to theirs?" asked Paul. And Möllhausen had answered: "The right of the stronger" (Möllhausen, 1861, p. 332). Might makes right. The duke didn't buy it.

His young companion was gradually persuaded by example. He experienced repeatedly what gallantry meant, and how it behaves, and what it does. He also learned that the Sioux and the Kiowa and members of other tribes on the Great Plains recognized and respected personal courage. He tasted this himself when a galloping warrior stole Möllhausen's hunting knife. Möllhausen had carried the big knife on his back. The Indian came from behind and grabbed it with bravado. The duke suggested that Möllhausen ride after the thief to get his blade back. Möllhausen wasn't charmed by the idea. In fact, he thought it was crazy and a fine recipe for losing his scalp. But the duke insisted that he should do this, and in the end he had no choice but to go or look like a coward forever after. So he went to see the chief at the camp a few miles distant.

He entered the lion's den. He used mostly sign language and pantomime. The chief understood and saw to it that he got his knife back. The daredevil who stole it and lost it again was furious and fired a shot after Möllhausen as he rode away. The bullet hit his cap and blew it from his head. He jumped from the horse, picked it up, and calmly continued on his way. No further shots followed. Möllhausen still had his scalp.

It is remarkable how news and mail traveled up and down the rivers and across enormous distances in those days, so when spring came and travel became possible once more, Möllhausen and the duke found each other again. A long and joyous letter, written in New Orleans on March 10, 1852, reached the young Prussian in Bethlehem, on the River Missouri. Yes, wrote Paul, he had organized a rescue mission, but the winter was so severe that it couldn't break through. Grieving, he had given up hope of seeing his companion ever again. How happy he was now to hear that the Otos (a tribe he knew and valued) had saved Möllhausen's life! In any case, he had faithfully fulfilled his promise to assist in transforming the young explorer from a greenhorn into an old Western hand. Therefore, it was a special pleasure to invite his countryman to stay with him at his home in Louisiana.

Möllhausen traveled by boat to New Orleans. He stayed for several months, helping the duke with work on his collections. In addition, the two Germans roamed through the region until, in the fall of 1852, Möllhausen received a job offer from the Prussian Consul in St. Louis. Would he be interested to serve as the guardian-supervisor for a consignment of American animals during their voyage to the Berlin zoological gardens? Möllhausen accepted. After three years of explorations and travel, this was a wonderful, all expenses paid opportunity to go home and see Germany again.

The animals and their custodian arrived in Bremen on January 6, 1853. From there they continued on to Berlin, where the precious cargo was delivered to the director of the Berlin Zoo, Professor Martin Lichtenstein. Everything had gone well. Lichtenstein was pleased, took a liking to the young traveler, and showed much interest in his experiences and his drawings of American landscapes, animals, plants, and inhabitants. He told his good friend Alexander von Humboldt about this new acquaintance, and very soon Möllhausen was introduced to the grand old man.

This was another big stroke of luck. As a companion-helper traveling with Duke Paul, he had learned a great deal in the best school possible: directly from a practiced explorer, natural scientist, and exceptionally well educated man. This around-the-clock schooling was intense, and despite, or partly because of, the hardships he experienced, young Möllhausen grew up in leaps and bounds. There was much curiosity in both America and Europe about the mostly unknown and so far unseen Western lands. Although his training as a draftsman was limited to the art classes he had taken at school, he had a passion and a considerable talent for drawing. During his travels with the duke he drew and sketched as much as he could, and had, as a result, produced a sizeable collection of drawings. Humboldt liked what he saw and encouraged the young man to refine his technique during his stay in Berlin. Soon the aspiring artist received private instructions from Eduard Hildebrandt, who was one of the city's best-known painters at the time.

Humboldt's mentorship opened doors to Berlin's scientific community and to the royal household. King Friedrich Wilhelm IV was delighted to see the young traveler's drawings, heard about his exploits, and finally asked to meet him personally. These were eventful months: Before he left for his second American trip, Möllhausen also met Caroline Seifert, daughter of Humboldt's secretary-butler-factotum, promptly fell in love, and was confident she would become his future wife. There were some silly rumors that Caroline was Humboldt's own illegitimate daughter, raised in his household by the loyal Seifert. And indeed, later photographs show a certain family likeness in Humboldt's and Caroline's facial features. But nothing has been proven. It was just gossip.

―

Stimulated by his experiences in Berlin, Möllhausen decided that this time around he would write a detailed journal about his upcoming travels with Lieutenant Whipple's Railroad Survey expedition along the 35th parallel. His two volume *Tagebuch einer Reise vom Mississippi nach den Küsten der Südsee* has a rare introduction by Alexander von Humboldt and was first published in 1858 by Hermann Mendelssohn in Leipzig. The English translation, titled *Diary of a Journey from the Mississippi to the Coasts of the Pacific,* followed quickly, also in 1858, from Longman, Brown, Green, Longmans, and Roberts in London.

I will use the English translation whenever I quote from the Diary. Incidentally, I didn't own an English language set, so I borrowed a 1969 reprint copy via Interlibrary Loan. It arrived from the University of Alaska and was last checked out in 1993, which can indicate that Möllhausen's work is pretty unknown, as is Humboldt's. In a biographical note added to the 1969 reprint, Peter A. Fritzell of Lawrence University wrote:

Very little scholarly work has been done on Möllhausen. There are only two readily available sources of information on this European popularizer of the American land. Preston Albert Barba has written a full-length study of Möllhausen ... William H. Goetzmann has included several paragraphs on Möllhausen in *Exploration and Empire: The Explorer and the Scientist in the Winning of the American West* (McKenna, 1936/1969).

Barba, who had titled his study *Balduin Möllhausen, the German Cooper,* wrote his book in 1914, while Goetzmann published his in 1966. I found one other text: an unpublished 1970 dissertation by David Henry Miller, who earned his Ph.D. in modern history at the University of New Mexico. His title is *Balduin Möllhausen, A Prussian's Image of the American West.* Given these details, I began to feel like someone who was joining the long forgotten young Prussian as a latter-day fellow traveler setting out across the great Southwest.

Compared to the earlier two-man expedition of Duke Paul and Möllhausen, the Railroad Survey under the command of U.S. Army Lt. Amiel Weeks Whipple was a large, impressive undertaking. He had assembled a

FIGURE 14. *Native Americans in the Valley of the Colorado River by Balduin Möllhausen, 1861.*

158

wagon train and about seventy men. The members of the survey were organized according to their rank, seniority, and duties. In addition to the soldiers,
teamsters, herders, cooks, and servants, it had a group of junior professionals
and a core group of scientists. A few of them of them could do more than one
thing: Lt. Whipple, for instance, leader of the expedition, was a member of the
Corps of Topographical Engineers, a capable astronomer, and someone who
nurtured an interest in ethnology. Dr. John M. Bigelow was the expedition's
surgeon and a passionate botanist. Balduin Möllhausen could draw, write,
and collect and preserve botanical and zoological specimens.

French-born geologist Jules Marcou, a graduate of the École Polytechnique,
was the expedition's senior scientist. He had taught mineralogy at the Sorbonne;
was well acquainted with Humboldt's friend Louis Agassiz at Harvard; had
published widely in the U.S.; and approached the geology of the Southwest in a
Humboldtian fashion. The Smithsonian Institution selected all of the scientists
and professionals with the exception of Albert L. Campbell, civil engineer and
surveyor, who may have joined due to a recommendation by Jefferson Davis,
the Secretary of War, who was in charge of the Railroad Surveys.

Möllhausen was pleased with the arrangements Lt. Whipple made for the
daily routine and functioning of the expedition. Dr. Bigelow and Dr. Marcou
shared a tent, while the Prussian, needing additional space for his drawing
equipment, papers, and paints received his own portable bedroom-studio.
The three men, soon called "the scientific gentlemen," had their own cook and
servants. There was also the group of the seven so-called 'young gentlemen.'
They lived in three tents, and also had cooks and servants to take care of them.
Actually, all the men participating in the expedition were young. Only Dr.
Bigelow was what today we would call middle-aged: He was 49 years old. In
his diary, Möllhausen affectionately called him the "gray-beard."

The luxury of having his own tent, and the convenience of enjoying the
services of a cook and servants freed the German artist-topographer from
much of the continuous manual labor he had performed as a travel companion of Duke Paul. His bouts with fever had ended, too. He could now take
pleasure in the upcoming journey of exploration to the fullest, sketching,

observing, writing, meeting native peoples, and collecting samples of plants, and perhaps animals, in the company of Dr. Bigelow.

—

About seven weeks after the wagon train started out from Fort Smith, Arkansas, it crossed the 100ᵗʰ Meridian, a line of longitude one hundred degrees west of Greenwich. This imaginary divide wasn't in the public eye until 1879, when John Wesley Powell, head of the U.S. Geological Survey, described it as a line that marked the boundary between the water-rich East and the arid West. East of that divide, irrigation was usually not needed because the land received more than 20 inches of annual rainfall. But west of the divide the terrain turned dry, irrigation for growing things became necessary, and population density dropped. Interestingly, the 100ᵗʰ Meridian also marks an elevation of approximately 2,000 feet. It doesn't stop at that: the Great Plains climb gradually higher, from the Mississippi River valley up to the foothills of the Rocky Mountains.

Lt. Whipple's survey team set up its first camp in Texas, on the edge of what was then called "Indian Territory." Luckily, the caravan didn't encounter parties of Comanches or Kiowas. The men saw their first herds of buffalo and large prairiedog towns.

After traveling westwards from Fort Smith through the arid, gradually climbing southwestern tablelands and the *Llano Estacado* to an elevation of about 5,000 feet, the expedition arrived on September 26 in Anton Chico, the first New Mexican village. Located near the Pecos River, the men found austere adobe houses nestled among colorful gardens. Irrigation ditches crisscrossed the hamlet, carrying life-giving river water to the fruit trees, vegetable beds, and corn patches. Bright red *ristra* strings of peppers decorated the house walls and looked beautiful against a deep blue sky. In the middle of it all stood a humble church and a dancing hall, or *fandango* salon.

Anton Chico had approximately 300 inhabitants and all of them, as far as the men could tell, came to welcome the strange and wonderful caravan.

It was a grand occasion for everyone. The surveyors were glad to have human contact and welcomed the chance to purchase fresh foods: eggs, milk, fruits, and also corn for their animals. The *alcalde* invited them immediately to a fandango to be held in their honor. The inhabitants had only necessities, but they sure knew how to celebrate.

But what to do? These explorers of the West had no fancy garments in their bags.

Möllhausen described how he used his stiff drawing paper to construct various improvements:

> Some of us wore somewhat creased, but extremely fashionable hunting coats on the upper part of our persons, terminated in leather leggings and heavy boots. Others showed civilization on their lower extremities, but a decided tendency toward savage life at the top. The majority boasted the paper linen I have mentioned (Miller, 1970, p. 9).

FIGURE 15. *Valley of the Rio Pecos at La Cuesta, after a painting by Balduin Möllhausen, 1861 Whipple Report.*

—

The village dignitaries and folk welcomed their guests at the door of the long, narrow dance hall with "very bad refreshments for very good payment," and the fun could begin. The Prussian noted that the "Mexican fair ones" used their seductive glances in a skillful manner with the aid of veils and shawls. The room was filled with a merry mix of languages. No one understood much of what someone else said. No matter. Spirits were high, supported by the orchestra of one violin and two guitars.

Compared to the surveyors, the Spanish dancers were in their element. Several of the travelers commented on the grace and verve of the señoritas, who indulged their dance partners with an additional exotic treat: During short breaks in the music making, they would light skinny cigarillos, take a few puffs, smile sweetly, and then pass them on Lt. Whipple's men. Imagine! What a difference to the prim and proper social etiquette on the East Coast! (Miller, 1970, p. 9)

—

When the expedition left Anton Chico, Lt. Whipple divided his group so that alternative routes could be explored. His own party continued via Galisteo and the pueblo of Santo Domingo to Albuquerque. Möllhausen was with him and appreciated the architecture at Santo Domingo, the handsome native people of the village, and the hospitality they provided. Finally, after passing through San Felipe and Algodones, the expedition reached the metropolis of Albuquerque on October 5. It was early fall, the most gorgeous time of the year.

Möllhausen had anticipated this moment. He was polite, but apparently felt disappointed about the town. To him, it was but a larger jumble of basic adobe houses, most of them with dirt floors.

Up to this point, the expedition had traveled through territory that was rough, but not completely unknown. What waited ahead however, west of the Rio Grande and all the way to California, was probably far more challenging terrain. Much planning and work had to be done during the weeks in town: Equipment had to be fixed; animals needed rest, reports had to be written; drawings completed and duplicated; supplies had to be replenished; and collections of plants, animals, geological samples and drawings required careful packing so that they could be dispatched to Washington from Albuquerque with a caravan traveling east.

Reinforcements under the command of Lieutenant Joseph Christmas Ives joined the survey team at this point. Lieutenant Ives and Möllhausen became good friends.

The reception in Albuquerque was extremely welcoming. Officers of the United States dragoons stationed in the city took the members of the expedition under their wings and provided helpful information about the ins and outs: The men learned details about the society, the best people, the best wine, and the things to avoid. The scientific gentlemen, Möllhausen among them, had rented small rooms in established households. This made it possible to get a lot of work done in relative comfort. The expedition's camp had been set up not far from the Rio Grande where the ground tended to be damp or even wet, especially after the rainy monsoon season of July/August. Given these conditions, it was difficult to keep men and materials dry.

Busy with their work during the day, Whipple's men looked forward to the evenings when they could enjoy the nightlife in Albuquerque. What the city lacked in appearance, it made up for with a warm hospitality and a lively social life. The church bell called out to the visitors to attend the fandangos, and they were only too willing "to perform their devotions to the fair and gaily-dressed Mexican ladies" (Miller, 1970, p. 101).

Meanwhile, Baron Gerolt, the Prussian ambassador in Washington, DC wrote a letter to Alexander von Humboldt in Berlin. It was dated November 28, 1853, and reported that he had recently received 400 dollars from Balduin Möllhausen, who was in Albuquerque and had saved the money from his salary to be forwarded to Caroline Seifert. She was the daughter of Humboldt's faithful butler/secretary. He had met her during his visit in Berlin. Möllhausen intended to marry her. Gerolt also wrote that he had seen beautiful drawings from the ongoing Whipple Survey, which the young artist had sent to the Smithsonian Institution.

While Whipple's men enjoyed their free time in Albuquerque, their commanding officer had a thorny problem to solve: How could he hire the most experienced, reliable guide and scout who knew how to proceed from the Rio Grande westwards? All kinds of rumors swirled around town. Whipple had to disregard them. The person he wanted was Antoine Leroux, a French-Canadian mountain man who lived in Taos and was growing old.

At first, Leroux refused to guide the survey expedition: He had been taken ill and was in no shape to do such a demanding job. But there was no one else with his extensive experience. Whipple increased his salary offer, and at last succeeded to persuade the veteran guide to accept. Möllhausen would soon enjoy listening to the stories the old trapper told around the evening camp fires in the months to come.

—

A detachment under Lieutenant Ives that included Möllhausen left Albuquerque on November 8 to investigate the area around Isleta Pueblo, south of town. Was it suitable for building a bridge across the river? The party forded the Rio Grande and met up with the main expedition at Laguna Pueblo. From there it traveled across the lava fields and the Continental Divide to El Morro, the Inscription Rock. It is located on the ancient west-east trail that was used for centuries by native peoples, conquerors, explorers, settlers and traders. They and their animals depended on a deep pool of year-around fresh water at the foot of the bold cliff that juts out into the gently rolling land. As they rested there, the visitors carved messages into the smooth, cream-colored face of the rock. It became a graffiti-cliff, with about 2000 inscriptions carved into sandstone.

Möllhausen's imagination traveled through the centuries, seeing conquistadors in his mind's eye. Yet even the sensible and pragmatic Lieutenant

Whipple wrote in his journal that El Morro was "grand and interesting far beyond my expectations" (qtd. in Miller, 1970, p.108).

⁓

Unfortunately, exploring the pueblo of Zuni could not be accomplished according to plan. Arriving on November 23 the surveyors found the little town ravaged by smallpox. They met only a few of the elders and had to keep a cautious distance to avoid contagion.

Möllhausen was disappointed. He entertained the idea that the Zunis were somehow descendants of the ancient Aztecs, and he was eager to investigate possible connections. On a bear hunt with a Zuni guide he did see a ceremonial site and later made a sketch of it. This exotic drawing became very popular. Thousands of copies, lithographed or in woodcut, were produced both in the U.S. and in Europe during the 19th century. Most of the prints did not give any credit to the draftsman.

⁓

On December 2, the surveyors found the fossilized remnants of a large ancient forest dating back to the Late Triassic Period. These massive tall trees had been alive and growing some 225 million years ago. Hundreds of petrified trunks, fallen and broken into segments, covered many square miles of ground. Their multi-colored, gem-like surfaces glistened in the sunlight. Möllhausen made sketches. They were probably the first ones ever made at the site. He also wrote about it, and published the details in 1853. Today, the place is the Petrified Forest National Park.

⁓

Supported by knowledgeable and still-healthy Zuni guides, the Whipple Expedition continued to travel with relative ease until it reached the Hopi settlements and found out that a severe small pox epidemic had stricken these pueblos too, and was still doing its devastating deeds.

Most adults were either ill or dead. With the Zuni guides returning home, and no Hopi guides available at all, the expedition was forced to go on without local guidance. It reached the San Francisco Peaks near present-day Flagstaff, set up camp, and celebrated Christmas. Hidden bottles of alcohol came out into the open. A huge kettle was soon bubbling with a tasty mixed concoction, and Möllhausen told his Diary that the men filled their tin mugs and began to feel warmth take the bite out of the freezing mountain temperatures.

"Toasts and jokes followed rapidly," he wrote. "Hearts became lighter, the blood ran more swiftly in the veins, and all present joined in ... a lively chorus" which "echoed far and wide through the ravines" (Miller, 1970, p. 112).

Rugged and insufficiently known high country awaited the travelers. Planning in advance, Lieutenant Whipple gave orders to lighten the loads on the wagons. Large amounts of gunpowder were given to the teamsters, who promptly fired salvos to celebrate Christmas, and, with permission, even set fire to isolated stands of pine trees, which outshone any decorated tree they had ever put up at home. With this festive scene illuminating the cold winter night, the Spanish speakers among the travelers burst into song, performed a customary New Mexico folk pastoral, and entertained everyone splendidly. There were even two stand-up comedians, one a Crow Indian serving with Leroux, the other one a herder. The two of them used unabashed free speech, saying whatever was on their minds, being funny and not terribly respectful.

In 1851, during an earlier exploration, Antoine Leroux had already advised Captain Lorenzo Sitgreaves that traveling further north from this point on would be useless because the Grand Canyon blocked all passages. Therefore, Whipple wanted to follow the 35th parallel west and a little to the south as closely as possible, and the only aids he could rely on were a Sitgreaves map and the experience of his guide Antoine Leroux. However, there were errors in the Sitgreaves map, which is perfectly understandable given the largely unexplored and jumbled geography. A river on the map suddenly disappeared.

To search for a way out, the expedition split. Each party tried to find a passable route. First there was bitter cold, snow, and ice, then followed waterless desert, cracks, canyons, lava fields. The caravan broke down. There was no forage for the animals. Cattle were shot, mules died, and supplies had to be abandoned. Food was growing scarce, and by February 10 everyone had to make do with half rations. Only two wagons and one cart were left.

"I am troubled ... and doubtful how to proceed," Whipple wrote in his diary on February 17 (Miller, 1970, p. 116). A day later, on February 18, Möllhausen also expressed his concerns. He called this the hardest day of the journey. They had dragged the remaining wagons "along a riverbed [that] alternated from marshy grounds to thick woods and tangled bushes, and where progress was frequently all but cut off by rock outcroppings and rim rock (Miller, 1970, p. 116). Nonetheless, on February 20, after the confusion, struggle, and forced detours due to forbidding topography, the expedition finally reached the settlements of the Mohaves and the Colorado River. "It has taken 52 days to travel 260 miles," noted John P. Sherburne, another diarist of the team (Miller, 1970, p. 117).

—

Worn out and hungry, both men and animals finally got a break. The Mohaves irrigated land along the river, were good agriculturists, and had surplus supplies of corn, beans, and other foods available for trading. They were skilfull fishermen too, using rafts and poles to reach the best fishing spots in the river. And to Möllhausen's delight, the tribe remained almost untouched by white men and their methods of refinement. Not even the intrepid Spaniards had seriously penetrated this area for any length of time. They had tried to navigate the unpredictable and often-violent river in this great desert, dragged some boats upstream for 15 days, and then traveled downstream in just 2½ days. It was all too much trouble.

—

Wagons were unfit to cross the powerful, as-yet-untamed Colorado River, and pack animals could not be overburdened, so Lieutenant Whipple still had goods to unload. They were valuable for his business dealings with the Mohaves. Lively bargaining activities followed, and the surveyors were astonished about the clever trading talents of the Natives. Whipple wrote down: "We found the Mohaves more than a match for us" (Miller, 1970, p. 118).

But replenishing food supplies was not the only trading activity. Möllhausen observed that the Natives trapped all kinds of small animals and carried them hanging from the waistband of their loincloth. On one evening, he noted, "Our visitors had rats, squirrels, and frogs dangling from their girdles, and wished to roast them at our fires, but as they were new specimens we exchanged them for mutton, and added them to our collection" (Miller, 1970, p. 118). In addition, artifacts were acquired: bows and arrows, lances, and shell beads.

What didn't work too well was the effort to collect some of the short skirts the Mohave women wore. The ladies were more than modest and didn't wish to part from their garments, which the visitors called petticoats. They were made out of bark and looked somewhat like the tutus of ballet dancers. The only problem was that the Mohave females were "so fat as to border on the comic" (Miller, 1970, p.123). Möllhausen wasn't alone with such an opinion. It was widely shared by his fellow travelers, all men who were generally appreciative of seeing females after months on the trail. The men had been more than ready to admire the Hispanic and Native American women they had so far encountered along the way.

In contrast, Möllhausen was impressed by the stature, athleticism, agility, and physical beauty of the males. Many grew taller than six feet. And coming from a country that not too long ago had made a big deal out of re-discovering and admiring the art of ancient Greece, to him they almost looked like copper-colored Greek gods. The males wore a little something around their loins, but otherwise remained nude. What they lacked in clothing was made up for by elaborate blue cactus ink tattoos decorating their bodies.

Möllhausen truly liked these good-natured people, and they liked him. He spent much time with them, watching and sketching, making pictures showing their daily activities and their housing—probably the first white man to do so. He observed their hoop games, noting that "they came bounding towards us in immense leaps over stones and bushes, with the agility of black-tailed deer" (Miller, 1970, p. 121). He was worried and wondered what would happen to the Mohaves in years to come.

> "On seeing how happy and contented these people were in their primitive state," he wrote,
>
> > one might have wished that civilization, with its errors and sufferings, should never find its way into the valley of the Colorado; though on the other hand, looking at the matter from a different point of view, one might regret that a race so physically and morally gifted should be strangers to the blessings of civilized life (qtd. in Miller, 1970, p. 122).

Yet our civilization didn't treat the Mohaves kindly. In 1859, a U.S. military camp was built on the east bank of the river. It was soon named Fort Mojave (the English spelling) and guarded the river crossing for the immigrants heading to California. More and more of them came. The natives were no longer happy. There were some fights. The decline of the tribe progressed. The military fort was closed in 1891 and the buildings then became one of those bullying boarding schools where little Native Americans were allegedly transformed from copper-colored primitives into civilized Anglo-Saxons. Except for an odd character like Möllhausen, dubbed a "romantic" just a few years later, no one was greatly bothered about this brave new world of 19th century America, and about the now-unwanted Enlightenment invention of the Noble Savage.

In 1863, prospectors began to roam the nearby Cerbat Mountains. Lead with a low silver content was discovered, then more silver, lead, zinc, and even some gold ore. The improvised town of Cerbat grew as fast as a ragweed after a rain, and prospered, and died, and now lingers on as a ghost: one of the many abandoned dwelling places that litter the wilderness of the West. Today, a smaller number of the Mohave people still live near the river. They are slowly making a comeback. They retained some water rights—absolutely vital in the desert.

—

On March 21, the Whipple Expedition reached Los Angeles and greeted it with a spirited "hurrah." The men could stay in a hotel, clean up, sleep in a real bed, and enjoy all those comforts after many months traveling through the big emptiness. It was the end of the survey project. Everyone was paid; the teamsters and other helpers were released; and the scientific gentlemen and other professionals gathered, organized, and packed their materials, notes, drawings, and collections for the long land and sea voyage back to the U.S. East Coast. Only three days later, on March 24, some of the artists, scientists, and officers of the Corps of Topographical Engineers boarded the steamer *Fremont* for San Francisco, and from there planned to continue on an ocean-going ship to the Isthmus of Panama. Möllhausen liked the sailing trip up the California coast, and he was thrilled about San Francisco.

"The town itself," he wrote,

> exhibits a perfect chaos: ... wooden sheds, tents, palace-like shops, and dwelling houses.... The streets are constantly filled with busy crowds, amongst which may be seen representatives of all the nations of the earth; carts, wagons, and coaches are driving about, doing their best to avoid coming in contact with one another, and the productions of the ends of the earth are offered for sale in all quarters (qtd. in Miller, 1970, p. 136).

The curious Prussian had the chance to visit and sketch the gigantic Sequoia trees, and next sailed on April 2 on the *Oregon* down the Pacific coast. There was a short stop in Acapulco, then the passengers disembarked in Panama on April 15. And even though Thomas Jefferson and Alexander von Humboldt had discussed the scientist's idea of building a canal across the Isthmus, that undertaking had to wait many more years before it became a reality.

Möllhausen still had to cross on land from the Pacific side to the Atlantic shore. He did so by rail and with mules, boarding yet another ship—the steamer *Illinois*—and arriving on April 28 in New York City. He went two days later to Washington, DC, where he needed to complete some of his sketches and drawings before he could travel home to Berlin. This work required several weeks, and he was happy to see Lieutenant Whipple and some other expedition members once more. They had remained longer in California to finish all the tasks involved in disassembling the caravan. Whipple gave Möllhausen a small collection of cacti as a gift for Humboldt.

⌣

Back in Berlin, Möllhausen was invited to live in Humboldt's household for a while. He married his Caroline Seifert, met King Frederick William IV, who was interested in hearing first-hand accounts about the American West and even bought some of the sketches. He found multiple open doors in society and at court, gave talks to the Berlin Geographic Society, and in early 1855 was appointed curator of the libraries in the royal residences in and around Potsdam. It was a preferment-type position, one that was mostly decorative and left much time for the pursuit of one's own interests. For Möllhausen, it meant he had gained the freedom to lead the life of a writer and have a family too. He started out by preparing the two-volume manuscript of his *Diary* for publication, and was even lucky enough to have Humboldt write a preface for it. This was something the old man rarely did, and it was a fine endorsement that helped to secure a favorable reception for the book.

Was Möllhausen now ready to settle down? Not yet. He had a bad case of the notorious German Wanderlust, or lust to roam, joy to wander. It's a bit like that Open Road syndrome Americans know so well. (Or like that travel urge of my brother, who has been everywhere on earth except in Japan and Korea. This year he has plans to do Mongolia, and then take the Trans-Siberian Express across the entire Asian continent to Russia). Unfortunately, little old Germany didn't have that much room to roam. Instead, it was still fragmented, and had been since the Peace of Westphalia in 1648. It was surrounded by many neighbors: nice neighbors, mostly, but not always. The newly united "empire" Bismarck was about to make was still slumbering in the near future.

Everybody else who was anybody had long gone out exploring and conquering and expanding across the big wide world. England, France, Spain, and Portugal, and Holland all had colonial empires, some of them exceedingly big. We know: the sun did not set in one of them. America, too, was growing rapidly: It was Manifest Destiny. First the Louisiana Purchase, then half of Mexico, and soon more to come. Oh, yes, there were bold minds among those Germans at that time. But conquerors they were not.

In the old days, if a young man became an apprentice, and learned a trade within the framework of the guilds, and finished his training, he earned a diploma, the *Gesellenbrief, and* advanced to the rank of journeyman. Now the world became his oyster: He left town to travel for a minimum of two years, depending on his field. It wasn't easy, but it fed his need to see, to learn new things, and to have adventures. Arriving in a new city or town, he would look for work in his trade, was well treated, and often employed for a time. It was a way of spreading know-how, refining skills, and meeting different people. It worked by dispersing knowledge in both directions: from master and his crew to traveling journeyman, and from journeyman to master and his household/firm. If there was no work, the guild rules and traditions specified that a modest monetary donation was to be given to the wanderer, so that he could eat while hitting the road again.

—

It's easy to make fun of the German fascination with the American West, but doing so serves no purpose. What's wrong with being enthusiastic and curious about a continent with endless vistas and about a land that offered things unavailable at home? Möllhausen loved it, and he later made a career out of that affection, and very many of those who shared his language wanted to read what he had to say. He wrote many popular books. In time, he was called the German Cooper. Can you imagine what today's public diplomats (new term for propagandists) would pay to get even a partial public relations' success of such a magnitude?

In any event, in June 1857, Möllhausen, now a married man with a young son, received an invitation to participate in another government-funded expedition to explore and survey the navigability of the Colorado River, this time under the command of Lieutenant Joseph C. Ives. The two men had traveled and worked together during the Whipple expedition and became friends. Ives had been impressed with the Prussian's talents as an artist and a naturalist.

For Möllhausen, a return to the Colorado and the chance to explore the Grand Canyon was, as he put it, the "fulfillment of my wishes" (Miller, 1970, p. 141). It would be his last trip to the United States. Congress published the report of the 1857–1858 survey in 1861 under the title *Report Upon the Colorado River of the West.*

—

Photography in the field was still in its infancy. The equipment was heavy and hard to handle outdoors. Lieutenant Ives took cameras with him, intending to have two sources for pictures: work done by the artists of the expedition and photographic plates. But as it turned out, the sketches and watercolors were sturdier. After setting up an elaborate photo studio under a protective tent in the Colorado River delta, a gust of wind blew it all into the water. Therefore, Möllhausen and another German became the first persons to produce hand-made images of the Grand Canyon.

The second artist was Baron Friedrich Wilhelm von Egloffstein, from a Franconian family of *Uradel,* or ancient nobility—first found in the written record in the year 1187. One Egloffstein was a prince-bishop of Würzburg and founder of the university in that city in 1402. Others were free Imperial Knights who had been granted Imperial immediacy. They served the emperors directly and avoided being vassals of powerful regional nobles. When Napoleon deleted the Holy Roman Empire in 1806, Imperial Knights were no longer needed. They became unemployed.

Friedrich von Egloffstein left the village by the same name near Nuremberg, and the very old, very bold family castle on a cliff above it, plus centuries of tradition behind him when he traveled to the United States. He arrived in 1846, 22 years young and already well trained as a topographer and mapmaker. As a Prussian officer candidate, he had passed his exams at age 17, then served for nine months before taking a second exam that included tests in Latin, French, German, mathematics, history and drawing (Rowan, 2012, p. 6).

For the first years after arriving in the U.S., he worked in New Orleans and St. Louis, then returned briefly to Germany to resign his commission as a lieutenant in the Prussian Army and to marry Irmgard von Kiesewetter. Back in St. Louis, he lived as "Fred Egloffstein." (Some members of the German nobility shed their titles during the crossing of the big pond.) He was busy with surveying and map-making, developed a friendship with the botanist Dr. George Engelmann, and was invited to become the topographer for the ill-fated 1853–54 John Charles Fremont survey expedition. Ill and half-starved, he parted from it in Utah, recovered, and joined the remnants of the Gunnison-Beckwith expedition.

His innovative maps, striking panoramas of Utah, Wyoming, Nevada, and California, and his illustrations were published in the *Pacific Railroad Reports*, vol. 11. The panoramas were folded into the inside of the books, and readers/viewers could unfold them to a length of about a yard, and they could instantly grasp the vast western landscapes in a real and surprising way.

The shaded relief map Egloffstein produced of the Grand Canyon was far ahead of its time. It presented a bird's eye view, or the view from a plane flying overhead long before such an aircraft was invented. It makes the incredibly complex, confusing, rough, jumbled terrain of the inner canyon clear and visible.

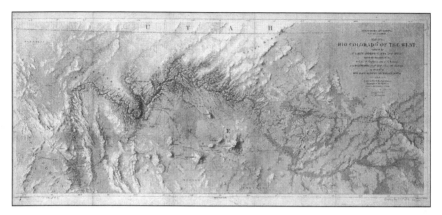

FIGURE 16. *Rio Colorado of the West, map by F.W. Egloffstein, 1858. Library of Congress.*

That wasn't possible before. No one could get an overview. The landscape was too gigantic, too broken up. Carl Wheat, in his authoritative *Mapping the Transmississippi West 1540–1861*, called Egloffstein a genius. The map is three-dimensional and uses the first commercial half-tone process in the U.S., a technique invented by Egloffstein for which he eventually obtained a patent. In his paper *Envisioning the American West,* J. B. Krygier (1997) wrote: "I suggest that one must recognize the map's scientific and cultural context—European Enlightenment ideas and Alexander von Humboldt's vision—all based on an explicitly visual way of knowing, a visual epistemology."

Various scholars and writers praised the map, but they ridiculed the illustrations. The pictures didn't look like the Grand Canyon. Condemnation was vigorous. Wallace Stegner said in a 1953 interview that Egloffstein's images were "markedly inaccurate; they are pictures of the artist's dismay" (qtd. in Hepworth, 1998). Other critics said the images looked like scenes from Gustave Doré's underworld, expressed excessive romantic fantasies, or a decadent "gothic" imagination, and even signs of schizophrenia. This malignant nitpicking occurred later, first came, due to the Civil War, a general lack of attention for the reports that were published in 1861.

Egloffstein was in the war. By 1861, he lived in New York, was elected colonel of the 103rd New York Volunteer Infantry, saw action, and was severely wounded in North Carolina in late April of 1862. He resigned in 1863 and was granted a brevet commission as a Brigadier General in 1865. He and his family left the U.S. in 1878, returned to Germany, and lived in Hosterwitz near Dresden until he died in 1885. He was 61 years old.

An autopsy was performed to provide evidence that this veteran of the Civil War died from an infection from his war wound. Only then was the disability/cause of death claim accepted by the United States Commissioner of Pensions. Egloffstein was one of more than 200,000 Germans (they were the largest group of foreign-born soldiers) who fought in the U.S. Civil War for the Union. He was soon completely ignored and forgotten. As to all those Germans who had enlisted, I have not researched how many died or were crippled and damaged. Considering that today's medical care for veterans is often insufficient, one can suspect that things weren't all that fantastic in the 1860s either—apart from the fact that medicine has progressed since then.

And that was that until in January 2012, *Harper's Magazine* contained an article on Egloffstein by Jeremy Miller, a media fellow at the *Bill Lane Center for the American West* at Stanford University. It's titled *The Long Draw: On the Trail of an Artistic Mystery in the American West.* The piece had the goal of restoring Egloffstein's reputation. One of the artist's images was named *Black Canyon,* and supposedly depicted the Colorado River near today's Hoover Dam, which didn't exist back then. It was this dark, brooding, almost-grim abyss of the Grand Canyon that had caused harsh criticisms and accusations of failure. This picture with its soaring vertical black walls, which almost suffocate the narrow whitewater river between them, is stunning and strong. But it is not beautiful. How could it be that a natural wonder like the Grand

Canyon looks so forbidding? Only a disturbed mind was capable of presenting such a distortion.

Well, in 2001, Jeremy Miller visited an exhibition at the New York Public Library. It was named *Heading West: Mapping the Territory* and contained Egloffstein's *Black Canyon*. Miller recognized instantly that this was not a picture of the Grand Canyon, but one that looked like the Black Canyon Gorge of the Gunnison River in Colorado, about 500 miles to the northeast from the Grand Canyon. Miller knew the area: He had hiked there for years. So he asked the curator of the exhibition "whether some grave injustice had been inflicted on the poor German mapmaker" (Harper's, Jan. 2012). Further investigations showed that indeed, the drawing was not made at the Grand Canyon, but on the canyon of the Gunnison River, and things really looked as grim and "gothic" as shown. Miller verified in the field, and risked breaking his neck while clambering through nearly impassable Gunnison terrain in search of Egloffstein's actual point of view.

Back in the 1860s, Congressional staff, inundated with an overabundance of material, had misfiled the images in a big file tagged "Grand Canyon." From there, the error continued and multiplied with a life of its own in publications etc. until 2001. Mistakes can happen. Yet the tongue-lashings for Euro-romanticism, schizophrenia, and artistic fraud remain real. The gallant effort of rehabilitation initiated by Jeremy Miller came much too late for the soldier-artist Egloffstein. His Civil War wounds and whatever else claimed the man.

—

Balduin Möllhausen lived a good, long life. He had two sons and died in 1905 at the age of 80. It has been estimated that he made about 300 pencil sketches and watercolors during his travels and explorations on the Western Frontier. Many images have been reproduced as lithographs in various books and survey volumes. In his *Pictorial Record of the Old West*, Robert Taft wrote that in 1939, the *Staatliches Museum for Völkerkunde* in Berlin had a sketchbook with 99 pencil drawings and 83 watercolors in its collections. But much of Möllhausen work was destroyed during the Battle for Berlin in April of 1945. In the United States, some of his artwork can be seen at the Smithsonian Institution in Washington, DC; the Oklahoma State Historical Society, Oklahoma City; and at the Amon Carter Museum, Fort Worth, Texas.

There was a *Caesur*, a historic break caused by the Civil War. But it is possible to follow specific railroad surveys almost step by step and day by day by reading the journals, diaries, letters of the participants, and the official reports. This gives the impression of men who were dedicated, educated, skilled, courageous and resilient. They had different backgrounds and worked well together. They were hungry for learning as much as they could about the world of the Frontier, and there was an almost innocent, eager spirit that permeated their undertaking. From the start, even the idea of these railroad surveys was intensely political and driven by competitive rivalry. But once the idea matured to take shape as an actual expedition, the Whipple Survey, for instance, it left all this behind and became an important, scientific, and multidisciplinary task. For that reason, it is a pleasure to follow these men, and to travel, listen, observe, and experience with them. From their points of view, America was vast, and wild, and (mostly) full of promise.

11

Being a Territory and the Coming of the Railroads

While we maintain the unity of the human race, we at the same time repel the depressing assumption of superior and inferior races of men. There are nations more susceptible of cultivation, more highly civilized, more ennobled by mental cultivation than others—but none in themselves nobler than others. All are in like degree designed for freedom.

—*Alexander von Humboldt,*
COSMOS 1849 (E. C. Otte, trans.)

With the railroads came the good, the bad and the ugly. But first came the Civil War and the Indian wars against the Navajos and the Apaches. Most of the actual Civil War fighting did not occur in the Southwest, but nevertheless, the conflict touched New Mexico intensely. The territory still included Arizona and parts of southern Nevada and Colorado and would soon be rearranged. Struggles for and against slavery, for and against languages and cultures, fights against Native populations, fights for land and work and natural resources, and fights over much more troubled the Southwest.

Yes, there was the 1848 Treaty of Guadalupe Hidalgo to settle hostilities after the Mexican-American war. But there were also continuing problems in the new border region between Mexico and the United States, for example in the fertile Mesilla Valley. The Mexicans claimed it was their land; the Americans did the same. No one protected the settlers, who were targets of increasing attacks by Native American bands especially after U.S. troops were withdrawn and reassigned to participate in the Civil War. No one offered compensation for their hardships and losses. It was quite a mess. The disputed area was called "No Man's Land."

Actually, business-friendly U.S. Southerners wanted to build a transcontinental railroad that could connect the Atlantic and the Pacific along the southernmost edge of the country. To do that, an additional relatively level strip of land was needed. The topographical features had to be unimpeded by mountains to make such an undertaking possible. Initially, the U.S. had wanted much more acreage, but finally settled on the Gadsen Purchase (named after James Gadsen, U.S. ambassador to Mexico at the time) of 29,670 square miles across an area that later became part of the modern states of New Mexico and Arizona.

The deal was signed on December 30, 1853. The price was $15 million. After much haggling, the U.S. Senate revised the treaty, ratified it on April 25, 1854, and reduced the price to $10 million, or 33 cents per acre. I guess the Mexicans were not informed about unilateral changes, but Mexican President Antonio Lopez de Santa Ana was hurting for money and signed it on June 8, 1854. Mexico calls the treaty *Venta de la Mesilla*—sale of Mesilla. This was another real estate deal with human inventory as part of the bargain.

The most grievous result of this was the creation of a new international border and the division of the old Tohono O'odham Native American people in the Sonoran Desert. Eventually, the land was cut apart by a cousin of the Iron Curtain, a barbed wire fence. For many years, members and families of the tribe who suddenly found themselves living on both sides behind the American and Mexican borders, could still cross that dividing line. But in the 1980s the actual fence went up. Now entry is illegal except at official checkpoints, and these are up to 150 miles away from the reservation. Personal contact remains difficult. Yet these issues are seen as minor.

~

In the Civil War, parts of southern New Mexico sided at first with the Confederates, who saw the territory as the vitally important link or route to California. With a small force of Texans, Lieutenant Colonel John R. Baylor occupied Mesilla in July of 1861. He declared that conditions in town and in the vicinity were close to anarchy and he took possession of both on behalf of the Confederate States of America. Mesilla was instantly named the capital of the Confederate Territory of Arizona, and Baylor became its governor. Remaining, but by then mostly empty Union military forts were dismantled. This did not reduce anarchy, but emboldened Apache warriors to increase their raids. White settlers fled to Tucson for their lives.

Congress debated a bill introduced by Texas Congressman John Reagan in November of 1861 proposing the creation of the Territory of Arizona. The bill passed and the new territory became official on January 13, 1862, when Confederate States President Jefferson Davis proclaimed it to be ready and functioning. Soon a Confederate army from Texas advanced deeper into New Mexico, intending to capture Santa Fe and then take the campaign north to Colorado. The Confederates won the Battle of Valverde in February 1862, but lost decisively in the Battle of Glorieta Pass in March. With this, the Confederate invasion of New Mexico was at its end. Now it was under Union control.

The U.S. Congress, which no longer had Southern delegates due to the war, changed things once more: It passed the Arizona Organic Act in February of 1863 with a new north-south border dividing big old New Mexico into two states. President Abraham Lincoln signed the act on February 24 and prohibited slavery, thereby following Mexican law valid in the Southwest prior to the 1848 Treaty of Guadalupe Hidalgo. Mexico had abolished slavery of black persons in 1829, and did so even in Mexican Texas in 1830.

The funny thing is, as soon as the independent Republic of Texas was established in 1836, slavery was made legal again. In any event, most New Mexicans never welcomed military visits from Texas. Slavery had long been illegal in New Mexico. But humans are inventive when it comes to taking advantage of their fellow man: A small scale, mostly informal commerce in human beings was a regular feature in the frontier province during the 18th and most of the 19th century. Children were stolen, and captives ransomed. Most were abducted from tribes of the Great Plains. The Navajos, for example, then sold their young hostages to the highest bidder. They were raised and re-educated as Christians by Hispanic families, and later in demand as domestic servants, shepherds, and laborers.

These non-pueblo Indians were called *genizaros*. The *Encyclopedia of the Great Plains* describes them as "detribalized Indians." What a term! Just as genizaro is a strange word that must have traveled around the world (perhaps from Habsburg Austria's long struggle against the Turks who advanced all the way to the gates of Vienna) to end up in New Mexico. It is the Spanish version of the English word *Janissaries*, name of the famed and feared elite infantry of the Ottoman Empire. Formed of Christian boys taken from their parents at the ages of 6 to 14, these captive children were first placed with Turkish families to learn the language, culture, and religion of the Islamic empire, and were then trained as the special forces of the Sultan's household and as his bodyguards. Especially gifted boys received higher levels of education, could advance into the ruling class as *viziers*, or become architects, engineers, or scientists. They received salaries and pensions, but could not marry. Their loyalty, discipline, and valor, at least during the centuries of their best performance, was legendary.

In contrast, New Mexico's genizaros had a low social status, were often abused, but also had legal protections, initiated through the 16th century work of the protector of the Indians, Bartolomé de Las Casas. The specific updated laws looking after them were part of the *Recopilation de Leyes de Reynos de las Indias 1681*, which permitted the purchase of prisoners under the Christian duty to ransom captive *Indios*. This became crucial after 1694, when a band of Navajos beheaded some stolen Pawnee children after the New Mexican Spaniards refused to buy them. The Spanish King Charles II was angered and ordered that in an emergency the royal treasury would pay to prevent the recurrence of such an atrocity.

Since slavery was forbidden in New Mexico, the *genizaros* served for a number of years, usually until their hosts had at least earned back the ransom money that had been paid for them. Once adults and free, they eventually received land in relatively insecure frontier locations, had to provide for themselves, and had to fight off hostile Native Americans during frequent raids. They did this to stay alive and to protect their families. Settled in places like Belen and Abiquiú (later of Georgia O'Keeffe fame), they began to intermarry, and eventually blended into their communities.

—

With the Confederates driven out of New Mexico, the attentions of the U.S. Army could return to the conflicts with the Apaches and the Navajos. In August of 1862, General James H. Carleton assumed command over the Army in New Mexico. As the American government advanced further into the West, a complicated set of laws was fashioned to keep things in order. The Indian Trade and Intercourse Act of June 30, 1834, which made it an offense to allow livestock "to range and feed on any land belonging to any Indian or Indian tribe, without consent of such tribe" was extended to all tribes in New Mexico by the Indian Appropriation Act of 1852 (Bailey, 1998, p. 30). The livestock industry was not pleased with that and pressured lawmakers in Santa Fe to change it. In the winter of 1853–54 the territorial legislature "ruled that under the laws of Congress there was no Indian country in New Mexico" (Bailey, 1998, p. 30).

Most ingenious: Navajo acreage was open now, and the herders lost no time in taking advantage of the finest grazing lands in the Territory west of the Rio Grande. Sheep and wool had been very important in New Mexico's economy for 200 years. Up to a million sheep were owned, and there were steady increases in the number of animals being exported and driven down to Mexico. By the 1840s, about 500,000 sheep, split up into small herds of around 15,000 each, were transported on the hoof (Bailey, 1998, p. 17). After the Mexican-American war, the trade with Mexico was disrupted.

Then came the U.S. Civil War and wool was in great demand. Big hopes of fabulous mineral riches also pushed the expansion forward.

Carleton himself started to pressure Washington as soon as he assumed command in New Mexico. He sold the idea of establishing a reservation and finally succeeded on January 15, 1864, when President Abraham Lincoln approved and signed a document that made the 40 square mile Bosque Redondo camp official. Lincoln probably had no idea how miserable the place was. It must have looked fine on paper.

—

For a long time, Hispanics and Navajos had maintained a difficult balance. While the settled pueblo dwellers had accommodated themselves slowly to living next to the Spaniards, the Navajos had not. But as long as they kept their large traditional areas for themselves, coexistence was possible. All this was now being disturbed, and the Navajos had grown restless, and irritated, and far more aggressive. Their pastoral way of life was threatened. In addition, bad years have always been part of life in New Mexico, when weather with droughts, flash floods, or abnormal winters could wreck the harvest and disrupt the food supply. Earlier, General Carleton had been promoted to colonel during the Mexican War, served under Colonel Edwin V. Sumner in New Mexico, pursued Apaches with Kit Carson for several years, and had ridden through the eastern parts of the Territory to inspect what was there. That was how he had found Bosque Redondo.

Interestingly, in 1856 Secretary of War Jefferson Davis set up "a commission to study the tactics of European armies fighting in the Crimea. Major Carleton was assigned the study the Russian Cossacks" (Bailey, 1998, p. 57). Fast forward: As the year 2014 arrived, the Crimea was once again in the news. In any case, what the general learned about the Cossacks influenced his strategy in the New Mexican campaigns against Apaches and Navajos. He was 47 years young when he returned almost 10 years after his first visits, and what he found was pretty grim. Lynn R. Bailey (1998) put it this way:

"What means he used to stabilize the situation depended on how much time he had and on his sense of humanity and manifest destiny, two incompatible concepts" (p. 63). Incompatible, indeed.

The Mescalero and the Gila Apaches were worn down first, and about 400 of them were marched initially to run-down Fort Stanton and from there to Fort Sumner, where they performed forced labor to get the Bosque Redondo reservation started. They dug an irrigation ditch to bring river water to the camp. Prior to Carleton's arrival the small-scale war between Apaches and ranchers, prospectors, and miners had been extremely brutal on both sides. For example: In an open letter printed later in the Santa Fe *New Mexican* on April 14, 1865, Judge Joseph G. Knapp of Mesilla

> blew the whistle, alleging that Mangas Coloradas had been lured into Fort McLane under pretext of consultation and confined to the guardhouse. While the Indian slept, he was attacked by soldiers, shot, scalped, and decapitated. The next morning his lodge was attacked, and his wife and daughter killed. The flesh was boiled from Mangas's head and the skull 'exhibited as a badge of honor', while the scalps of himself, his wife and daughter were worn as ornaments (Bailey, 1998, p. 71).

Mangas was an aged Apache leader. Indescribable atrocities were also committed by Indians.

—

Fort Sumner at desolate Bosque Redondo was quickly set up as a—very primitive—Indian reservation. General Carleton then met with Navajo leaders at Fort Wingate on the eastern border of the Navajo areas. He told them to give up their homelands and move voluntarily to Bosque Redondo, almost 400 miles away. If they failed to do so, the U.S. military would deal with them and show no mercy. The Navajos rejected the ultimatum. Wouldn't you?

This brings General *Nuts* to mind. During the Battle of the Bulge in December of 1944, Anthony McAucliffe was the acting commander of the 101st Airborne Division and under siege in Bastogne, Belgium, from a much larger, last effort German force commanded by General von Lüttwitz. The Americans were encircled. The German sent a delegation offering a solution that would save the U.S. troops from annihilation. He suggested "honorable surrender." If the proposal was rejected, German artillery would do the rest, which was not healthy for the civilians trapped in town. The American general's answer was one word: Nuts! It remains widely admired to this day.

I have a friend who is nicknamed Med Flower. She's a practical, young working mother with two small children and a husband. She is funny. We have lively conversations. I told her about the Navajo and General Nuts ultimatums, and asked why we approve of one but not the other. She laughed and said, "We Americans are like toddlers, we must win. Anything more complicated than getting and keeping is of no interest whatsoever, especially to our rulers."

That sounded plausible. I would feel better if we had more comparative history in the U.S. It is a problematic field, not yet widely done, and definitely needed. Being polyglot could be useful in getting up to speed, but how many historians or politicos are fluent in languages these days? As things stand now, almost everyone prefers to tell nice, safe, narrow national narratives, hero-stories, and orthodox tales over and over again. Or, if one works in academia, perhaps one can specialize in opening one single window with a detailed view to the past. To see research investigating anti-imperialist thinkers from the Enlightenment era is a recent development. Such a topic had been taken off the table for nearly 200 years.

〜

Under orders from Carleton, Colonel Kit Carson, fur-trapper, ailing scout, local New Mexico expert, and veteran of the Battle at Valverde, began the campaign against the Navajos in July 1863. The demand was simple: Surrender or die. With some 700 soldiers, Carson was to hunt down Navajo men, shoot to kill those who did not capitulate, and take all the women and children prisoners. There seems to be no evidence of killings, but the troops certainly used scorched earth methods, which will kill slowly. They destroyed crops and dwellings, and confiscated horses, mules, and sheep. Yet the results were unsatisfactory. Only 180 Navajos gave themselves up, while others were still out and about raiding, desperate for food.

General Carleton was not happy. Next he ordered a direct attack against the beautiful Navajo heartland of Canon de Chelly. This was total war. The U.S. Army razed, burned, and cut everything in sight: hogans, food supplies, and the precious 1,000–1,200 peach trees growing in the fertile bottom soil of the canon. Other Navajo enemies, among them the Utes, joined in the manhunt. Winter came. Hunger and cold drove 3,000 Navajos to surrender. They were imprisoned at the nearby forts, began to die in droves from dysentery and exposure, and were then forced to go on the notorious "Long Walk" across New Mexico to the barren paradise of Bosque Redondo.

FIGURE 17. *Soldier guarding interned Navajos at Bosque Redondo, ca. 1864.*

Thousands more followed later. Already weakened by the tactic of starving them into submission during the attacks of the preceding months, many of these unfortunates died during the forced winter marches. Women gave birth in the cold and during blizzards; young and old collapsed from hunger and illness. Moccasins were torn to shreds; clothing turned into rags. Coyotes soon followed, and crows and vultures circled, waiting for the next roadkill. After arriving at Bosque Redondo, the Navajos continued to perish. There they found nothing except several hundred Apaches, archenemies of the tribe, and a mutual source of friction during the captivity for years to come.

The Army leadership believed both Native American nations spoke the same language: they did not. General Carleton had a starvation problem at his hands. He hurried to get emergency supplies so the camp's inmates could survive the winter and spring. It was tough, because it had been a bad year for harvests elsewhere, too.

Never before had there been so many Native Americans crowded into such a limited plot of land. Exposure was another severe danger. There were not enough tents; some were cut up to make sacks for the transport of corn and flour. People dug holes into the ground, covered them up with grass mats or whatever they could find, and huddled like animals. What little wood had grown on the site was rapidly used up. Soon the only firewood was mesquite roots, and to dig these up these one had to walk for 12 miles. Sure, 12,000 trees were planted near the river in the winter of 1864–65, but with lots of luck it would take many years to grow this fuel for the future. As to the water in the man-made ditch, it had turned brackish, was almost foul. And the soil was alkaline. The land wasn't fit for growing grain, yet for three years, ground was broken up and crops were planted. They failed year after year, devoured by cutworms, beaten down by rainstorms and hail, parched by heat.

There was rationing, malnutrition, and illness. The interned suffered from pneumonia, and from malaria (a new disease for the Navajos) caused by mosquitoes breeding in the standing water and in irrigation ditches. There were epidemics of mumps and a milder form of small pox, plus dysentery year round caused by bad water and bad food. And there were venereal diseases: Syphilis was rampant. The camp's prostitution shacks were called hog farms. Soldiers and destitute Navajo females fraternized there. Often, the women were available in exchange for a handful of food.

General Carleton was a capable can-do officer with clear objectives: He wanted to make New Mexico (and the new Arizona) safe for progress and development, and he wanted to civilize the Apaches and the Navajos. They were seen as wild tribes. He made plans about feeding the nearly 9000 incarcerated Native Americans. He wanted to educate them; he wanted to see them live in villages designed by the white man; he wanted them to work, grow food, be self-sufficient, and be more like the Pueblo Indians. And most of all, he wanted them to behave. This was a grand social experiment, a project of radical social engineering (although that concept hadn't been fabricated yet). It failed. It was all wrong. Nearly one third of those marched to, and kept at gunpoint within Bosque Redondo, died.

First of all, as we have seen, the land was unsuitable for the project. It could not feed or provide clean drinking water to those contained on it. (Critics soon mocked it as "Fair Carletonia.") And from this basic fact the wrongs accumulated: putting enemies who spoke different languages together in one reservation; planning to build 12 villages for a people who didn't want to be in communities but lived in hogans in family groups; picking 12 village leaders—all men, when the social Navajo structure was matrilineal; ignoring customs, beliefs, traditions, and tearing the social fabric apart. Navajos, for example, did not stay in rooms or dwellings where someone had died. The village concept was abhorrent to them, and so was the small hospital. Those who go in there, they said, never come out.

"The road to hell is paved with works in progress," quipped Joseph Roth, and so it was in this case. After long delays, bureaucratic obstructions and negotiations, a treaty was signed on June 1, 1868, between the U.S. government and the Navajos. None other than General William Tecumseh Sherman, he of the devastating 1864 March to the Sea, signed the document together with Navajo leader Barboncito and others. The Navajos could return to their homeland, and received about 10 percent of it as their new reservation.

The treaty had all kinds of rules and provisions. The impoverished returning people would get some sheep, and food staples for the first winter. Much of the promised goods subsequently vanished at points between federal delivery and the designated Indian agents in the field. The sad saga was not over then, and went on and on. Yet today, the Navaho Nation has approximately

300,000 enrolled members, of which nearly two thirds live on what is now the largest reservation in the U.S. It is located in the FourCorners region, where four states meet: Arizona, New Mexico, Utah, and Colorado. It has now a size of 27,000 square miles, and it was and is rich in coal, oil, natural gas, and yellow dirt. It sits on the second largest uranium deposits in the U.S., with 70 million tons. This fueled the atomic arms race of the Cold War. Navajo miners paid a price for the lack of safety precautions.

I knew a young boy who grew up next to the tailings of a uranium mine in New Mexico. It gave him leukemia. This can be treated now, especially in kids. But you must be a tough little warrior to get through it. Many adult Native American miners perished or fell seriously ill from digging the yellow dirt. Those left standing had to fight for help and compensation for many years. For some, the legislation came too late. As to the little boy with leukemia, he is in remission, but received nothing. Kids growing up next to uranium waste dumps were not part of the program.

—

According to Tomas Jaehn, who to the best of my knowledge wrote the only study on the subject, there were 224 Census-counted Germans in the New Mexico Territory in 1850. That's 0.3 percent of a population of only 61,547 persons living on 235,000 square miles (or 510,000 square km) of land (Jaehn, 2005, pp. 29–30). New Mexico was big, and the settler population sparse. And even later on, with the massive influx of German immigrants to the U.S. during the second half of the 19th century, the numbers in New Mexico (and newly created Arizona) remained Lilliputian: 1.1 percent at most. There were not enough Germans to aggregate into an ethnic group. But there were individuals. Intriguing individuals. The book will look at just three of them:

- Herman Ehrenberg, Prussian, soldier in the Texas Revolution and mining engineer.

- Albert "Al" Sieber, from Baden-Wuerttemberg, soldier in the Civil War at Antietam, Fredericksburg, and Gettysburg. U.S. Army Chief of Scouts during the Apache Wars.
- Franz Huning, from Hannover, bullwhacker on the Santa Fe Trail, New Mexico merchant, mill operator, land-speculator, castle-builder, and city-planner/developer in Albuquerque.

⁓

The birth of a boy named Hermann Vollrath Ehrenberg was registered on October 17, 1816, at the Lutheran Church in the village of Steuben, Prussia. Just 18 years old, the young man immigrated to New York in 1834 and traveled on to New Orleans in October of 1835. The city was aflutter about news from the Texas revolution. Ehrenberg attended a rally and quickly joined a volunteer militia company called the New Orleans Greys. Led by Captain Thomas H. Breece, the unit sailed by steamboat up the river to Natchitoches, Louisiana, and from there it marched into Texas and joined the Texas Army in San Antonio. A siege was laid, and then the Texans attacked. They came under Mexican fire and advanced by fighting from house to house. After three days of urban warfare, the Mexicans retreated into the countryside.

In March of 1836, Ehrenberg participated in the Battle of Coleto led by Colonel James W. Fannin. On the 20th, Fannin ran out of water and ammunition. He had to negotiate for surrender. His soldiers were worried about this since they had heard rumors that the Mexicans had executed Texas troops earlier at the Alamo. And anyway, how could the parties talk? The Mexicans didn't speak English and the Americans didn't understand Spanish. Fortunately, a Mexican captain, Juan Jose Holzinger, spoke German like Ehrenberg did on the Texas side. So these two men parleyed in German about the terms.

Fannin gave up all weapons, and General Urrea offered to let the Texans go, provided they agreed to never fight the current Mexican government again. Ehrenberg said later that this was an easily acceptable condition: Times were so unsettled that no one anticipated that the Mexican government would last very long.

Waiting to be released, the 300 to 400 Texan soldiers were—temporarily, they thought—locked into the little church at Goliad. It was very crowded in there, and the men could neither sit down nor stretch out to rest. Before he had to leave, Urrea left word that the Texans should be treated well, but his arriving superior General Santa Ana had other ideas and ordered the execution of the rebel captives.

Then, on March 27, the men were divided into groups and had to march from the church for about a mile towards the San Antonio River. They were barked at to kneel down. Most of the Texans didn't understand the command, yet the first and the second volley came quickly and mowed the men down. Covered in a thick cloud of gun smoke, his eyes filled with sights from the writhing or already-dead bodies of his friends and comrades, Ehrenberg bolted and ran. He could move. He was not wounded. He sprinted through the smoke towards the sound of rushing water to the edge of the river, and jumped into the water, yelling "Texas forever!" (He later wrote an account about it, telling us that this was what he shouted (Ehrenberg, 1845).

The book was published in Germany in 1843 under the title *Texas und Seine Revolution.* (The University of Texas has a typescript copy of it). A hail of bullets came down around him, but he swam to safety. He was one of the 28 survivors of what became known as the Goliad Massacre.

Yes, now he was safe, but also humgry and weak from thirst. The countryside was empty and inhospitable. People had fled. The only humans he could find were Mexican soldiers. When one reads these old stories, amazement hits. How resistant, inventive, bold, and witty people in almost hopeless situations behave! I come across this often enough, and it happens regardless of origin or languages spoken by those involved. In any case, our 20-year-old massacre survivor now audaciously turned to the enemy General Urrea, saying that he was a lost Prussian traveler who needed protection in this theater of war.

The Mexican general was of the chivalrous sort, as we have already seen from his orders given earlier. Now he permitted Ehrenberg to travel along. This the young man did for several weeks. Yet on April 21, after Santa Ana was defeated by other units of Texans, Ehrenberg faded away from General Urrea's troops, reached Matagorda, which was controlled by Texans, and was properly discharged from the Texas forces on June 2, 1836.

Perhaps then Ehrenberg's appetites for fighting had disappeared. He returned to Germany, attended Freiburg University—yes, it was Freiburg, not The Technical University Freiberg (I wrote to this school and checked), which is the famous mining academy in Saxony where Humboldt studied. Ehrenberg wrote and published his book about the Texas Revolution, and by the early 1840s taught English at Halle University. Comparing this to Charles Blümner's unfulfilled desires to return to Prussia for a visit to his family, I wonder how young Ehrenberg was able to finance all these travels and studies.

In any event, by 1844, Ehrenberg was back in the United States and worked as an explorer, surveyor, cartographer, prospector, and mining engineer. He joined a fur-trapping party on its way to Oregon, and from there sailed to Hawaii in May of 1845. The government hired him to survey Honolulu, and draw a map of the city. He then visited various Polynesian islands and traveled as far as Tahiti. Returning, he was in California during the Mexican-American War and witnessed the conquest. He was also present during the gold rush of 1848–49, and active in mapping parts of the Gadsen Purchase and areas in New Mexico, California, and Arizona.

In 1856, together with Charles Poston, he set up the offices of the Sonora Exploring and Mining Company in Tubac, Arizona. His articles were published in the *Journal of Geology,* the *Mining Magazine,* and *Arizona Weekly.* He never married. He had a home in San Francisco. During the years from 1863–66 he was an agent for the Mojave (or Mohave) tribe on the Colorado River Reservation and spent much time among the people that Möllhausen had liked so much. That was almost the end of the road, and what a road it was:

As reported in *Daily Alta California, Volume 18,* Number 6064, 18 October 1866, Herman Ehrenberg was murdered at Dos Palmos, California, on the road from San Bernardino to La Paz. The Arizonians, the articles stated, "consider him one of the leading pioneers and most prominent citizens of the Territory. Mr. Ehrenberg was a very modest, taciturn, brave, kind, honest, and in every way worthy man" (*Daily Alta California,* 1866). He was 50 years old when he died.

Mineral City, Arizona was renamed Ehrenberg in his honor. Today it is another ghost town. There is also a summit called Ehrenberg Peak in the Grand Canyon National Park.

—

The Apache wars were fought in the mountains of New Mexico, Arizona, and even across the border in Mexico's *Sierra Madre.* They mirrored the terrain: choppy, fractured, implacable, and visually impenetrable. Usually, you just saw the cruel results. People today talk about asymmetrical conflicts, and if there ever was one, this was it. It lasted for a long time, from the end of the Mexican-American War in 1849 against the Jicarillas of northern New Mexico, to the final battle that concluded with the surrender of Geronimo in 1886. But it still continued in small skirmishes after that. It was a war that can make you feel nauseous and distressed, and almost sorry that you belong to the human species.

Most wars will do that if you look closely enough, but this one had its own merciless logic and it masquerades as being inevitable. The conflict stands like a symptomatic sign of the times, which were fueled by the drive for Manifest Destiny and the mindset of survival of the fittest. One of the key players on the American side was a German, Albert "Al" Sieber, a veteran of the Civil War who became the Chief of Scouts for the U.S. Army during the Apache Wars.

Albert Sieber was born in Mingolsheim near Heidelberg on February 29, 1844, as the 13th of 14 children. His father died only a year later, and revolutionary disturbances in 1848 and 1849 drove his mother, Eva Katharina, to leave Baden and to immigrate to the United States. The eight children who had survived the childhood illnesses and hardships traveled with her. I try to visualize this. How could any woman, alone in the mid-19th century, manage to do such a thing? The family settled first in Lancaster, Pennsylvania, among other Germans, and later moved to Minnesota. It somehow ate, and slept, and lived.

The minute he turned 18, Al Sieber enlisted in Company B of the Minnesota Infantry and served in the Civil War. He fought at Antietam, Fredericksburg, and Gettysburg. He was badly wounded during the Cemetery Ridge fight at Gettysburg, and never fully recovered for the rest of his life. He merely collected additional wounds and permanent injuries in the course of his career.

At Gettysburg, his regiment was 60% German and fought against an adversary five times superior in strength. Out of 262 men, 174 were wounded. Sieber received an open head wound from a shrapnel and was shot through his right leg. He healed for six months in an Army hospital, served as a warden in a POW camp, was promoted to corporal, and honorably discharged with a bonus payment of $300 on July 15, 1865.

Readjusting to civil society after a big war seems to be a recurring difficulty, and so it was after the Civil War. Many men did not wish to stay in the frenzied developing East, so they drifted westward and grabbed whatever work they could find. Sieber did some prospecting in California and Nevada, and then found a job running a ranch in the brand-new town of Prescott, Arizona. He must have learned by doing. Indian fighting became part of the working day.

In 1863, gold was discovered near Prescott and a stampede of would-be miners arrived. Farmers followed, taking hold of the Verde Valley. This changed the situation for the native Yavapai people rapidly and drastically: Game was killed; seed-bearing plants were munched by cattle. The Yavapai began to go hungry. To prevent that, they raided. White settlers fought back. Managing a ranch, Al Sieber learned about dealing with Indian attacks and retreats first hand. It turned out that he was a natural.

Within two or three years, Al was widely known for his unusual scouting skills. When the local wars over land and resources became ever more intense, cries for help were finally heard and the U.S. Army under General George Crook began to deal with the Apaches. In 1871, General Crook hired Al Sieber as his chief of Scouts. It was one of the most dangerous positions within the U.S. government. Sieber was wounded 29 times by knives, bullets, or arrows, and served for most of the Apache wars, beginning with Crook's Tonto Campaign from 1871–1873. The Apaches called Al the paleface who didn't know fear. He negotiated and translated. He was out in the field for weeks on end as the only white man among his Apache scouts.

FIGURE 18. *Al Sieber with Apache Scouts,*
photo by J.C. Burge, 1870's. Wikimedia Commons.

Apacheria, as it was called, was the home of various subgroups, bands, and clans of people who all had their own names. Al Sieber was confronted by, and involved with many of them over years of service. The historian Dan L. Thrapp wrote a comprehensive account of the scout's life and activities in Arizona (Thrapp, 2012). Sieber had become a formidable Indian fighter. He could out-track, out-last, out-smart, and out-fight even the most skillful Apache leaders in a contest that required above all the abilities of stealth and endurance. He participated in more missions than Daniel Boone and Kit Carson combined. He was tough, and killed many Apaches. But he was also honest, and respected his adversaries. He came to know their way of thinking, and understood the psychological basics of their behavior. This worked on both sides: The Apaches respected Sieber and his word.

Dan L. Thrapp's book contains a chapter titled "A Man of Note." And that is what Sieber became: a man with a good reputation, a record of campaign successes, and a permanent job on the U.S. Army payroll. Others were hired part-time for specific campaigns, but Al was the full-time Chief of Scouts and General Crook worked well with him. When Al participated in a campaign (essentially, they were complicated search and destroy missions and demanding manhunts through the mountains) it usually turned out well for the U.S. Army. Once the army had pacified an area, the Apache population was transferred to a reservation, first to Camp Verde and then to San Carlos.

The Verde Valley had provided water, riparian vegetation, shade, and good soil. But scarce fertile land was desired by incoming whites. Accordingly, the Camp Verde reservation was closed only a few years after being established through a presidential decision, and in February of 1875, Sieber was ordered to move about 1,500 people of several tribes in the dead of winter to a new place.

His commander during this operation was the cocksure Levi Edwin Dudley who decided that the longer and safer dirt road should not be used. Instead, the people on the forced march of 180 miles had to walk on foot on a shorter route which took them through narrow canyons and swollen creeks, over mountain passes, and through steep-sloped forests all covered with snow and ice.

I have driven through the mining town of Globe, now a pleasant little place with some signs of gentrification. The Apache called it *Bésh Baa Gowah*, the place of metals. Indeed, silver was discovered there, lasted only a few years, and then came a copper boom of sorts. A stagecoach route connected this mining hamlet with another one: Silver City in New Mexico. I also drove through the forests and mountains to San Carlos, which is a large reservation to this day. On July 7, 2014, it had a population of 15,392 persons.

These days, San Carlos Apache Chairman Terry Rambler is adamantly opposed to the land "swap" bill HR 687, which passed Congress on December 12, 2014. It will give 2,400 acres of core Apache land, site of a massive copper belt, to the giant British-Australian mining corporation Rio Tinto. This multinational group is headquartered in Melbourne, Australia, and has operations across the globe. The land in question contains such iconic places as Apache Leap, where families jumped from a cliff to their death rather than await being killed by settlers, and the extraordinary Devil's Canyon.

HR 687 was attached as a rider to the National Defense Authorization Act with the support of Senator McCain (R-AZ) and therefore became practically untouchable and assured to pass. The Sierra Club and other environmental organizations had fought against the mining plans for more than a decade, arguing that the making of a mining hole two miles in diameter would devastate the area's aquifers and that the anticipated block caving, or drilling the land more than a mile deep would turn the earth underground into something resembling a Swiss cheese with the danger of collapse. Without a veto from the White House, the "swap" will go ahead.

But back to the San Carlos beginnings. At first, conditions were very bad. The place was scorned as Hell's Forty Acres. The initial residents were the Chiricahuas. They were soon deported to Florida, which was even more dismal for them: Many wilted and perished in the climate. Within three years, 20 percent had died.

Next it was the turn of the Rio Verde Natives who were ordered to a new location after Camp Verde was closed. Sieber had an almost impossible job on his hands during this removal trek. The old, the young, and the weak began to collapse. Two dozen children were born under appalling conditions. In addition, as at Bosque Redondo, a combination of ignorance and arrogance sentenced old enemies to become living or traveling companions. It didn't work. Near the Mazatzal Mountains someone yelled "Kill the Tontos!" and the tensions between two hostile groups erupted in instant vicious fights. Sieber and his men leaped into the middle of it, struggling to separate the two sides, trying to prevent a bigger massacre. With improbable bravery, in this they succeeded. Many people were wounded, but "only" five Apaches died.

The anecdotes, or rather legends (because that is what they became) of the Apache Kid and Al Sieber have a pull and a fascination that's hard to resist. No one knows for sure where the Kid was born, or how and when his life ended. But everything in between is packed full with drama, daring, and pain. According to Dan L. Thrapp, the tall, handsome, lean, and intelligent Apache "had greatness in him, and the tragedy of the Kid is that of lost greatness" (Thrapp, 2012, p. 320). His life, as far as we can know about it, provides an overlooked lesson on how a man can become radicalized. Maybe it is useful to remember this, since there are so many examples of radicalization in today's world.

The Kid had allegedly up to a dozen Apache names, and most of them were a yard long and unpronounceable for the white people in Arizona. That's why they simply called him the Kid, and later, after he had turned outlaw, he was the Apache Kid, with deeds, crimes, and tall tales galore heaped upon his life.

As a child, the Kid was the boy about town. He ran errands in Globe, did jobs for soldiers, and was helpful to residents. One could see him, always following Al Sieber like a puppy. Al became friendly with him, and some say that he treated him almost like an adopted son. The youngster learned quickly, spoke English early, and paid close attention to everything Al Sieber did. He even picked up Al's way of cooking. After a few years he had grown so skillful that he successfully enlisted in the U.S. Army's Apache scouts and, still a teenager, participated in campaigns under General Crook and with Al Sieber.

It had been General Crook's idea to use Apaches to subjugate Apaches. Who else understood and could read or track them better? They were furtive and wily, and very hard to pin down. The dilemma with this approach is that it must produce conflicting feelings. We Americans were the intruders and occupiers. We had the resources, and we were winning. Hiring those Natives who were already defeated, or pacified, or contented to live under our guidance, and employing them against their own still resisting freedom fighters created a delicate dynamic. There were setbacks. There were outbreaks when Apaches fled the reservation. And there were also desertions and betrayals.

Didn't we recently spend huge amounts of treasure to train and equip armies in Afghanistan and Iraq? Haven't we found out from history what usually happens to those who collaborate with liberators, invaders, and occupiers if the tide turns? And didn't the American-trained Iraqi army just recently dump most of its expensive and superior U.S. hardware and ran away? Now all these goodies, including tanks, help the Islamic State radicals to make things difficult for us.

In any event, the Kid became a scout in 1881 and did so well that he was promoted to sergeant only a year later in 1882. The 1885–1886 campaign against Geronimo took him as far as the *Sierra Madre* in Mexico. He was noted for his incredible eyesight. In one instance, operating in desert terrain, he could see a group of riders 15 miles distant. The Southwest is known for its far and clear vistas, but the Kid could also report to his field-glass wielding officer how many white men were in that party, and how many Indians, and the number of horses, and mules. This could be discerned from the different body language of the riders and their animals, and even from the dust clouds they stirred up. The officer saw nothing but moving specks, even with his strong field glasses. He could, however, confirm later that the Kid's observations had been completely accurate.

The Kid was outstanding, but in general, whether "pacified" or still "wild," the Apaches were tough mountain people on their own turf in extremely difficult terrain. They could make use of everything on their own land, and any guerilla to this day could learn from their masterful tactics of resisting and of becoming virtually invisible within their surroundings.

The troubles for the Kid began when he was left in charge of his fellow Apache scouts in May of 1887. The unit's commanding officer Captain Pierce and Al Sieber were called off on an assignment. This presented a wonderful occasion for the Apaches to brew *tiswin,* a highly intoxicating drink made from fermented corn or fruit. It was an illegal concoction on the San Carlos

Reservation, but as the saying goes, when the cat is away, the mice will play. A wild party followed.

One Apache killed the Kid's father, and was in turn killed. The Kid himself then went out to dispatch the father-killer's brother. Yet when he and his companions came back to San Carlos, Captain Pierce and Al Sieber had returned and were waiting. The officer ordered the scouts to disarm. The Kid obeyed first, and immediately. As Pierce then told these men to enter the guardhouse where they would be locked up, a shot was fired from the group of spectators that had assembled to watch the scene. More shots followed. Al Sieber was hit in his ankle, which injured him badly and semi-crippled him permanently.

During the scuffle that broke out, the Kid and several other Apache scouts fled. It's not known who fired the shots or injured Al. Only one thing is clear: It wasn't the Kid or one of his fellow culprits, because this little group had already been disarmed. The Army reacted fast as lightning, sending out troops from the Fourth Cavalry to find the Kid and the other escaped scouts. The soldiers needed two weeks to locate the fugitives. Their horses were taken, and the hunted men scrambled off into rocky canyons.

The Kid sent a message to General Miles, who had replaced General Crook: If the general decided to recall the Cavalry, the Kid would surrender. Miles agreed. The Kid and seven others gave themselves up. They were court-martialed, found guilty of mutiny, and desertion, and sentenced to death. Miles was troubled about the verdict, asked for reconsideration, and got a new verdict of lifelong imprisonment. In the end, this was further reduced to ten years. The men were soon shipped off to the prison rock of Alcatraz in California.

But that wasn't all. Extreme prejudice among the officers was found regarding the earlier court-martial proceedings, so the convicted men were returned to San Carlos and set free. This enraged the white residents of Gila County and led to the re-arrest of four scouts, which included the Kid. This time these Apaches were indicted on a bogus charge of assaulting Al Sieber to commit murder even though they had had no weapons to shoot with at the time. The travesty of justice continued with a new guilty verdict of seven years to be served at the Territorial Prison in Yuma, Arizona. The prisoners traveled to this place under guard, escaped, fought, and fled yet again. One guard was killed, one died from stress or heart attack or such, and the third, Eugene Middleton, lived to tell the tale. He testified that the Kid prevented his death by restraining the others from bashing his head in. It was now October 1889.

This was the last time anyone actually saw the Kid in person. For years, stories about sightings, about his tuberculosis, and his numerous dastardly deeds were told, but there was no proof or hard evidence. A $15,000 reward was placed on his head by the Arizona Territorial Legislature. However, the kid was never captured. Only the legends surrounding him grew and grew. Geronimo was a leader and a fighter who had resisted for years and was finally brought down and exiled. Only the Kid remained hunted, yet free and undefeated.

Al Sieber continued to serve at San Carlos, but grew increasingly grumpy and bitter. In December of 1890, Major John L. Bullis fired Sieber on the spot after the old scout gave his superior a piece of his mind. Sieber felt that the Apaches were being mistreated. Indian agents lined their pockets while the newly dependent Native people didn't receive most supplies. They were hungry. They were also used as unpaid prison-labor to construct roads, and when the prisons were empty Bullis filled them with innocent men on trumped-up charges. The major was said to be a millionaire who had amassed thousands of acres of land in Texas by driving out long-established Mexican settlers with the help of Seminole Indian Scouts and then buying the vacated land for cents per acre (Thrapp, 2012, p. 400).

There were other incidents when Bullis and Sieber didn't see eye to eye. In any case, after his firing Al left San Carlos within a few hours after serving more than 20 years. He was crippled now, and growing frail. He returned to prospecting in the area around the town of Globe.

Meanwhile, U.S. progress marched on: By 1907, Roosevelt Dam was being built on the Salt River in the Tonto Basin. Old Al Sieber was asked

FIGURE 19. *The Apache Kid*

to be the manager for Apache work crews that constructed roads needed for the Dam project. After all, he knew his Apaches. On February 19th, Al's men had tried all day to deal with the problem of a huge boulder on a steep slope. It blocked the way. It had to be removed and weighed an estimated five or six tons. About thirty workers had tried everything, but the rock would not budge.

Sieber crept up the slope with his injured leg to inspect the situation. He pushed himself into a space under the stone, which suddenly shuddered and rushed down the slope. It crushed the body of the old fighter. He made no sound. A moan went up from the work crews, although some people later said the Apaches pushed the rock on Al (Thrapp, 2012, p. 401).

His grave is in the cemetery of Globe, Arizona, and his Apache laborers made another memorial for him near the spot where he died. They used the fawn-colored stones of these hills. There is also a Sieber Creek named after him, and a Seiber Point (misspelling his name) on the northern edge of the Grand Canyon National Park.

—

In contrast to Herman Ehrenberg who was murdered and Al Sieber who was crushed by a rolling boulder, Franz Huning died on November 6, 1905, in Albuquerque, in his bed, and as a wealthy man. Born in Hannover in 1827, he had left his home during the time of the revolutionary tide and sailed for the United States. In 1849, he signed on as a bullwhacker on the Santa Fe Trail, arrived in New Mexico, liked what he found, and stayed on. Soon he was hired as a clerk by one of Albuquerque's first American merchants, Simon Rosenstein.

Only five years later, Huning opened his own store on the plaza and from then on his career as a sort of pioneer merchant prince of territorial New Mexico took off. He seemed to do everything right. First of all, he invited his brothers Louis, Karl (Charles), and Henry to join him in New Mexico. The four brothers worked well together. By 1871, they had opened six stores and sold and traded widely in the area. One of the stores in Los Lunas, south of Albuquerque, operated from 1860 until 1994.

The Hunings also had substantial government contracts. Their livestock holdings were immense. They included 60,000 head of sheep and about 8,000 cattle. The wool business boomed during the Civil War, and even afterwards. In a good year, the Hunings could sell about 200,000 pounds of the warm natural fiber.

Ever enterprising, Franz Huning bought the needed machinery and built a new flour mill and a saw mill in Albuquerque. Both were highly successful. He eventually owned 700 acres of land on the edge of town and built himself a castle in the middle of it. That was what people called it: the castle. It was a grand palatial villa with a square tower surrounded by manicured gardens. Huning Castle was the finest residence in town, and Franz raised a family in it.

More than 20 years had passed since Lieutenant Whipple, and with him Balduin Möllhausen, visited Albuquerque during their important work on the Railroad Survey. What happened to the big plans for building a railroad to the Pacific? Well, the Civil War happened. Eventually, the railroad came to New Mexico from the north, and Franz Huning was ready for it. He had bought up land for some time. Together with Elias Stover and the attorney William Hazeldine, Huning made a discreet deal with the railroad for the right of way. This made Albuquerque a (soon booming) railroad town, and by 1880, the tracks were finally laid two miles east of what was soon named the "Old Town."

The Atchison, Topeka, and Santa Fe Railway arrived and a whole "new" town grew up almost over night. Many people came to New Mexico. For a while, almost one third to one half of the town's male workers were employed at the rail yards. Fairly soon, the benevolent climate triggered a wave of visiting tuberculosis patients who came hoping for a cure and often stayed on. Clinics and sanatorium facilities opened up. Next, New Mexico's tourism was invented. Beautiful posters and brochures advertised the scenery, the architecture, and the exotic cultures of the area. Artists followed, discovered Santa Fe and Taos, settled in, and turned both locations into art towns.

The railroads were not constructed according to the fine pre-war surveys. They were built in bits and pieces, but that too worked. The infrastructure of the railway networks was absolutely necessary for the most basic development of the huge country. They became the arteries that supplied what was needed in sufficient quantities and with a speed that had been impossible up to this point. It wasn't an easy or painless process. It aided progress and disrupted or hurt long-established patterns of life. Yet the well-being of the men (many of them Chinese immigrants) who did the hard labor of putting down tracks under the harshest conditions was not a matter of concern.

I am sure it will not be very popular if I say this, but I can't help of being reminded of Russia's forced development and industrialization somewhat later under the communists. In both cases, you had huge countries that needed immense amounts of hard work, and you couldn't accomplish that by pussy-footing around. Russia punished persons by sentencing them to do hard labor in Siberia and then in the Gulag. The U.S. had immigrants who came voluntarily but had no safety net. For many, this meant that if they wanted to survive in 19ᵗʰcentury America, they had to work. It didn't matter how hard, hot, cold, brutal, demeaning, and bone-breaking the job was; it got done. The German language has a word for the process: *verheizen*. You would be *verheizt:* ill used as fuel, or become fuel.

There is too much material to cover it within the scope of this book, but New Mexico had its own railroad stories and ballads. The land grant way of looking after the common good was under assault with the coming of the railroads. Speculators known as the Santa Fe Ring used elaborate schemes to liberate locals from their property or communal lands. Squatters settled whereever they liked. It was a tactic that had already been successful in Texas and Florida. They even sold acreage that they didn't own to begin with. Land wars broke out as ranching empires were assembled and legends flourished around Billy the Kid and his days and deeds. New Mexicans were asked to show ownership in English language documents (which was impossible) even though they had farmed the same soil for generations and had done business in Spanish for hundreds of years.

Times were hard across the countryside. Barbed wire restricted the freedom of movement across the land, and that produced the short-lived but fierce resistance movement of *Las Gorras Blancas,* the White Caps. They were organized in San Miguel County during the spring of 1889 by the brothers Juan José, Pablo, and Nicanor Herrera. Supporters and participants came from surrounding small communities. The White Caps rode on horseback, mostly at night, and were camouflaged by wearing white caps. They fought against Anglo land grabbers by tearing down barbed wire fences, driving livestock away, burning barns, and disrupting ranching operations. They also demanded better wages for Hispanic laborers, and when the Atchison, Topeka, and Santa Fe Railroad refused, Juan José Herrera led a group of White Caps to set thousands of railroad ties afire.

The men even formed their own political party named *Partido del Pueblo Unido*, ran for office, and succeeded in having three members elected to the state legislature. Pablo Herrera, one of the elected, soon resigned and gave a parting speech in front of his colleagues. He said that he had served time in the penitentiary and was in the legislature only for 60 days. But the time in prison was more enjoyable than his work among the lawmakers because there was far more honesty among the inmates at the penitentiary.

Soon, the activities of the White Caps ceased. Pablo was killed by the sheriff in Las Vegas, New Mexico—at the time a wild railroad town. Juan José moved to Utah and lived a few years longer. I did not see a reference on Nicanor.

~

As for the Railroad Survey along the 35th parallel, its proposed route was to a large part incorporated into what John Steinbeck called the "Mother Road," the road of flight, in his famous novel *The Grapes of Wrath*. It ran from Chicago to Los Angeles. It was 2,448 miles long. Refugees from the suffocating Dustbowl of the 30s, the Beat generation, the footloose and the restless with their songs and stories, all traveled along this road until the huge Interstate system was built and bypassed it. Now only sleepy sections, the legends, and the romance linger on.

12

Meet My Grandfather

The crisis that brought war in 1914 was the fruit of a shared political culture.

      — Christopher Clark (2012), The Sleepwalkers

Does patriotism mean support your government?
No. That's the definition of patriotism in a totalitarian state.

      — Howard Zinn (2008), Denver Speech

The amiable Baron Gerolt took his leave from the United States and President Grant on June 29th, 1871. This happened only about six months after the reunification of Germany as the Second Empire. (The first empire was terminated by Napoleon in 1806). The baron had served as Prussia's ambassador or Minister Plenipotentiary in Washington for more than a quarter of a century. He had been in Washington, DC during the U.S.-Mexican War and the Civil War. No German diplomat served longer. On May 17, Gerolt was honored with a formal state banquet attended by numerous illustrious guests giving short speeches (*The New York Times*, 1871).

We have come across a few small examples of the diplomat's activities in earlier chapters of this book, for example when Balduin Möllhausen sent $400 of his saved salary to the ambassador, asking him to please forward the money to his sweetheart, Caroline Seifert, the daughter of Humboldt's secretary/butler, in Berlin. Gerolt did this, and also wrote to Humboldt about Möllhausen's artistic work and about the overall progress of the Whipple expedition. The diplomat had studied mining and geology as a young man, knew Humboldt well, and shared interests with him and with the explorers of the survey team. It is also worth noting that there was still a personal and caring touch available back then.

And indeed, despite some grumbling from Benjamin Franklin about too many Germans with their language in Pennsylvania (no one could or would pronounce "*deutsch*, so these early immigrants morphed into the Pennsylvania Dutch), relations with the United States had been friendly and smooth from the start. The first treaty signed with a European power after the American Revolutionary War was the Treaty of Amity and Commerce between the United States and Prussia. Thomas Jefferson was then ambassador to France and helped with the negotiations. George Washington and Frederick the Great signed it on September 10, 1785. It declared peace and friendship between the two countries.

Among other beneficial things were a Mutual Most Favored Nation Status, Mutual Protection of Vessels when under U.S. or Prussian jurisdiction, the right of each country's citizens to hold land in both nations, and unconditionally humane treatment for war prisoners. This last provision was a newfangled one after the excesses of the 17th century Thirty Years' War over there and the more recent Savage Wars between Native North Americans and Europeans over here. Frederick, a valuable ally during the French and Indian War, was probably well informed about the conflict on American soil. He wasn't interested in scalps and such.

That war was also fought on a larger scale and has multiple names: The French Canadians call it the War of Conquest; Germans, The Seven Years' War; and for various historians it is a world war of sorts. It involved Europe, North and Central America, West Africa, India, and the Philippines.

There has actually been a tall statue of Frederick, nicknamed "Freddy the Great," standing for more than a hundred years with interruptions on a stone pedestal in this country. It is now at the U.S. Army War College in Carlisle, Pennsylvania. Maybe Freddy would have tolerated the irreverent renaming, which nicely combines the ridiculous with the sublime. After all, he was a king who remarked, "a crown is merely a hat that lets the rain in."

As a young man, shortly before he ascended the throne of Prussia, he wrote an essay titled *The Anti-Machiavel*. As a king-to-be, reading Machiavelli's *The Prince* was part of his education, and so he wrote his own essay as a rebuttal of that famous book, chapter by chapter and point by point. His friend Voltaire participated in the editing and publishing. A king, argued Frederick, is mostly charged with maintaining or building the health and prosperity of his subjects.

Incidentally, Frederick the Great visited Humboldt's home, Tegel. The children were introduced to him. The king chatted about Alexander the Great and asked the boy Alexander if he was also interested in conquering the world like the ancient Macedonian. "Yes, sire," answered the boy, "but with my head" (Helferich, 2004, p. 5).

Frederick cared about education for all. In 1763, he mandated free public education in Prussia for children aged 5 to 13/14. Out of this developed the Prussian Education System, so-called in the English-speaking world. It was developed by Alexander von Humboldt's older brother Wilhelm von Humboldt, who became minister of education in 1809, was a philosopher, diplomat, linguist, founder of the Humboldt University in Berlin and of the Gymnasium, and a reformer of education, as well as a proponent of academic freedom for young and old alike.

The Prussian model worked and spread to Austria and the Scandinavian countries. Even Russian-ruled Estonia, Latvia, and Finland adopted it. France and England were slower to reform: They finally established compulsory education in the 1880s. There was also much interest in the United States. In 1843, the Massachusetts politician and reformer Horace Mann visited Germany to study tax-supported Prussian education. He returned fired up, and worked tirelessly until the Prussian model was accepted for his state in 1852. New York and other northern states followed. By 1918, the United

States reached the point when the schooling of all children, at least at the elementary level, was required.

But back to the Freddy statue. Its fate reflected the changing Zeitgeist and the yo-yo- relationship between the two countries by narrowly escaping a first bomb attack in 1905, and a second one in 1918. After that second attempt, Old Fritz (the German nickname) was put into storage, taken out in 1927, and made to disappear once more at the start of World War II. It's really no way to treat the man who never harmed a hair on a single American head. Anyway, he had to wait until the 1950s to leave the darkness to see some American light of day again. In contrast, the trials and tribulations of his real body and bones, over there, during and after World War II, were far more bizarre. But for this story, it's sufficient to know that the Treaty between the U.S. and Prussia was renewed in 1799 by young John Quincy Adams, sent to Berlin by his father. In 1828, it was confirmed again. It endured for about a century.

It is not surprising that President Ulysses S. Grant saw things in a favorable light. On February 7, 1871, he greeted developments by saying "The union of the States of Germany into a form of government similar in many respects to that of the American Union is an event that cannot fail to touch deeply the sympathies of the people of the United States" (Jonas, 1984, p. 16).

Grant had first-hand knowledge of the contributions German immigrants made during the Civil War. Their enlistments by far exceeded their percentage within the total population. Even Carl Schurz, a politically prominent 48er who later served as a U.S. Senator and Secretary of the Interior, fought as a major general of volunteers for most of the war (Jonas, 1984, p. 23). And not only that, an American mission in Europe to sell U.S. government bonds fell flat in England and the Netherlands, but raised funds in Frankfurt. Overall, about $800,000 in bonds had been sold in German lands by the end of the war. One can only guess that the Germans were in a unification mood and supported the U.S. struggle to stay together.

In 1867, George Bancroft, an admirer of Prussia, was appointed as minister (ambassador) to Berlin. He remained in this post until 1874 and his retirement. Like many young Americans—some before and many after him—he had studied in Germany. His doctorate was from the University of Göttingen, and he had also done work in Heidelberg and Berlin. He was a scholar, politician, historian, and Germanophile, something that was not uncommon at the time, existed quite naturally next to Anglophiles etc., and is nearly unthinkable today: Modern wars never end. In any case, he met almost every person of import, from the Humboldts to Goethe to Bunsen.

And yet, eventually Bancroft himself and his work fell out of favor. The writing of history appears to have ups and downs, with various trends and fashions. It's strongly dependent on political winds. I once acquired an aged multi-volume set of Bancroft's *History of the United States of America* at a yard sale and tried to plow my way through it. But I couldn't stay with it.

Since the revolutionary uprisings in Europe, millions of Germans had come to the United States. Many were frugal and hard working. On Sunday they usually frolicked, thereby annoying their puritanical fellow citizens. Nevertheless, *The New York Times* wrote in January of 1869 that these persons were "undoubtedly the healthiest element of our foreign immigrants" (Jonas, 1984, p.20).

My husband's family arrived in the 1850s and bought a small farm in Ohio. They didn't have much, but it was enough to start a new life. When we attended his mother's funeral there some years ago, we toured the area. There were neat towns and villages that looked like copies transported from the old country. One was called New Bremen: all light red bricks and white trim. There were lovely little country churches and graveyards filled with withered Civil War headstones and chiseled German names. Strange.

—

Alexander von Humboldt died on May 6, 1859, nearly ninety years old. He had still worked every night until three in the morning, and made do with little sleep. On April 19 he delivered the last volume—number 5—of his big work *Cosmos* to his publisher, remained in bed two days later, and soon closed his eyes for good. His funeral was a grand affair not because of pomp, but for the participation by the people of Berlin. Only one funeral could match it in size: that for the revolutionaries who had died in 1848. At that time, old Humboldt himself had marched in front of the mourners with the wind ruffling his white hair—now they marched for him.

Four royal chamberlains came first, then the hearse with twenty students carrying palm fronds surrounding it, then family, friends, academics, German and American students, bureaucrats, politicians, scientists and artists, and thousands of workaday Berliners. He included them in his work and life, and they included him.

All the major American papers wrote wonderful things on the occasion of his death, and even ten years later, on the September 15, 1869, centennial of his birth, *The New York Times* devoted the entire front page to Humboldt. A bust was dedicated in Central Park, about 25,000 people attended, and there were banners and celebrations throughout the country. Well, after noting all these German-friendly goings-on, I felt as if I had eaten a dessert that was far too rich.

—

So now it's time to meet my grandfather:

Cool. A rock star. Evil and dripping blood.

What happened?

The United States declared war on Germany on April 2, 1917.

But why?

—

There will be a look backwards over the years between 1871 and 1917, but first I want to remember my real grandfather. I never knew him in person, only from stories and photos. He was said to be a mild-mannered man, an engineer in Berlin, married, and the father of three young children. Since the

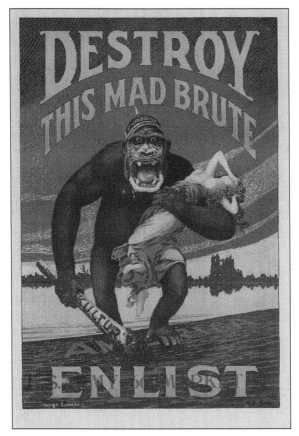

FIGURE 20. *U.S. Army World War I propaganda poster by Harry R. Hopps, 1917. Library of Congress.*

insatiable soldier-eating war machine in Europe required ever larger amounts of fresh human fuel and ran out of very young recruits, family men like him were also conscripted to serve.

He survived the trenches on the western front, but his heart was not so lucky. It was badly damaged. He came home. His family was happy. My mother, age seven, was the oldest, and she used to wake up early, sneak into her parents' bedroom on bare feet, and cuddle gently against her precious father. One morning he was ice cold.

215

My mother grew up fast and, during the years of the Hyperinflation and the Depression she was the substitute man in the house, going to school, helping my grandmother, and then being the bread-winner. She was good with languages and able to find work as a French & English secretary. I still have some 10, 50, 100 billion Mark banknotes from these years. She gave them to me. Things were so wild and crazy that in the morning you needed a shopping bag filled with paper money to buy a loaf of bread, and by the time the sun went down you needed a suitcase.

～

In 2014, the First World War was 100 years old. My father, who had an enduring appetite for history and read widely, probably stimulated my own passion in this direction. When I asked knotty questions, he told me to wait a hundred years. History didn't begin to take shape until a century had passed. I objected fiercely: But by then we are all dead! That's the idea, he said.

He liked Mark Twain, read him in translation, and shared Twain's old age view that "none but the dead are permitted to tell the truth."

Accordingly, Twain's *The War Prayer* was not published until 1923 when its writer was safely buried. And even today, when there is a TV documentary on his works and life, I noted *The War Prayer* is missing. How free are we if we censor one of our finest writers well into the 21st century? Do we accept our perpetual wars so much that we can't listen to an anti-war prose poem that tells it like it is?

My mother, on the other hand, with a cheerful disposition and her repertoire of songs and rhymes, used to sing comforting little verses when we kids were hurting or sad. The charming song exists in many variations from nursery rhyme to Carnival song to post-World War II love ballads for destroyed cities. This is the semi-nonsense refrain: "Heile heile Gänschen, wird alles wieder gut. / Heile, heile Mausespeck, in hundert Jahren ist alles weg." (Inadequate translation: "Get well, little goose, all will be good again. Heal fat little mouse—in a hundred years, it's all gone anyway.")

So here I am, with a father who told me that one must wait 100 years to catch a glimpse of history, and a mother who sang that everything will heal and that a 100 years from now it's all gone and forgotten! Both were right. I can deal with contradictions, but sometimes I feel I am suspended in a field of tension between the two statements. And one fact always intrudes: our short human lifespan. The great wars lapped up entire generations. Whole populations can be harmed, crushed, changed, and ruined by the raw and rowdy course of history.

─

To date, the literature on the First World War, this granddaddy of all modern wars, has become inexhaustible. As Christopher Clark wrote in his bestselling book *The Sleepwalkers* (2013),

> There is virtually no viewpoint on its origins that cannot be supported from a selection of the available sources. And this helps in turn to explain why the World War I origins literature has assumed such vast dimensions that no single historian (not even a fantasy figure with an easy command of all the necessary languages) could hope to read it in a lifetime (p. xxiv).

Clark tells us that twenty years ago, an overview found 25,000 books and articles on the subject. Imagine how many more were added since, and especially during, the anniversary year of 2014! The physical-visual remembrance was especially stunning in the UK, where nearly 900,000 tall man-made poppies, one for each of the fallen, formed a lake of red flowers around the Tower of London. It was a beautiful, moving concept and made me recall the British poets who lost their lives on the western front. Paul Fussell wrote about them in his *The Great War and Modern Memory*, which won both the 1976 National Book Award for Arts and Letters and the National Book Critics Circle Award for Criticism. I have an autographed copy of that book and also had the experience of sharing more than a lively hour of time during his visit to our school with Fussell and my English professor. The two men knew each other well.

Yet English-speakers are unaware of the artist-soldiers on the German side. They were expressionist painters. Two of them died on the western front: August Macke as early as September 1914, and Franz Marc in 1916 at Verdun. Actually, during and after the war, communication was pretty much a one-way street. English could travel; German was quarantined or worse. Those outside of Germany could not hear what these men and others had to say.

Britain cut all of Germany's international telegraph cables on August 5, 1914. They had crossed the ocean floors to the rest of Europe, to North Africa, and to North America. Britain knew how important the battle for public opinion was going to be, and intended to win it.

Franz Marc served in the cavalry. He was a friend of Klee and Kandinsky, and an astute, emphatic individual who had co-founded the artists' group *Der Blaue Reiter* in Munich. I have owned his *Briefe aus dem Felde 1914–1916* since I was a teenager and even hauled the book across the Atlantic. In 1938 and 1944, censorship prohibited the publication of these letters. They were unspoiled by bigotry, hatred, and jingoism. The orientation was toward the universal, with wide interests, and a deep affection for the homeland. The writing made you feel, hear, and smell the war; it raised questions and stimulated thinking.

No English translation existed until 1992, when Peter Lang published one: Franz Marc— *Letters from the War*. Now, many years after it was written, this remarkable book has become one more of the tens of thousands of items in World War I literature and it will slumber in that pile. How can any working, multi-tasking, time-starved present-day individual hope to cope with a tsunami of materials, provided he or she is even interested in that bygone old war of our grandparents or great grandparents? And how can any citizen and voter cope with history by and large, specifically in our country, which has been nicknamed the United States of Amnesia?

Well, never mind. Such questions can't be answered. I will have to focus on how I can deal with the issue. I am interested in that war. I have to be. The United States is my home and the home of my children. And just now I have to look at that poster of the brutish Hun-Ape once more. Its message eradicated German memories in the U.S. It wiped the slate clean. There is no such thing as a German or German-American community any longer. No one uses the term "German community." You hear about the Hispanic, the Jewish, the Black, the various Asian, the Italian, the Muslim, and the you-name-it communities. Yet you never hear anything about the "British community" either, but for different reasons. Barely post-Brexit, for the time being the British habitually remain the special relations. The Germans, in contrast, are the ideal Americans. They have no past.

It's fun to note, however, that Americans like to self-identify their descent. In the Census of 2000, "four out of five people specified at least one ancestry … 58 % of the population specified only one … 22 % provided two ancestries" (U.S. Census Bureau, 2004). Away from the Census, the people I meet or know increasingly joke and call themselves "American Mutt," listing the most delightful mixtures of descent within their own families. Even the aristocratic 138-year-old Westminster Kennel Club has now stooped to admitting mixed-breed dogs into some the country's most exclusive tournaments. So far, they had been reserved only for impeccably pedigreed dogs. And that's not all: Starting out, one of the mutts promptly earned three first places. Little things like that make me happy.

The numbers fluctuate somewhat depending on the way the Census people structure politically correct or desirable questions, but the noncommunity of persons with a German background remains the largest ancestry group in the U.S. as of the 2009 Census: 50.7 million people. It is such a big number that one can hardly call it a minority. The English group is listed with 27.6 million individuals. As things stand, I wouldn't be surprised if Members of Congress and political plotters soon begin to worry, after an intermission lasting a century, about the German vote once more .

Meanwhile, it is likely that the diverse Latino-Hispanic community will overtake all others. A good real-life demonstration of this would be a weekday visit on a summer morning to our attractive local zoo. It's green, and in full bloom with flowers, animals, birds, babies, and very young Hispanic women. Most of the pristine mamas are beautiful. I have never seen so many flourishing females pushing baby carriages in one place. This must be a meeting point. There are hardly any other visitors on such mornings. And somehow, even though life may be hard soon, for them having babies early seems to be the natural and joyful thing.

—

How to look at the time period from 1871 to 1917, leading from peace to war? From high regard to hate? It is impossible to contend with tens of thousands of already existing publications, and with books written by scores of international historians. The blame business has subsided, but understanding remains elusive. Over the decades, few historians were ready to agree that the "Sunday school theory" comments made in 1926 by their prominent colleague Charles A. Beard, who remarked sardonically that the tall tale of

> three pure and innocent boys—Russia, France, and England—without
> military guile in their hearts, who were suddenly assailed while on
> their way to Sunday school by two deep-dyed villains—Germany
> and Austria—who had long been plotting cruel deeds in the dark
> (qtd.in Borning, p.111)

was rather fanciful.

So do I begin with local events here in the U.S. Southwest, or with the big picture? I will start with a larger canvas. Let's visit England first.

There were several vigorous movements, factions, and schools of political thought active during the last third of the 19th and the first decade of the 20th century. One can investigate the liberal imperialists, the Fabians, the tariff reformers, internal and external social Darwinists, socialists, and more. Essentially, it was a struggle between Free Traders and those who wanted to protect English workers from lower-priced imports and job losses. The U.S. and Germany had industrialized rapidly, almost simultaneously, and began to outperform the world leader, Britain. In 1895, super-imperialist Cecil Rhodes described how he visited the East End of London and attended a meeting of the unemployed. He listened to passionate speeches which all seemed to shout and cry out for bread. He couldn't stop thinking about the scene, and he became convinced that imperialism provided the answer. This is what he came up with:

> My cherished idea is a solution for the social problem, i.e. in order to save the 40,000,000 inhabitants of the United Kingdom from a bloody civil war, we colonial statesmen must acquire new lands to settle the surplus population, to provide new markets for the goods produced by them ... The Empire, as I have always said, is a bread and butter question. If you want to avoid civil war, you must become imperialists (qtd. in Semmel, 1968, p. 4).

He didn't say what would happen to the native populations in the newly acquired lands.

A delegation from the Birmingham Chamber of Commerce told the Government, "We are being ruined. We work as hard as ever but without profit" (Semmel, 1968, p. 77). They told the authorities that America now produces her own guns, and that it even gets orders for foreign wars. The Midlands used to have a monopoly for screws and nails, they reported, but now the U.S. and Germany have built their own factories under the shelter of tariffs. Even Asia buys German nails, and buttons, and iron wire. And you can also buy these items right here, under our noses, in Birmingham.

Many of these concerns somehow came together in the life and work of Sir Halford Mackinder, a pioneer in the field of geopolitics and in geographical studies. He was appointed as the director of the first English university-level school of geography at Oxford. Active in politics and a MP for several years, he gradually changed his mind and joined the ranks of the protectionists, fearing that the 20th century would be a violent one.

In 1902, Mackinder suggested that imperialism and democracy were two antagonistic systems, but given the conditions in the international economy, even democracies needed to acquire empires. For Britain, this pairing was possible because there were oceans between the systems. (Similar ideas were apparently adopted in the U.S.) Later, his rationalizations had matured into a neat construction of his thinking:

> The separation of the tropical Empire from the European island, although perhaps a source of weakness from a military point of view, has had the supreme advantage, that
> ... imperial rule in the dependencies has not corrupted the freedom at home (Semmel, 1968, p. 167).

Next, in his famous 1904 essay *"The Geographical Pivot of History,"* he introduced the Heartland Theory. Mackinder warned against "the threat which a great land-based power, whose strength was in its armies and its industry [read Russia and Germany] posed for a sea-power on the periphery of the pivot, whose principal interest was peaceful trade."

England was a great sea power. It ruled the waves and trade. Things were not all that peaceful, however, out there in the Empire and away from home. Queen Victoria's Little Wars erupted one after the other, starting around 1837. This continued all through the 19th century until there had been nearly 100 conflicts worldwide throughout the British imperial possessions (Farwell, 1985).

Just in time for the Peace Conference at Versailles in 1919, The Pivot of History or Heartland Theory had been expanded into a book called *Democratic Ideals and Reality.* Mackinder's basic message was: "Who rules East Europe commands the Heartland; who rules the Heartland commands the World-Island; who rules the World-Island controls the world" (Mackinder, 1942, p. 150).

It was sea power versus land power: the World-Island was land-based Europe-Asia-Africa, all interconnected. The Heartland-Pivot was in the middle: Russia and neighboring areas. There were offshore islands, namely the British Isles and Japan. And finally there were the outlying islands, North and South America, and Australia. The World-Island contained more than 50% of the world's resources. Its Heartland was inaccessible by ships, and it was located in the planet's strongest defensive position. Intercontinental missiles had not been invented yet.

Mackinder lived a long life, from 1861 to 1947. His ideas remained influential in World War II and during the Cold War. And one glance at the 21st century Ukrainian conflict shows that the ghosts of the Heartland obsession are still spooking around in Anglo-American minds.

—

And then there was the twin theorist, this one the American strategist of sea power, Alfred Thayer Mahan, born at West Point in 1840, lecturer, president of the Naval War College, and friend of Theodore Roosevelt. He was older than Mackinder, and more focused specifically on naval matters. His book *The Influence of Sea Power upon History* (1890) became an international success. Kaiser Wilhelm II made the book required reading for all his naval officers, and ironically, Admiral Alfred von Tirpitz used Mahan's arguments in his struggles to get funding for a shiny new German fleet.

Mahan was an American imperialist, a variant of the species Mark Twain, as a vice-president of the Anti-Imperialist League, detested. One of Mahan's key ideas was the control and protection of commercial shipping. This was a radical new idea for Americans. Didn't they have already enough to do with expanding from sea to shining sea? And their leaders had desired even more and acquired it, across the oceans: Hawaii, the Philippines, American

Samoa, the Panama Canal Zone, and various islands in the Pacific and the Caribbean. This neo-colonial strategy was designed to secure access to dependent, and all other, foreign markets. Fueling (coaling) stations for ships and bases were required, but not too many, warned Mahan, because maintenance would be expensive.

So here we have it: Fierce competition for international markets. Squabbles about tariffs and land for fueling stations and military bases. It was the beginning of discord between the U.S. and Germany. American Samoa and German Samoa can serve as one example. As a trading nation, the Germans wanted fueling stations too. Their exports had steadily increased and, by 1913, reached 12.3 percent globally, while Britain's share had decreased from 22.4 percent in 1880 to 14.2 percent in 1913. Then there were unsubstantiated (Mitchell, 1999) American fantasies about German challenges to the Monroe Doctrine in South America. And with all this overheated competition going on, rivals were afraid of anyone who would become the dominant sea power of the future. Such a power could put a stranglehold on the economic life of other countries and did so during World War I.

Location, location, location. Germany is a central piece of real estate very close to the "heartland"— mostly flat—and with many neighbors. It's convenient and suitable as a playground or a battlefield. Thus, in the Thirty Years' War, which began in 1618 and ended in 1648, everybody in the neighborhood came to do his bloody business on this battlefield. At first it was about Catholics against Protestants. Soon it was meaningless. And then it turned into a long, ferocious fight for power in Europe. It was the time when Nation States were born, like planets, from violent swirls of gases and hot air.

The endless war trashed the playing field. Back then, people we know today as the sensible and civilized Swedes, apparently destroyed dozens of castles, hundreds of towns, and more than a 1000 villages. That many? In the course of doing this, Sweden became a great power. For a while.

Almost half of the male population in Germany perished. There were regional differences: Some areas lost up to 66 percent of their inhabitants, others far less—from war, disease, and hunger. Overall estimates range from a depopulation of ¼ to ½. For the United States today that would be like losing 85 to 170 million of its people. Unimaginable. It's mentioned here not to fish for empathy for that country, but only to set the stage.

When the treaties for The Peace of Westphalia were signed in 1648, Germany was a collection of countless little shards lying around like the remnants of a shattered majolica vase. Such a state of dissolution was probably a blessing in disguise because it made a long-lasting recovery period absolutely necessary and prevented German colonial conquests across the globe. The Germans were not among the bad guys. The splintered country did lie low, for the most part. When Bismarck finally glued the shards together, it came as a surprise to some. People and powers seem to be creatures of habit: The neighbors really had no use for a biggish patched-up vase.

—

In any case, by 1908, things in Britain had progressed to a point that made the daily diet of the German working class an issue of hot debate. Their workers eat better than ours! was the accusation. Not only the press beat the drums. The Tariff Reform League and other political groups printed and distributed enormous amounts of material. "The British worker," wrote Bernard Semmel (1968), "was assailed from all sides with leaflets, pamphlets, posters, diagrams, cartoons, and sheets of statistics" (p. 103). In 1906, 1,603,000 items were published by the League; in 1907, the numbers doubled and increased every year until they reached 6,034,900 in 1908. By 1910, the Tariff Reform League had distributed more than 53.1 million printed pieces (Semmel, 1968, p. 104). At that moment, the situation seemed to indicate that having huge colonial possessions did not necessarily guarantee a good return on investment (ROI) for the working population at home.

The tariff reformers said the German workers ate nothing but fine white bread and fed horseflesh only to their dogs, while lowly rye bread and horsemeat cost too much in England. A quarrel broke out over prices and the quality of bread: "Estimates for a 4 lb. rye loaf in Berlin in February of 1908 ranged from the *Economist*'s 8d, to the Board of Trade's 7½d, to the Tariff Reform League's 5¼ d." (Semmel, 1968, p. 110).

Actually, I have long felt that history has an impish sense of humor. Today's wellness gurus tell us that white bread, refined carbs, and gluten can be detrimental to our health. Therefore, the contemporary health conscious eater prefers rough rye to decadent white bread. Furthermore, when I was a kid, horseflesh literally saved me. Escaping, according to today's standards, fashionably super-thin from the Soviet Zone of Occupation after World War II, the children of our family looked like stick people. Today, during the winter, when I see the visiting sandhill cranes here in New Mexico, I think of my own kiddie legs back then: very long, bony, and with prominent bulb-like knees.

My father's friend in the West took us in because we didn't have a home yet on that western side of the new Iron Curtain where every bigger city looked liked Aleppo. He ran a small hotel and pub in the country. He served horseflesh stews. It was the only meat he could get. Fortunately, I didn't know what it was. I like horses. But I ate—pardon me—like a horse until a weight appropriate for my age was regained.

Since no agreements on food prices could be reached in anno 1908, English workers called "tariff-trippers" were dispatched to Germany to find out for themselves. They came home with much information about the happy conditions of the working stiffs over there. Sometimes these travelers exaggerated a bit, but all agreed that German blue collar guys had a better life. They had higher wages, better terms of employment, old age pensions, health insurance, and they ould afford some decent food. Today, with our dismal squabbles about healthcare and jobs/jobs/jobs, perhaps we Americans should dispatch some of our workers to investigate conditions elsewhere around the world.

Actually, England displayed evidence of poverty and wretchedness. Not everyone in Britain was pleased about these journeys. Some looked at the tariff trippers as if they were traitors or rebels.

~

Meanwhile, back home in the U.S., people lived in the Gilded Age. Mark Twain wrote a book with that title, and the title gave its name to the entire era. It lasted from about 1870 to 1900, roughly the time period that interests us here. But let's add the first decade of the 20th century, and then the World War I years to that.

Gilded doesn't indicate that something is solidly golden. Instead, it is only covered with a hair-fine layer of gold. One can watch how it is done when a craftsman gilds a picture frame.

Yes, it was like a gilded U.S. frame that showed a painting of great riches and luxury. Enormous fortunes were made. National wealth increased fivefold. At the same time, there were those who supported or condemned the era's Social Darwinism. Survival of the fittest was very much in vogue, although Darwin himself wanted to have nothing to do with it. "If the misery of our poor be caused not by the laws of nature, but by our institutions, great is our sin," is what he said (Darwin, 1839, XXI).

Indeed, millions of working people lived in squalor and had trouble putting food on the table. It was an intensely dynamic time filled with rapid, massive progress and profits, but also full of appalling human misery and labor strife. The financial panic of 1893 didn't help. A railroad bubble burst, 500 banks and 1500 companies failed, unemployment rose almost instantly and reached record levels in some states, for example 35% in New York, and 43% in Michigan. Small farmers were hard hit, too. Agricultural commodity prices fell, and many hard-working families had to mortgage the properties they had acquired through the Homestead Act not long ago. Soon they fell behind in payments and many lost everything they had..

Falling into this time period, just north of New Mexico, the 1913/14 Colorado Coal Strike became the deadliest labor conflict in the U.S. up to that date. Officially, about 75 people died, although fatality estimates were much higher. It was like a local civil war, lasting for more than seven months. In the worst incident, security guards of the Colorado Fuel & Iron Company (partly owned by the Rockefellers), and the National Guard attacked the strikers in the Ludlow Massacre. About 1200 strikers and their families had lost their company-owned shacks and survived the harsh winter conditions in tents. Machine gun volleys started the fires in the tent camp. Two women and eleven children were suffocated by smoke or burned to death. In response, hundreds of miners exploded and went to war in southern Colorado, assaulting mines and the hired hands/mercenaries of detective agencies employed by the owners until President Wilson dispatched federal troops, who disarmed all parties to the fight.

—

With a ferocious war going on in Europe and beyond since August of 1914, a Preparedness Movement sprang up in the United States. Ex-President Theodore Roosevelt, ex-secretaries of war Elihu Root and Henry Stimson, and General Leonard Wood were the main promoters. Big business and prominent members of the East Coast establishment joined them. They told the country day and night how weak it was with its tiny force of 100,000 men in the U.S. Army, plus a mere 112,000 National Guardsmen. That was a ratio of 20 to 1 compared to the German military. That would not do.

But the American people were not interested in far-away conflicts and President He-Kept-us-Out-of-the-War Woodrow Wilson did not fall for the Preparedness crowd until, on March 9, 1916, the Mexican revolutionary leader Pancho Villa attacked the American border town of Columbus, New Mexico, with 1500 guerillas. The raid killed 19 Americans and burned parts of the place to the ground. Pancho Villa felt let down by the U.S., but that is another story.

Now things happened very fast. Just a week later, on March 14, the U.S. Army launched a military campaign against Francisco "Pancho" Villa on orders from President Wilson. The objective was to catch Villa, but that failed. The expedition ended on February 7, 1917. General John J. "Black Jack" Pershing had been in command and continued his career soon thereafter by being put in charge of the entire World War I American Expeditionary Force going to war on the western front in Europe.

Operations in Mexico against Villa were like a dress rehearsal for the Great War. Up to 10,000 troops gained valuable experience. New weapons and equipment, including airplanes, were put to the test in the field. The reluctant American public grew used to a daily diet of military news. It was as if the Preparedness Movement managed to reach its goals after all. Anyway, after the unsuccessful chasing of Pancho Villa, the Preparedness supporters promptly faded away. Now it was curtain up for the real business of war, and for conscription, and the new income tax, an ever-larger military, and for other kinds of improvements. Most of these marvelous things have been with us ever since.

—

"Once lead this people into war, and they will forget there ever was such a thing as tolerance," said President Woodrow Wilson on the day before he declared war on Germany. "To fight, you must be brutal and ruthless, and the spirit of ruthless brutality will enter into the very fiber of our national life, with infecting Congress, the courts, the policeman on the beat, the man in the street."

Woohoo—and so it happened. When I have a bad dream at night, it seems as if that ruthless and brutal spirit has become our permanent characteristic, openly displayed or just barely hovering underground. But then, after waking up, comes a sad merriment. Perhaps he was still fortified from viewing the pro-Ku-Klux-Klan film *Birth of a Nation* in March of 1915 at the White House, but what the good president recommended to the American people was to practice precisely what he detested in the allegedly-evil Hun: frightfulness.

The merry-go-round goes like this: According to John Quincy Adams, "America does not go abroad in search of monsters to destroy." Sorry, sir—but now she does. In 1917, she arranged things as follows:

- First, America manufactured the alien monsters with the help of an official government-launched propaganda program and an Orwellian character like George Creel;
- Then a peace-loving leader affirmed that the country's people would likewise transform themselves into monsters who must be brutal and ruthless for the fight;
- And last, you could watch how America went abroad in search of monsters to destroy.

It was in the news and in the movies. It was everywhere.

～

On April 13, 1917, a few days after the U.S. declared war on Germany, President Wilson had created the gigantic organization Committee on Public Information (CPI), with George Creel as its head. The CPI recruited 150,000 academics, business people, and talent from the media and arts to promote the war to the voters. Up to 20,000 newspaper pieces per week were printed based on "voluntary censorship" and CPI hand-outs. That probably was the birth of "embedded."

Hollywood contributed its share by producing masterpieces like *The Kaiser: The Beast of Berlin* and *Wolves of Kultur.* Super-patriotic volunteer groups joined in, whipping up a tidal wave of war hysteria, hunting for imaginary spies or saboteurs which did not exist, and seriously violating civil liberties—all with the goal of making the world safe for democracy. Only one German miner named Prager was lynched. Many books were burned, citizens tarred and feathered, German names of places, streets, foods, and objects removed. Bach became a person *non grata.* Schools were closed and the German language itself was treated like a terrorist weapon. Teaching it in school was outlawed in more than a dozen states.

A performance of *Wilhelm Tell,* Schiller's play (premiere 1804, in Weimar) for freedom and against tyranny, which was influenced by the American and

French Revolutions, was cancelled because the poet was a German *Wolf of Kultur*. This was the same play W. E. B. Du Bois had read in German at Fiske University before he studied in Berlin where his "first awakening to social reform began." In 1895, he became the first African-American to earn a Ph.D. from Harvard (Hutchins Center, 2013).

Schiller also wrote the *Ode to Joy* used by Beethoven in his 6th Symphony. It is cherished by freedom-seeking persons across the globe. And, by a comical concurrence, it was this same Schiller who penned: "Against stupidity the gods themselves contend in vain" (qtd. in Wikiquote: The Maid of Orleans, 1801, act III).

—

Today we have laws against hate speech and hate crimes. The dictionaries define the first of these as follows: "Hate speech is speech that offends, threatens, or insults groups, based on race, color, religion, national origin, sexual orientation, disability, or other traits" (Hate Speech, 2016).

What about the Statute of Limitations? I didn't find anything on stupidity, but according to the *U.S. Code § 249*, it is seven years for hate speech, and there is apparently no time limit if the result is death. Seven years? That fits our speed. Mistakes were made—let's move on.

—

In 1919, World War I was already over, but the hysteria was not. Once you whip up this great country in a campaign against all things German or whatever, don't expect this to disappear quickly or at all. Fortunately, however, the Supreme Court case *Meyer v. Nebraska* decided in 1923 that a 1919 Nebraska law restricting foreign-language education violated the Due Process clause of the 14th Amendment.

Robert T. Meyer was a teacher in a one-room Nebraska school. He taught a fourth-grader by reading to him from a bible Martin Luther had translated into German. Luther had also nailed his theses to a church door, thereby triggering the Reformation. That was 500 years ago: the anniversary date is 2017.

In a US state, however, in 1919, teaching by using Luther's blessed book was considered illegal if not a crime. The teacher Robert T. Meyer was convicted and fined. The Nebraska Supreme Court upheld the verdict 4:2, stating that the harmful effects of letting immigrants educate their children in their mother tongue was hostile to our own safety. Well, the one-room schoolteacher was a fighter, and so was his attorney, Arthur Mullen. The case went up all the way to the Supreme Court of the United States. Meyer won. In his decision, Justice McReynolds explained to the Nebraska courts, "Mere knowledge of the German language cannot reasonably be regarded as harmful" (*Meyer v. Nebraska*, 1923).

You have to love it. Hallelujah.

But it was too late. Lasting damage had been done.

—

In any case, this whole campaign against a language and a group of people smacks of another grand experiment with human beings. Starting in the 1870s, the U.S. government opened about 150 boarding schools to re-educate Native American children. Richard Pratt, an Army Officer, developed the program in a prison for Indians. Pratt held that the goal was to "kill the Indian, and save the man" (Pratt, R.H., 2016). Thousands of children were brought to these schools, in some cases by force. Other public schools were closed to Indian youngsters for racial reasons.

Once at the boarding schools, the kids were transformed from the inside out. The well-intentioned curriculum had to turn them from uncivilized persons into dressed-up little Anglo-Saxons who could function well in U.S. society. They could not speak a word in their own language without being punished. The process of eliminating someone's way of being and speaking is not necessarily based on the color of skin or the shape of the eyes. Almost anything will do. A determined practitioner of human engineering can even make an evil Hun out of a Beethoven. The grand Indian transmutation effort failed, as such efforts must. "Time is the old justice that examines all such offenders," said Shakespeare (*As You Like It*, Act 4, Scene 1).

Accordingly, in an interesting recent twist, the Navajo Nation presidential candidate Chris Deschene was not permitted to run because he was not fluent in the Navajo language. This was the decision of the Navajo Supreme Court. And as *The Guardian* pointed out in an article on October 3, 2014, for this largest Native American nation on the largest reservation in the U.S. "the language issue goes beyond the election. It centers on how to preserve what the federal government once tried to eradicate and what parents were ashamed to teach their children" (Guardian, 2014, Oct.3).

Further north, in Canada, on May 31, 2015, the appointed Truth and Reconciliation Commission presented a landmark study after six years of research; access to 1.5 million documents archived by the government; interviews; and investigations of the files of 150,000 native (First Nations) children who, from 1955 to 2002, were forced to live in 130 residential schools so that the Indian could be taken out of the child. I happened to be in Vancouver on vacation when the study results were announced. All the major news programs covered the story extensively for several days, and I saved the Globe and Mail National Newspaper of June 2, 2015 with the blazing headline: *'Cultural Genocide' Cited as Goal of Residential Schools.*

The Commission leaves no doubt that its research proves cultural genocide. The highest ranking official who has used the term to date is Supreme Court Chief Justice Beverly McLachlin. So far, as of September 30, 2013, the Canadian government has paid $1.6 billion in compensation to former forced students. This covers 105,548 cases. (CBC News, 2015, June 09).

The term *cultural genocide* for the killing of a culture was coined by Raphael Lemkin in 1944, but was excluded as a (controversial) category in 1946 from the newly created United Nations and also from the U.N.'s 1948 Genocide Convention.

—

After the military expedition chasing Pancho Villa in Mexico, New Mexico was quiet until there was one incident, and after that, the Bisbee Deportation. In the mining town of Van Houten, an enraged mob accused a German miner of supporting the land of his birth, forced him to kneel, kiss the American flag, and yell "to hell with the Kaiser." The man lived, but what have feudal kneeling and flag kissing to do with the United States and its constitution?

The discontent of labor had been rising for years, and in early 1915 it found official expression in hearings held by the United States Commission on Industrial Relations, an arm of Congress. It dealt severely with people named Rockefeller, Morgan, and Carnegie. In August, the Commission found that wages were kept artificially low. It stated that

> The workers of the nation, through compulsory and oppressive methods, legal and illegal, are denied the full product of their toil … Citizens numbering millions smart under a sense of injustice and oppression. The extent and depth of industrial unrest can hardly be exaggerated (Karp, 1979, p. 217).

The miners of the town of Bisbee, Arizona, knew all this only too well. They were men from more than twenty countries. They performed back-breaking and dangerous work in the copper mines of the area and wanted more safety and better pay in an industry that was booming and important to the war effort. The miners did not share in the prosperity. Nothing trickled down to them.

Various unions were active in town, among them the anti-war Industrial Workers of the World, called the Wobblies. In late June of 1917 they went on strike, impairing work at Phelps Dodge, the Calumet & Arizona Mining Co., and Shattuck Arizona Copper—with around 5000 employees altogether. All of the the strikers' requests and demands were rejected.

"There will be no compromise because you cannot compromise with a rattlesnake," said Walter Douglas, president of Phelps Dodge. Mr. Douglas blasted Spaniards "from the anarchical provinces of Spain" as troublemakers nearby. He added, "I believe the government will be able to show that there is German influence behind this movement" (Bisbee Daily Review, 1917, July 11).

To make matters truly absurd, a U.S. propagandistic genius accomplished something no one else could do: He merged the Kaiser, the top German aristocrat, with the International Workers of the World (IWW), who were damned as socialists or even as commies.

And this is the nice little anti-Wobbly and anti-German drawing the cartoonist H. T. Webster created for the New York Globe newspaper in 1917. The International Workers of the World (Wobblies) acronym "IWW" replaces the Kaiser's facial features:

IFIGURE 21. *"The I.W.W. and the other features that go with it." Propaganda poster by H. T. Webster, 1917.*

The members of the IWW experienced much repression for the sake of war-time security. In the fall of 1917, federal agents raided all their offices across the country. About 300 leaders were arrested and charged with espionage and sedition. Six months later, two thousand were in jail and awaiting trial. The labor leader Eugene V. Debs was among them. He was convicted and sentenced to ten years in prison on November 18, 1918, for his anti-war stance. At his trial, he spoke for two hours in his own defense. His speech was so eloquent that it is now regarded as a classic in the English language. In 1920, Debs ran for president while imprisoned in Atlanta. He received 919,799 votes. His sentence was commuted in Dec. of 1921. Fifty thousand people cheered him upon his release. In 1924, he was nominated for the Nobel Peace Prize. But by now he was worn out. In the fall of 1926, he died at the age of 70, from heart failure.

Back in Bisbee, on the early morning of July 12, 1917, 3,000 armed citizens who had been deputized by Sheriff Harry C. Wheeler the night before, formed a huge posse and captured the striking miners. They even fished them out from barbershops or diners. A total of 1,186—only 20 of these were German (Webster, 1917)—were herded into waiting boxcars enriched with sheep-dung, and shipped off 170 miles through the sizzling hot desert to Columbus, New Mexico, the same little border town Pancho Villa had attacked earlier. It was a long, fiery ride. There were a few soon-emptied water barrels, but no food or water for most. Columbus didn't want the "deplorables," so the train had to lurch back to Hermanos, some 20 miles to the west. There the engine was decoupled, left for El Paso, and the cattle cars filled with the exhausted men remained standing there in the middle of nowhere. Help arrived eventually. There were slow government investigations and legal proceedings, but nothing much came of them.

On July 13, the local paper had summed up that the deportation was "a question of beating these foreign terrorists and professional agitators and strikers to it" (Bisbee Daily Review, 1917, July 13). And that was that.

―

When reconsidering all this today, I feel an acute unease and even a sense of *déjà vu*. During such moments, I sometimes flee to Harold D. Laswell's 1927 classic *Propaganda Technique in World War I*. Laswell understood what it takes to manufacture extreme hostility:

> So great are the psychological resistances to war in modern nations, that every war must appear to be a war of defense against a menacing, murderous aggressor. There must be no ambiguity about whom the public is to hate. Guilt and guilelessness must be assessed geographically and all the guilt must be on the other side of the frontier (Laswell, 1938, p. 47).

This state of affairs produced various reactions. The British poet Lt. S. Sassoon wrote in *Memoirs of an Infantry Officer*, "The newspapers informed us that German soldiers crucified Belgian babies. Stories of that kind were taken for granted; disbelieving them would have been unpatriotic."

Rudyard Kipling, head of the British Propaganda Section, said in a 1915 speech that, "However the world pretends to divide itself, there are only two divisions in the world today—human beings and Germans" (qtd. in Gilmour, 2002, p.250).

And Professor Vernon Kellogg, a prominent participant within the Committee on Public Information, eloquently expressed his opinion in one of the CPI publications, writing:

"Will it be any wonder if, after the war, the people of the world, when they recognize any human being as a German, will shrink aside so that they may not touch him as he passes, or stoop for stones to drive him from their path? "

—

All of this was incredibly shabby. Shameful. The Wilson Administration's campaign of demonization and hate against Americans and immigrants of German descent during World War I was never rectified. Since 1917, after a collective bite into a poisoned apple, a silenced population with its language lingers on like a version of that stricken young woman who had fled to the Seven Dwarfs, and then slumbered on in a hundred-year trance. Maybe in 2017 a wakeup call will come, or a kiss. My father, who expected a century-long waiting time before one could catch a glimpse of history, would've liked that.

—

It is possible to love a language or languages. I do. This is what Jorge Luis Borges wrote in *To the German Language*:

> My destiny is in the Spanish language,
> the bronze words of Francisco de Quevedo,
> but in the long, slow progress of the night,
> different, more intimate musics move me.
> Some have been handed down to me by blood—
> voices of Shakespeare, language of the Scriptures—
> others by chance, which has been generous;
> but you, gentle language of Germany,
> I chose you, and I sought you out alone.
> By way of grammar books and patient study,
> through the thick undergrowth of the declensions,
> the dictionary, which never puts its thumb on
> the precise nuance, I kept moving closer.
> My nights were full of overtones of Virgil,
> I once said; but I could as well have named
> Hölderlin, Angelus Silesius.

Heine lent me his lofty nightingales;
Goethe, the good fortune of late love,
at the same time both greedy and indulgent;
Keller, the rose which one hand leaves behind
in the closed fist of a dead man who adored it,
who will never know if it is white or red.
German language, you are your masterpiece:
love interwound in all your compound voices
and open vowels, sounds which accommodate
the studious hexameters of Greek
and undercurrents of jungles and nights.
Once, I had you. Now, at the far extreme
of weary years, I feel you have become
as out of reach as algebra and the moon.
(Borges, transl. Alistair Reid, 1977).

13

Shadowless

Yet can the Grey Man boast not that he had me *Fast* by my
shadow! Nay! He must resign His claims on me, my shadow's
mine ... I had it from the first, and never lost it.

—*Adelbert von Chamisso, The Shadowless Man*

There is a crack in everything. That's how the light gets in.

—*Leonard Cohen, Anthem*

Each year in early May, the desert garden behind our house turns into a
field of gold. It is a low-water xeriscaped space, lush with native plants and
wildflowers. The deep yellow, almost orange-colored California poppies like
it there and faithfully bloom their little hearts out, living on almost nothing
and only on small amounts of water. The Spaniards called the flower, which
has a diameter from 2.5 to 5 cm., *copa de oro,* cup of gold.

Every crack and hot, sandy spot is sufficient for them. They reseed themselves for the next year, and require only minimal care. All there is to do is
pull them out after they are spent, and wait for another spring.

As it is my habit, when I suddenly get curious about something, I look
it up. These days that's easy to do online. So some months ago I checked up
on the golden California poppy, which is that state's official flower. I found

it, and with it I found, quite unexpectedly, Adelbert von Chamisso. I had not known that he named the poppy scientifically, or that he visited California in 1816. Yet, by searching for the flower, I rediscovered a poet and scientist, and he made me the gift of a most meaningful story. But more about this later.

Chamisso was in San Francisco Bay with a Russian expedition and named the golden poppy *eschscholzia californica* after his friend and fellow traveler, the Baltic-German physician and naturalist Johann Friedrich Eschscholtz.

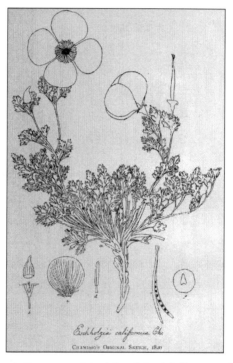

FIGURE 22. *California Poppy—original sketch by Adalbert von Chamisso, 1820.*

Americans noticed the varied spellings of the name: the original Escholtz changed to Eschscholtz via transliteration to the Russian and back to our alphabet. (The Estonian city of Dorpat where he was born and lived had been a Catholic diocese and a Hanseatic trading center for 300 years, then it became part of the Russian empire.) Eschscholtz returned the courtesy and also classified/named plants after his friend, for example Chamisso's Lupine or Silvery Beach Blue Lupine (*lupinus chamissonis*); the genus *camissonia* or sundrop; and several arnica and coast hedge nettles along the American Pacific Coast.

In any event, the two young explorers were sailing around the world with the 1815–1818 Russian Romanzov Expedition on the brig *Rurik,* commanded by Otto von Kotzebue. The three-year voyage searched unsuccessfully for a polar passage from the Pacific to the Atlantic, but researched productively throughout the Pacific. Many specimens were collected in Brazil, Chile, the Marshall Islands, Hawaii (then called the Sandwich Islands), California, the Bering Strait, Kamchatka, and the Aleutian Islands.

The map of Alaska shows discoveries and names from this expedition. There is a Kotzbue Sound, an Eschscholtz Bay, and Chamisso Island, now part of the Chamisso Wilderness. Far away, in the Marshall Islands, there was also an Eschscholtz Atoll which was renamed Bikini Atoll and gained a sad fame as the testing ground for atomic weapons. The residents were resettled to another island that could not produce enough food for them. Out of a total of 67 tests, in 1954 the U.S. dropped a 15 megaton hydrogen bomb on the unfortunate atoll, many times more powerful than the atomic bomb that destroyed Hiroshima.

The islanders were allowed to return home in 1970, but were removed once again in 1978 because the crops they grew were still highly contaminated. In March of 2016, the Republic of the Marshall Islands sued 9 nations in the International Court of Justice in the Hague for violating the 1970 Nuclear Non-Proliferation Treaty (NPT). Hearings are ongoing. Nothing much happened in the last 45 years: 190 countries had signed the treaty. Yet the weapons are still with us, and those nations with the biggest atomic arsenals are planning to invest large sums to bring their aging inventories up-to-date.

—

Eschscholtz and Chamisso spoke German with each other, although one was a German from Russia and the other a German (Prussian) born in France. It was the tumultuous time of the Napoleonic wars, and it produced an unusual number of multi-talented people, and even geniuses, in several countries. In Germany, it was as if something had been mended, and was now bursting at the seams from sheer energy. This produced not only an outstanding era in literature, philosophy, and music, but soon in the sciences as well.

Chamisso was one of the era's multi-talented persons. He enriched the fields of botany, zoology, geography of animals and plants, anthropology, ethnography, and even linguistics. In addition, he was also a poet and writer of importance. And not only that; his mother tongue was French, but he became a German poet. Being able to write poetry in a second language is rare.

He was born in January of 1781 at the ancestral Château of Boncourt in the Champagne, France. His parents were members of the nobility, lost their land and possessions during the French revolution, and fled to the Low Countries in 1792. By 1796 they settled in Berlin, where the boy became a page in waiting to the Prussian Queen Luise and a student at the city's French school.

There was a whole French neighborhood in Berlin, the Gendarmenmarkt, with its newly-built French Cathedral, where Protestant Huguenot refugees found a new home after being invited to live in Prussia. This began in 1685, when French King Louis XIV issued the Revocation of the Edict of Nantes. In response, Elector Friedrich Wilhelm of Brandenburg published the Edict of Potsdam, offering peace, religious freedom, and safety from persecution to the Huguenots. About 20,000 arrived, many of them highly skilled. For a while, French immigrants outnumbered Berliners. In any case, the undertaking was a success, and it added a desirable new flavor to the city.

In 1798, Chamisso became an ensign (flag-bearer) in the Prussian Army, and in 1801 he was promoted to lieutenant. His schooling had been erratic. His parents had been practically homeless, and were on the run for years until they decided to stay in Berlin. Young Adelbert joined the military as one route open to him, but with little interest in being a soldier. He was drawn to the natural sciences and to literature. Since his regiment remained in Berlin for several years, he used every free minute too study intensively not only through readings in the natural sciences, but above all he came to know the work of Rousseau, Voltaire, Schiller, and the German Romantics. He also learned Greek, joined a group of poets, became co-publisher of the *Gruener Musen Almanach,* started some writing of his own, and formed warm friendships. Until 1805, when his regiment was transferred to the fortress-city of Hamelin—the place of Pied Piper fame.

1806 was perhaps the worst year in Chamisso's life. In October, Napoleon defeated the Prussian Army at Jena. In November, Chamisso's regiment surrendered Hamelin without a fight, and he became a prisoner of war permitted, on his word of honor, to travel to France to find his parents, who had returned home (pretty decent and gallant military conduct compared to our modern behaviors). However, his mother had died, and shortly afterwards his father died too. Meanwhile, Napoleon occupied the capital city of Berlin. The king and queen fled to the farthest eastern corner of Prussia. A year later, at Tilsit, Queen Luise pleaded unsuccessfully with Napoleon for better terms after Prussia's crushing losses. She was very beautiful and died young, only four years later, which prompted Napoleon to remark that the king had lost his best minister.

In 1808, the hapless soldier Chamisso officially resigned from the Prussian military service, found work as a private teacher, and soon also as a translator of Schlegel's work into French. In 1810, he traveled to Paris and meets Alexander von Humboldt, an event that would be valued throughout his life. 1811 found him as one of the founders of a literary *Tischgesellschaft* or roundtable, together with a whole group of budding literary men, among them Achim von Arnim, Clemens Brentano, Heinrich von Kleist, and Friedrich de la Motte Fouque. Then followed a long 15 months stay with a steadfast opponent of Napoleon's politics, Madame de Staël, at castle Coppet near Geneva, Switzerland. It was a productive time. Chamisso discovered and pursued a passion for botanical research, returned to Berlin, and enrolled as a student of medicine and botany at the university.

In between came the enormous 1813 Battle of the Nations, when from October 16th to October 19th, a coalition of the countries of Europe, including Russia, in a combined force of 430,000 men fought against Napoleon's Army near Leipzig, Germany, and decisively defeated the great conqueror for the first time. The Allies suffered 54,000 casualties, and the French an estimated 45,000. Napoleon soon lost his throne and was exiled to the island of Elba.

Also in between came the writing of a slender masterpiece. Consider Chamisso's situation: Born a French aristocrat and fleeing a revolution with his parents as a child; a Prussian by necessity and choice; a Prussian soldier and POW of the French Army; and a defeated French-born Prussian person in occupied Berlin. His distressed and conflicted state of mind must have been something to behold. His friends were afraid for him, and convinced him to stay out of sight in the countryside. He was welcomed as a guest at the *Kunersdorfer Musenhof,* a notable country salon in Brandenburg with companionship and lodgings for artists, poets, intellectuals, scientists, and all kinds of intriguing people. The Humboldt brothers were guests, and many others. The estate had gracious hosts, a castle, a unique little church, gardens, and a library with 30,000 volumes.

During the summer of 1813, Chamisso botanized and wrote his famous novella *Peter Schlemihls Wundersame Geschichte,* or the story of *The Shadowless Man* in Kunersdorf. I knew this tale as a child. Like *Gulliver's Travels,* this one can also be read at a young age. The style is deceptively simple, but it works on several levels and has puzzled critics, scholars, and interpreters in various languages for 200 years, or ever since it was put on paper in a few short weeks.

It was a time when the *Kunstmärchen,* or literary fairy tale, flourished. In contrast to the collected folk stories of Grimm's Fairy Tales (published in 1812), these new ones were written by individuals. They contained elements of the fantastic, the uncanny, of social satire, complex psychology, and of magical realism. They foreshadowed Kafka, and Gabriel Garcia Marquez. In our part of the world they live on in the *Nutcracker* ballet, the operatic *Tales of Hoffmann,* or the *Puss in Boots,* with the voice of Antonio Banderas.

246

FIGURE 23. *Peter Schlemihl loses his Shadow. Plate by George Cruikshank, London, ca. 1861.*

Chamisso's story deals with the naïve young Peter Schlemihl who travels across the sea to a foreign country and, with a degree of innocence, sells his "lovely, lovely" shadow to the devil in exchange for a magic fortune purse that always contains coins of gold.

The evil one is a modern Beelzebub. No fire and brimstone from him; he is elderly, tall, thin, nearly nondescript. He wears a grey coat, could be a bureaucrat or someone who works for a big insurance company, and he is called the Grey Man throughout the novella. As Peter lives a life without his shadow, ostracized wherever and whenever people notice what is missing, he develops survival tactics. He uses his gold, loses his love, matures, goes through numerous adventures, and, from time to time, encounters the Grey

Man, who pulls his lovely shadow out of his coat pocket, unrolls it, shows it off, and tells him how easy it would be for Peter to get it back. All he has to do is sign over his soul, and the exchange will be made. There is no other way.

It's a Faustian bargain, but not quite. This Peter will not do: sacrifice his soul to get his shadow back. In the end, he gets rid of the gold-spewing magic purse, tells the Grey Man to go to Hell where he belongs, acquires a pair of seven-league boots and a dog, selects solitude, and devotes himself to scientific work all over the world, much like his role model Alexander von Humboldt. The book is deeply serious, wonderfully playful, and dryly humorous throughout. In a few pages, Chamisso even sketches a good-natured parody of Humboldt's career for his own protagonist, Peter Schlemihl. The magical boots carry him across the continents, as fast as thought, and he has to take the boots off to get some rest. A newly purchased pair of slippers are his footwear at home. And where is home? At Thebes, in a cave. He describes his new life as follows:

> Instead of my departed fortune, I enjoyed my tobacco—it served instead of the good opinion of mankind. And then as to my affections: I had a love of a little dog that watched my Theban cave; it sprang forward to greet me, making me feel the spirit of humanity within me, and that I was not quite alone on earth (Chamisso, 1910, pp. 105–106).

In another witty twist pipe-smoking Schlemihl addresses Chamisso, the author, in the last paragraph of the story:

> And you, my beloved Chamisso—you I have chosen to be the keeper of my marvelous history, which, when I have vanished from the earth, may tend to the improvement of many of its inhabitants. But, my friend, while you live among mankind, learn above all things first to reverence your shadow, and next to that your money (in Chamisso, 1910, pp. 105–106).

⌒

Almost immediately, the little book written during the 1813 summer of massive war and political turmoil became a remarkable success. It was translated into English and other languages, and printed and illustrated through several editions. From the start until today, readers and scholars have been busy with interpreting the story, trying to break its 'code,' and figuring out what it means. This amused and annoyed Chamisso even during his lifetime.

The loss of the shadow is a big thing—does it signify losing one's identity? Or does it turn the shadowless person into an outcast from society? In a letter to Madame de Staël, Chamisso once wrote that in Berlin he was a Frenchman; in France he was German; under aristocrats he felt a Jacobin of the French Revolution; and under democrats, like a person from the ancient regime. I empathize with that, but I don't want to analyze the story. I like it as it is. It speaks for itself, makes an impact, and delights.

⌒

What is amazing is the fact that soon, reality mimicked fantasy. By July of 1815, Chamisso was one of the two natural scientists on board the Russian ship *Rurik* (named after a Viking who explored Russia) sailing to circumnavigate, explore, and search to find the Northwest Passage. Now he was indeed traveling and researching around the world, for three years—from 1815 to 1818—via a ship that served as his seven-league boots. He wrote a wonderful book about it. *Reise um die Welt mit der Romanzoffischen Entdeckungs-Expedition* is regarded as one of the outstanding examples of travel literature. Henry Kratz, the English translator of *Reise um the Welt*, wrote that Chamisso "combines the interest of the humanist with the sharp eye of the scientist" and is "a master of literary style" (Perry, 2003, p.1). He was ahead of his time in understanding and insight, and was especially taken by Hawaii, or the Sandwich Islands, as they were still called.

The *Rurik* sailed into Kailua Bay on Hawaii Island in November of 1816. The village was the home of the warrior-king Kamehameha, who had unified the islands into one kingdom and initiated reforms, but intended to keep Westerners safely distant from meddling in local affairs.

The king invited the captain and the officers of the ship to a banquet, equipped with tables and tableware. They were served roasted pig. Kamehameha watched them eat, and only afterwards did he enjoy his own meal of broiled fish and taro, presented on banana leaves. Gifts were exchanged. The royal host received a cask of European wine, apples from San Francisco, and a mortar with ammunition. The gift for the Russian czar Alexander I was an *ahu ula*, a kingly cloak made from colorful bird feathers.

On a side-note: King Kamehameha had a liking for music of the islands, but he also wanted to hear western music. So far he had mostly listened to the hymns from American missionaries, but he knew that Germany had a reputation for music. So he wrote to the government in Berlin and asked for assistance. Eventually, a young army musician named Heinrich Berger arrived, on loan for four years. Berger worked for his four years in Hawaii, returned to Germany, asked the army to discharge him, and promptly sailed back to the islands.

For the next fifty years he organized the musical life of Hawaii, with much local support. He taught in schools, instructed members of the *alii* (royalty), worked closely with native composers, formed bands, imported string instruments and nurtured new orchestras, one of which eventually grew up to become the Honolulu Symphony. That happened in 1900. Berger had loved music and musicians. He stayed away from politics.

—

The *Rurik* sailed on to the big island of Oahu and anchored in Honolulu Harbor. Next to it was the pleasant little town, and much hinterland for Chamisso to explore and botanize in. He collected a treasure trove of plants and recorded charming little stories. One anecdote tells how the natives poked fun at him and laughed, because he wanted to show off his swimming skills and swam across a river that was shallow enough for walking. Why swim when you can cross on foot? In another incident, a noisy swarm of kids followed him and he marched on without paying any attention to them, when, at once, he turned around, faced them, and screamed and howled as loud as he could. They froze, terrified, until a smile came up and everyone started laughing.

In Honolulu, the ship's crew had the chance to see hula dances. Chamisso described the spectacle. "With movement and chanting they tell an epic story," he wrote, and "in the dance, the human form represents itself in a constant flow of easy, unrestrained motion in every natural and graceful position" (Perry, 2003, p. 1).

Hawaiian is a mellifluous language, and the poet in Chamisso must have responded to that. To him, it was sophisticated, subtle, pleasing to the ear, and consequently he wrote a monograph/dictionary on it. It was published in 1837. *Über die Hawaiische Sprache* (On the Hawaiian Language) was apparently the first grammatical work on that language. Then, in 1898, Hawaii became an American territory and progressed to becoming civilized. Soon, the native tongue was banned from schools. By 1983, it is said that only about 50 children still spoke Hawaiian. It was almost gone when, as elsewhere in the world, for example in Wales, in Australia, among the Maya, and the Native North Americans, concerned educators and activists began their work. In Hawaii, they created pre-kindergarten immersion schools called *punana leos,* language nests (PBS, 2015). Gradually, schools up to the 12th grade evolved. Today, the rich tongue, which has hundreds of names for the wind and the rain, is among the living once more.

⌣

In October of 1818, Chamisso was back in Berlin. He presented a *First Account About an Expedition* in December, received an honorary doctorate from the University of Berlin, became an assistant custodian at the Botanical Garden, and later its director/custodian. In 1819, he married Antonie Piaste, and in 1820 and 1822 his first two children, sons Ernst and Max, were born.

Chamisso led a peaceful, productive life filled with family and friends, constant scientific work and publications, and with the writing of poetry. One example from these years is a group of poems called *Frauen Liebe und Leben (A Woman's Love and Life)*. Dealing with thoughts and feelings from a female point of view, they were set to music in 1840 by Robert Schumann in a song-cycle, *Opus 42*. The Chamisso *Lieder* were a major component in what has been called Schumann's "year of song."

In 1835, Chamisso was elected as a member of the Academy of Sciences in Berlin. He fell seriously ill; still traveled shorter distances; took "the cure" at a healing spa; met Heinrich Heine; saw the publications of his major works; lived through the illness and death of his wife in 1837; and, unwell himself, died on August 21, 1838, in Berlin at the age 57.

—

The *Rurik* failed to find a polar passage from the Pacific to the Atlantic but 200 years later, on September 14, 2015, an international high-seas racing crew set a new world record by sailing through it, non-stop, in 12 days, 7 hours, and 3 minutes.

The 97-foot trimaran racing yacht *Qingdao China* left Murmansk and headed for the Bering Sea. The skipper Gua Chuan was Chinese. His small German-Russian-French crew included Boris Herrmann, a 34-year old top sailor from Germany, and Sergei Nizovtsev, a sailor and polar explorer from Russia. Experts said it couldn't be done. It was deemed as difficult as the first ascent of Mt. Everest. There were many icebergs and other dangers, yet climate change had diminished the ocean-covering ice. Although this helped the sailors, it was also troubling to them.

—

FIGURE 24. *Arctic Ocean First Non-stop World Record Challenge Completed by Guo Chuan Racing, Sept.15, 2015.*

Back to Chamisso and his shadowless man.

There is a yellowing old cartoon pinned with a magnet to my refrigerator door. I clipped it from *The Wall Street Journal* years ago. It is by Bob Schochet and shows two Native Americans with feathered headbands, watching a 17th-century galleon anchored in the bay, and two small boats with seamen rowing towards land. Remarks one Indian to the other: "more illegal aliens."

I still have to grin whenever I glance at this cartoon. Indeed, once upon a time we were all illegal. But today no one cares about that anymore. Only immigration itself is a never-ending story.

Perhaps the slow blending of different peoples from different parts of the world who speak different languages and have various cultures is in itself some type of evolution. It is influenced by good and by bad times, by attraction and repulsion. It can turn ugly, especially when the total number of people migrating is too numerous, when there is conflict, or when the economy isn't doing well. The acceptance process can be slow, at least if seen from the perspective of our short human lifespan.

Until recently, we and our scientists assumed, in good old survival-of-the-fittest fashion, that Neanderthalers perished from the earth because modern man arrived about 45,000 years ago in Europe, and out-competed and out-reproduced the clunky older creatures. Still, the two branches lasted about 5000 years living side by side, which is a good portion of our entire documented human history, if we start counting from the earliest civilizations of the Sumerians, Hittites, or Chinese.

But surprise! Eventually, we found out that the Neanderthalers didn't vanish completely, but live on in almost all of us in the West. Today's Caucasians have from 1 to 4% of the Neanderthaler inside of them. It's in our DNA. So if someone calls you a Neanderthaler, it's no longer an insult. And with the awareness that my own life is, relatively speaking, as supershort as that of a fruit fly, it's fun to time-travel back to the Neanderthalers.

When I was young, we used to go on leisurely Sunday hikes through the idyllic valley near Düsseldorf, especially in spring when the beech woods showed off their soft new green. The path meandered through meadows and woods along the little River Düssel to a garden restaurant by an old water mill. The entire area of the Neanderthal is now a nature preserve. The first bones were found in 1856 and, at the entrance to the valley, is a small museum about the ancients with bones, skulls, plans, models, texts, and life-size replicas of their persons. Neanderthalers buried their dead. If I recall it right, they also put flowers and ornaments into the graves, which counts as evidence for feelings such as grieving and caring.

—

Shadowless. *Once a colonial, always a colonial*—perhaps my joking friend was on to something. More and more often, I think that our society has things in common with other former colonies.

At the very least things are paradoxical, and puzzling. Tonight, for instance, I will watch PBS television. It's a Sunday, and all the shows are UK imports. We live, we are told, in the greatest, richest country on earth, but we can't produce our own middlebrow public not-for-profit TV shows supported by public funding? And why would we bother? We share a language. It's convenient to buy programs in the UK. The British quality is high, and the shows are enjoyable even if much of the material is upstairs-downstairs stuff or reruns.

If you are looking for other entertainment of the more popular and profit-making kind, you can browse through the entire U.S. media mainstream terrain. You may find a cool show or two. However, most programs are also predominantly mono: mono-cultural, monolingual, mono-ra ra ra, mono-scared, mono-everything, and never mind the actors' skin colors. Many books are not being translated from other languages either. "America has a famously poor record of publishing works in translation," wrote Alex Shephard in the October 19, 2015, issue of *The New Republic*. Pundits and academics have talked about this for years.

Yes, we know. English is our language, and that is wonderful. A country needs a language. (Or two, like Canada. Or three to four, like Switzerland). And after years of delay, there are now Spanish-language channels too, and Spanish is likewise an ex-colonial language. But what is astounding is that international mainstream offerings are missing, even if delivered in English. After all, the U.S. is an international society if ever there was one. We could make the best of it.

People from every nook and cranny on the planet came to live here. They were needed to do the enormous amounts of work that had to be done to develop this big lump of land after the original inhabitants were swept aside. But mental and emotional nourishment for the international roots of the incoming millions was, and remains, scarce unless it bubbles up from below, from the street level. It's an embarrassing dilemma. Yes, we need them, but we don't care much for the contents of their hearts and minds.

It is such a waste. Actually, only about 27 million people in the U.S. claim British descent, yet about 300 million are asked to march along following that antiquated drummer.

So, go on. Trade across the globe, but keep 'em down at the farm?

—

We are a varied, feisty, and vibrant society that is nudged to uphold a small-minded outlook. Being good citizens shouldn't mean we have to display closed minds to the rest of the world. And being American shouldn't sentence you or me to being one-dimensional. There is room in human hearts and minds to love more than one thing. OMG, to get just a taste of all the stories, connections, and cross-fertilizations that make life so much more interesting—among other beneficial things—nowadays you would have to browse daily in Fernand Braudel (1981) or race around the planet electronically. Racing around is being done anyway via social media, and there are Netflix, and even Amazon offerings, and international movies, and new ways of delivery. But the U.S. mainstream media and the official narrative maintain a firmly provincial orientation that seems to grow more rigid by the day. The error with this approach is that global connections cannot, and will not, work exclusively for the economy. The electronic media is global already, and this will affect the social and cultural life of humans and the physical health of the planet. Holding on, almost frantically, to a defensive nationalism will be of no use in the long run.

All these people from every region on earth who settled in the U.S. brought many cultural, practical, and mental abilities, plus their associated flaws with them, and all these casually found their way into daily life. But there is little acknowledgment. The United States as a nation is not terribly interested. Perhaps it cares foremost about keeping a lid of control on its assorted population.

—

I am still dreaming of an open-hearted society, but the possibility for it recedes rapidly. There is now so much conflict and hysterical fear of terrorism (real or invented) that it feels like being swept along by a powerful riptide. The lack of sympathy is everywhere, and palpable. Even prior to this new normal, it was a matter of attitude and habit to portray things outside of our borders in the service of politics, and more or less as "the other." We are told that we are exceptional; it follows that therefore *they* are unexceptional. They are not like us. They can be dangerous, and are definitely suspected of being unsafe. And once a massive terrorist attack happens, no language is adequate to describe the mood shift.

We actually know little about other countries and cultures apart from clichés, and never mind that *culture* became the Merriam-Webster word of the year in 2014, while a blood-dripping *Kultur* was written on the cudgel shown in a nasty poster about a 100 years earlier.

What's surprising about this behavior pattern is that nobody seems to consider that by now such almost instinctive or automatic social phobias towards other countries, their inhabitants, their stories, and perhaps even their religions, must be unpleasant to much of the U.S. voting public that itself has roots all over the planet. Even if you have become a convinced American, you still do not wish to see the place of your ancestry disparaged or belittled. That's humbug, anyway.

Yet, in an indirect and backhanded way, insults flow quietly and daily. Political correctness keeps them publicly in check, but that really fools no one. What counts is the fear-driven diet. Perhaps it is therefore no wonder when persons with upset or empty stomachs transform themselves into angry lone wolves or eventually even into homegrown terrorists, and go on bombing or shooting sprees that will routinely be explained as being caused by mental abnormality. (You could counter-argue that large parts of our country are sliding into a state of abnormality.)

Inevitably, after each U.S. mass shooting urgent voices can be heard calling for gun control laws. But other voices immediately demand: *We need more guns. More guns will make us safer.* It is like a refrain from our foreign policy: More weapons. Better weapons. More bombing. More drones. More antediluvian destruction. All producing ever more angry turbulences in the planet's climate.

These days I often think about my own sweet and plucky mother, who was full of songs, sorrows, and sayings. *Life is always life-endangering,* was one of her favorites. She would have have been well equipped to dwell in our USA, where the safety net is flimsy, full of holes, and the getting by is synthetically stressful. She also borrowed something from the English bard: *A coward dies a thousand deaths.* Shepherding her family first through the tough times after World War I, and then through the World War II carpet-bombing, Russian occupation, and the flight to the West with four little kids across a minefield of the new Iron Curtain gave her plenty of opportunity to put these words to the test. A father? Loving and absent. Serving at the front for the duration of that dinosaur of a war and kept in a POW camp for some years afterwards.

—

How can it be that the U.S., such a great country populated with resilient, hard-working, and mostly decent people, is so insecure? Does it have a bad conscience? Or is it possible that our powers-that-be are a bit afraid of their own inhabitants? And why don't we search for the buried reasons for our fear and for our violent tendencies? And must we grapple recurrently with racism, prejudice, injustice, discrimination, exploitation, denial, and inequality? For how long? Daily? For centuries? Longer? And each time we forge a new enemy, will we dehumanize an entire new group of people collectively? And will other countries follow our leadership?

—

Perhaps even the finest and most well-intentioned constitutions and political systems are rendered helpless against the human drive to construct hierarchies which, over time, congeal into rigid and smug ruling cliques.

~

It's possible that all the 24/7 disaster-data from around the globe lead to mental overload. Information used to travel within a local area, and then across one's country, but not around the earth in seconds. Long-distance mail along the trade routes, and news sailing across oceans, was slow. Now it is all very fast. And it offers too little information of the right kind.

~

The Economist sent me an email. It reads: "Dear ... get a grip on global events."
 Then it added: "The world is crazy. But at least it's getting regular analysis."

~

This much I know: I will not like living in a neighborhood or on a street where every house is a type of fortress, an island, armed to the teeth, with alarm systems, suspicious about all neighbors and their intentions, watching every move, and plotting how to out-earn, out-trade, out-compete, out-spy, out-shoot, out-bully, out-talk, out-win, out-incarcerate, and out-fear everyone of them.

I do not like living in a world like that either. In a world of gated communities, with ever- more new walls and fences, with excessive controls, unrelenting surveillance, endless war, desperate mass migrations, and homeless people on many street corners. Or in a dog-eat-dog world that doesn't exist to begin with. In reality, dogs almost never eat dogs.

All I want is try to do the best I can, respect the right of others to do the same, and employ a mutual measure of kindness. And no, liking every Tom, or Dick, or Harry isn't possible. But I do have a strong compassion for all of us who are in that shaky-yet-hard-wearing-state of being human. It's certainly not the most privileged or carefree lifeform to exist in.

~

Much is lost in translation. More is lost if there is no translation at all. But these days, who has the time or the money for linguistic luxuries? They might, however, be less expensive and time-consuming than unsuccessful wars, which could have possibly been avoided with better communications/translations. On September 10, 2015, Tom Engelhardt wrote in *TomDispatch* online about the four types of our responses to war failures. "The first," he wrote, "has involved simply stumbling along in Washington's fog of ignorance when it comes to strange peoples in far off lands."

—

Not too long ago, Americans still learned languages in high school. My husband took Latin, French, German, and Spanish, and continued with two of these in college. He remembered well, and used his skills on me and when we traveled. He even read books (slowly) or joked in a foreign tongue.

But anyway, the U.S. became a sole superpower, and all that foreign babble is now being ignored or forgotten except for Spanish, which is alive. English has grown into a world language, and is required in business, the sciences, publishing and technology. Some fields wouldn't even function any longer without English. Countless young people in many countries learn and speak it, ranging from fluent to bare-bones basic. Many refugees from Syria speak English. Some countries even invent hybrid variations: Spanish-speakers use Spanglish, and Germans Denglish. All that is fine, and helpful, and practical. We are used to this, and generally take an English-speaking world for granted, just like people once took Latin for granted. But there are also disadvantages to such complacency or self-importance. Locals might get uppity. They once translated the Bible into their own tongues. Latin faded away.

We had our *American Century* and our international leadership phase already, and the model now gives off a whiff of being *ewig-gestrig* or "forever yesteryearish." What the country that called itself the only superpower or the indispensable nation faces now is not too pretty, and the world isn't any safer for democracy either.

Globally, we now have to experience growing radicalizations and inequalities, terrorism and rampant violence, civil wars, outbursts of xenophobia, right-wing revivals, serious environmental degradations, wild weather and droughts, plus 65 million refugees— and that's only the short list.

In September of 2015, an online site unfamiliar to me (called the IPA/ Institute for Public Accuracy) named the destabilizing human tidal wave sweeping into Europe "Regime Change Refugees." That is unusual. The U.S. media try their best to avoid such wording. To be sure, just watching our TV personalities (I named one of them Uriah Heep) squirming, until the attention span fizzles, in front of new razor wire fences put up to keep the refugees out in the cold, demonstrates that our star reporters don't know how to perform in the face of such events. They are fashionably dressed for war but hardly mention the U.S. bomb runs flown over the Middle East and elsewhere although this hard information is available, for example, from the Council of Foreign Relations, where Micah Zenko reports 26,171 American bomb drops for 2016, most of them over Syria and Iraq.

It is an old story. In his *A History of Bombing,* Sven Lindquist (2001) wrote that Churchill didn't appreciate having to read a disgraceful report that told him what those cost-effective, no-boots-on-the-ground RAF bombing raids around Baghdad did to pacify the population. Terrified people, mostly females, the old, and kids, jumped into a lake to stay alive. Once in the water, they were "making a good target for the machine guns" (p. 43). Churchill suggested trials by court martial for the responsible officers. Nothing came of it. That was in 1920, when World War I-engineered mandates replaced the defeated Ottoman Empire with the imperial methods of Britain and France in the Middle East.

So much time, so much war, so many words gone. And overall, how little things have improved. Now that Russia is also in on the bombing, it's once again like a warmed-up variant of the antiquated Great Game. These old wars, hot or cold, are made to go on and on and on.

And then there is the terror, foreign and domestic. Back in 1949, Algeria-born Albert Camus wrote a play titled *Les Justes (The Just)*. My family loved the theater, so I saw the show when I was very young. It was based on a true story taken from *Memoirs of a Terrorist* by Boris Savinkov, and deals with of a group of youthful Russian revolutionaries who assassinated the Grand Duke Sergei Alexandrovich, son of Czar Alexander II, in 1905. It is said that all members of the royal family were targets, yet the duke traveled unprotected, alone with his driver. The bomb, thrown by Ivan Kaliayev, who is also the lead character in the Camus play, was launched from a few feet away and landed in the duke's lap. It tore him to pieces. Ivan the perpetrator was injured, imprisoned, and executed.

I will have to read this play again. It explores the moral and philosophical issues of killing through acts of terror. (Does this include state-sponsored terror?) With the exception of one member, the other four terrorists had all given up good lives to fight against tyranny and dismal conditions in Russia. Their credo was: If you kill, you must also die. The widowed Grand Duchess visited Kaliayev in prison. After telling him what kind of caring and humane man her husband was in private, he was touched. She offered him a pardon if he agreed to being a murderer, and not a revolutionary. He declined and told her: "Let me prepare myself to die. If I did not die, then I would be a murderer."

Today's suicide bombers do it too: Some of them elect to die. They kill themselves, or we kill them, but then they live on in legend among their people.

—

A key component in the tragi-comedy of U.S.-German relations and translations is a tale about Ranke—Leopold von Ranke, that is—professor of history and idolized by newly professional American historians. The American Historical Association was founded in 1884. It celebrated the German as the father of modern historical scholarship, and as someone who was "unsurpassed and unprecedented." Ranke became the first honorary member of the association, and "after his death in 1886 one of his former students arranged for the purchase of Ranke's library, including his portrait, study table, chairs, and pens, which were set up as a shrine at Syracuse University" (Novick,1988, p. 26).

Germans are raised with the familiar saying *Eigenlob stinkt* (self-praise stinks). And, living with the post-1945 re-educating mental GPS guidance system, high esteem (even if it originated prior to 1914) for anyone and anything from that country appeared to be absolutely abnormal. Nevertheless, the Ranke episode is part of this book, so it will be told. I feel it is symptomatic.

"That Germany possessed the sole secret of scholarship" wrote Bliss Perry, "was no more doubted by us young fellows in the eighteen-eighties, then it had been doubted by George Ticknor and Edward Everett when they sailed from Boston, bound for Göttingen, in 1814" (qtd. in Novick, 1988, p. 21).

And so they came, thousands of young Americans studying in Germany. They did so for various reasons. Graduate training hardly existed in the U.S. before the late 19th century. In England, universities produced primarily gentlemen, and until 1871, students had to sign their assent to the required 39 Articles of the Anglican Church. In France, study at the Sorbonne was suspected to include exposure to vice, infidelism, and popery. In comparison, study in Germany cost about a third less than attending a good American university; there was not much of a moral drill; little orthodoxy; and a great deal of rigorous scholarship with the goal of achieving academic excellence. Also, German academics served as role models with their high social standing and good incomes. The knighthood was within reach for successful professors.

The aspiring American historians among the students were attracted by Ranke's methods and reputation, and his introduction of the seminar. The funny part is that Ranke was misunderstood, mistranslated, and misinterpreted by his U.S. fans from the start.

"The misinterpretation of Ranke can be considered part of a more general phenomenon," wrote Peter Novick (1988, p. 31), who taught a lot to me. He quoted Allen Janik and Stephen Toulmin: "One of the greatest misfortunes that can affect a writer of great intellectual seriousness and strong ethical passions is to have his ideas 'naturalized by the English' " (Novick, 1988, p. 31).

That's it! I smirk.

Novick continues by pointing out that

> All German historians saw Ranke as the antithesis of a non-philosophical empiricism, while American historians venerated him for being precisely what he as not ... To American historians their mythic hero was empirical science incarnate. Frederick Jackson Turner [he of the *Closing Frontier*] explained Ranke's orientation 'as a result of his having grown up in an age of science' (Novick, 1988, p. 28).
>
> Apart from the fact that Ranke is not without his critics in today's Germany, here in the .

U.S. the whole charade once started with the mistranslation of one word: *Wissenschaft*. That's not the same as "science." With science (scientific objectivity, or whatever that was supposed to be), efforts ended for the American historians. Yet for Ranke these were preliminaries, and the real work of the historian began at the point where they finished. From here, he wished to penetrate to essences.

Goodness! How is all this possible? Ranke was admired for what he was not and for what he did not do. It seems Americans had no appreciation of the division between the "thoughtways, and as a result either distorted or disregarded what they couldn't comprehend" (Novick, 1988, p. 31). Ranke wasn't the only misinterpreted person. There were numerous others, among them the anti-imperialist political thinkers Herder and Kant, and eventually A.v. Humboldt, too.

The Ranke episode puts a spotlight on some of the farcical elements of Anglo-American and German relations specifically, and Anglo-American and overall foreign relations in general. American historians spent time in Germany, but "there was little understanding among them of the great gulf that separated the German and Anglo-American cultural and philosophical contexts, and this was even truer of the majority of professional historians who had not studied in Germany" (Novick, 1988, p. 31). Furthermore, courses in European intellectual history were not taught at U.S. universities until shortly before World War I, and we know that during those years peculiar methods of interpreting the world were dominant.

I have lived through ongoing tragi-comical misreadings or distortions for half a lifetime, seldom knowing if to laugh or cry or do both. But not any longer. Now I am done with that. It is what it is. A laugh-in.

Perhaps we must invent a new "science" of foreign policy. It would start with polyglots and people who are fluent in speaking the languages of foreigners and know at least the basics of their ways and their history before they are authorized to push for regime change and such. Looking for unicorns like Marco Polo and reporting we found them when they were, in fact, unknown beings—who will charge when angered—will not do. A Zulu proverb has some sound advice: Do not talk about a rhinoceros if there is no tree nearby.

—

Kurt Vonnegut wrote in one of his last slender books titled A *Man without a Country:*

> Many years ago I was so innocent I still considered it possible that we would become the humane and reasonable America so many members of my generation used to dream of. But now I know that there is not a chance in hell of America becoming humane and reasonable, because power corrupts us (Vonnegut, 2005, p. 71).

Sorry, I cannot, and must not, accept such a grim outlook. It has nothing to do with being credulous or gullible, but as a kid may be growing a bit braver against imagined monsters lurking in the dark, so I will have to tell myself again and again that the shelf-life of tainted power is not unlimited. If you look around in world history, it never was.

And if the country slides down into another period of Know-Nothingness or related aberrations, we will have to call on our inner and outer defenses, and resist to outlast such miseries.

It was moving to hear Vonnegut locally and in person a few years before he left our messy planet for good. He spoke for almost two hours to a packed house with a wildly enthusiastic, cheering audience. It was after 9/11. I guess he was heartsick, but he made us laugh.

14

Bold Blue

The disease of mutual distrust among nations is the
bane of modern civilization.

— *Franz Boas*

You know, when I was a girl, the idea that the British
Empire could ever end was absolutely inconceivable.
And it just disappeared like all the other empires.

— *Doris Lessing*

New Mexico has many caves. For example, erosion and humans were long
at work on the soft volcanic tuff at Bandelier National Monument in the
Jemez Mountains near Los Alamos. The cliffs there are dotted with caves and
cave dwellings, and evidence of humans living in the area goes back at least
10,000 years. The inhabitants could reach their homes with ladders rising
from the Frijoles Canyon floor. Incidentally, that canyon played a significant
role in Aldous Huxley's dystopian novel *Brave New World*. It is the location
of the Savage Reservation in New Mexico, and the birthplace of John the
Savage. John's live birth was seen as obscene and despicable in the *Brave New
World;* humans were grown and conditioned in bottles on assembly lines.

I often stumble over this: The state is so ancient and still partly pristine; it has such a huge unpopulated expanse of land. Yet at the same time, there are dystopian, even apocalyptic elements mixed in. After all, it was here, at Trinity Site, after the explosion of the first A-bomb, that J. Robert Oppenheimer recited a line from the ancient Sanskrit epic of the Bhagavad Gita: "Now I am become death, the destroyer of worlds" (Easwaran, 2007).

Among our many caves and one enormous cave system, a stunning group stands out: the sculpted underground spaces carved by Ra Paulette into the mountains of northern New Mexico near Embudo and Taos. No one else does what Paulette is doing. It seems he can listen, hear, absorb, and understand what a cave-to-be wants. Then he goes on to make it—beautifully. He calls it "intuitive engineering."

Born in Chicago, raised in northern Indiana, the cave-digger dropped out of college, served four years in Vietnam, came home, and then wandered the country working mostly as a farm laborer known as the human backhoe. He came to New Mexico in 1977. He got his idea while watching a bunch of teenagers chipping away on a tiny cave. His first carved project was completed in 1987. He has now sculpted soft *Ojo Caliente* sandstone for more than 25 years, literally moving mountains of debris and carving Gaudí-echoing wonders with openings that draw natural light into the belly of a mountain or a cliff. He uses no fancy machines, no dynamite, just his hand tools, his wheelbarrow, and an almost incomprehensible amount of patience and strength.

Once he had patrons who ordered carved caves from him, but that didn't work out. This is a type of project that cannot be commissioned or ordered. So Paulette remains just one man, in his late sixties now, growing tired, and still working alone, with his dog by his side—currently on his biggest and last project. California filmmaker Jeffrey Karoff's 2013 short documentary *CaveDigger* shows Paulette in his caves and at work. The film was nominated for an Oscar and won several other awards.

I like Chamisso's idea of the cave, and appreciate having one of my own. When you carry loads of life, living, working, and caring accumulated on

FIGURE 25. *Sandstone Cave by Ra Paulette, New Mexico.*
Photo by Kate Nelson.

your back, it feels good to come to a small hide-out, put down your baggage, sort things out, rest a little, and voilá, all can be well once more with your world. I was out there *Looking for Humboldt* for some time, snatching hours away from other tasks. So it was lovely to come back to the refuge, take off my hiking boots, put up my feet, and chill. Did I find Humboldt? Of course I did; he was always there. The planet has more than a thousand places, universities, an ocean current, plants and animals, a giant Humboldt Squid, a legal California cannabis product called *True Humboldt,* plus a crater on the moon named after him. And the other day my daughter came to visit, smiling from ear to ear. Look in your freezer, she said. I did. There stood a tub of Humboldt coffee chip ice cream, made in Fortuna, California, by the Humboldt Creamery. We both had a bowl of the good stuff.

It wasn't really Humboldt's doing that he was dropped down the memory hole here in the America he liked so well that he considered himself to be half American.

Although today Humboldt is largely invisible like Schlemihl's Shadow, and Americans forgot him like they forget and probably have to forget so many things in our fast-paced society, there is something of a slight reawakened interest in the man, his ideas, his spirit, and his work. To use a buzzword you could almost say he is *trending*, or rather that he was already trending more than 200 years ago but we lost interest in that, ignored him, and proceeded with activities that were detrimentally divergent from what he stood for.

Here in the United States, at least three outstanding new nonfiction books helped to bring some interest back to Humboldt. The first one, in 2006, was *The Humboldt Current*, by Aaron Sachs. I liked it very much. My own Humboldt project was then still in the preparation and early writing stage, and I was appreciative and surprised about the Sachs publication. Next, in 2009, came Laura Dassow Walls' *The Passage to Cosmos: Alexander von Humboldt and the Shaping of America,* and then, in September 2015, Andrea Wulf's *The Invention of Nature: Alexander von Humboldt's New World* appeared and was soon a national bestseller. It was one of the New York Times 10 Best Books of the Year, and Best Book of the Year of *The Economist* and *Publisher's Weekly.*

So why do I taste in some places the same stale flavors of misunderstanding that Peter Novick identified in his study *That Noble Dream?* He, as noted earlier in this book, said, "The misinterpretation of Ranke can be considered part of a more general phenomenon." Yes, and there is already so much mangled material layered between the cultural history of the Anglophone world and that of others, why add more? Andrea Wulf, who is fluent in German, explains Humboldt's vanishing act in her recent book *The Invention of Nature* by writing that "It is as though his ideas have become so manifest that the man behind them has disappeared." And in a September 27, 2015, *New York Times* Sunday review of the book, Colin Thubron pointed out that, apart from Latin America and his birthplace Germany, Humboldt's name "has receded into near oblivion."

That's right. But the invisibility didn't strike because Humboldt's ideas were so completely and magically absorbed in our Anglosphere that the man himself was dissolved in it like a spoon full of cream in a cup of coffee. My mental Geiger counter is wiggling: humbug ahead!

First of all, Germany and Latin America, where appreciation of Humboldt persists, are dismissed as if they are sideshows, which they are not. They certainly play a more vital role in this story than the U.S. or the UK. And secondly, it is charming, even elegant, to argue that Humboldt's ideas have become so "manifest" that they are present everywhere, while only the perishable man has vanished. Nice try. But I don't think this is what happened. Massive U.S. industrialization happened. There was a fork in the road, and folks followed, or were carried along to the right side of it with the Manifest Destiny crusaders, the White Man's Burden warriors, and the Social Darwinism crowd. Imperious Man must be in control, and Nature had to be subdued and utilized. The Gilded Age and Labor Strife were on the horizon. Then came the Great War. And the Great Depression. Humboldt's insights fell increasingly out of favor. However, as Aaron Sachs puts it in his *The Humboldt Current,* "The decisive blow to Humboldtianism in the United States was likely the rise of a rabid anti-German sentiment during World War I: there could be no Prussian heroes after 1917" (Sachs, 2006, p. 339).

Just so. Yet at the present moment, once again, history displays her sense of humor. She has the last laugh. Apparently it wasn't Humboldt who was stewing in the mystical romanticism he was accused of—he simply lacked a shortsighted vision which we usually have in abundance. Furthermore, the term *romanticism* (back then, persons who showed concern for nature or natives were routinely classified as romantics) is so loaded and misused that one scholar, E. G. Burgum (1941), warned that trying to define Romanticism is a hazardous occupation prone to produce many casualties. Another author,

271

F. L. Lucas, listed 11,396 definitions of romanticism in his 1961 book *The Decline and Fall of the Romantic Ideal*. In contrast, Manfred Frank, a scholar, compared *Early German Romanticism* to a beneficial philosophical supernova: It was that significant. Not only did it have a strong current of anti-imperialist thinking during the Enlightenment era, it is such a rich storehouse of ideas that even something as unromantic as today's Systems Theory goes fishing in it.

Whatever the case may be, Humboldt was not out of touch with the rapidly specializing modern worlds of science and industrial progress. Instead, he was ahead of his time and of his critics. He had a different mindset. His brother Wilhelm understood as early as 1793 that "He is made to connect ideas, to see chains of things that would have remained undiscovered for generations without him" (Sachs, 2006, p. 12).

Yet there is much more to the man. He was a democratic republican throughout his life; hated slavery; liked science to be free for the good of all, thought that very idea of a colony was probably immoral (Herder called colonialism the grand European sponging enterprise); attacked forced labor and plantation agriculture; was one of the first individuals who studied, honored, and documented the pre-Columbian cultures of the Aztecs and Maya; learned Hebrew as a young man and still fought for Jewish civil rights as an old one; and almost single-handedly secured a law that set free any slave setting foot on Prussian soil. Such legislation was mostly symbolic, since not many slaves had the opportunity to come to Prussia. But that was not the point. Slavery was still thriving in the United States. He found that most disappointing. And even though Humboldt was a man of his time and class, supremacy thinking and bigotry were revolting to him.

Come to think of it, not one of the German immigrants covered in this book behaved like a racist. Does this indicate I was cherry picking in finding these individuals? No. The plain reality seems to be that these newcomers to the U.S. had not been exposed to racial discrimination during their childhood and youth. Until the end of the 19th century, Germany did not have colonies, nor did it import slaves, and therefore there was no cause for inventing superiority complexes. That doesn't mean that these were better people, it simply means that they had other worries, like trying to rebuild their home turf as a country.

The following James Gillray political cartoon from 1805, the year after Humboldt visited Thomas Jefferson, shows William Pitt and Napoleon having a modest *"petit souper."* They are slicing up the plum-pudding of the globe, with the English gentleman cutting the biggest piece for himself. He took almost half of the planet! And no Prussian in sight! Not yet, at any rate. There was still much to learn—unfortunately.

FIGURE 26. *Carving Up the Plumb Pudding; hand-colored caricature by James Gillray, London 1805.*

Apparently, permanent oblivion is not in the cards for Humboldt no matter who wants to hide him in a trunk in the attic with the rest of the unwanted knick-knacks. Elsewhere, he is being prepared for the big time. Scheduled to open in 2019, the new *Humboldt Forum* in Berlin is a museum project on a large scale. It will serve as an international center of world culture and will be housed in the reconstructed royal city palace, which was destroyed in World War II and later completely carted away, probably to one of the new mountains made from rubble—now landscaped and used for various city winter sports during the cold season.

These artificial hills sprouted up around most big cities. Berlin has several of them. The house where I was born was also pulverized, removed, and most likely incorporated into a man-made mountain. The largest and tallest one is called *Devil's Mountain*. With an elevation of 260 feet, it is the highest point in Berlin. It contains 98,000,000 cubic yards of bombing debris. The view from its top is splendid, and on New Years' Eve hundreds of people watch the fireworks from their *Schuttberg* (rubble mountain). This time around the show is peaceful, instead of being destructive.

There is another Berlin rubble hill called *Humboldt Höhe*, and I hope the ruins from the house where I was born are part of that one. It would be nice, but I will never know. This new mountain is now green, forested, and located in a pleasant park. The space also has a public pool and playgrounds for children. When the project was completed, Berliners were asked how they would like to name the new peak. Nearly 1000 suggestions were mailed in, and the name *Humboldt Höhe* won. I hope that many children will have fun sledding down the slopes. Recycling the debris of devastation into places of enjoyment is a cool thing to do.

—

For years, the Palace Square (*Schlossplatz*), formerly in East Berlin behind the Wall, had been a post-unification empty space in the middle of the city. The government, various major institutions, the public, and an international commission of experts wrangled about the controversial project for more than a decade, wrote reports, and argued pros and cons. It was finally approved in 2002. Once completed, the triangle of the Humboldt Forum, the institutions of the Museum Island, and the scientific collections of Humboldt University will be an exceedingly content-rich sanctuary for global art, science, and culture.

Approval didn't stop the criticism and the debates. The arguments were political (No more Prussian glory. Prussia had been abolished by the Allies, remember?); architectural (What style—modern, historical reconstruction, mixed?); or they dealt with Berlin's dented identity. They were also related to many other issues. What will the role of the museum be in the 21st century? Was the *Kunstkammer* (cabinet of art) in this palace—as in other European palaces where collections began centuries ago— the prototype of a world museum? What about colonial history and the "collecting" of art/artifacts for the institutions of the hegemonic West? And was the pre-imperial phase of European museum collecting more cosmopolitan and less condescending in orientation? The Forum will have a theater, a movie theater, restaurants, and an *agora* inspired by ancient Greece as a venue for discussion and encounter.

There was a nice lull in the stormy weather around the project in the spring of 2015 when it was announced that Neil MacGregor, the highly regarded and successful director of the British Museum for more than 12 years, would become the artistic director of the Humboldt Forum. A few years earlier MacGregor had declined an offer to become the successor of Philippe de Montebello, Director of New York's Metropolitan Museum of Art. So now he will go to Berlin. Even the media seemed to grow temporarily quiet about such news, but then there were numerous articles in the major papers.

In talking to *The New York Times*, MacGregor said that the Humboldt Forum will unify all the surviving German collections which were *not* acquired during imperial conquest, but from "a Germany of the mind, that sees the world as connected and understandable through intellectual endeavor— the whole notion of *weltgeschichte,* of *weltkultur*" (Erlanger, 2015) or world history and world culture. "It's an intellectual inheritance that was shattered by the

Nazis, and the reconstruction of that idea, that cultures are both particular and global, contextual and connected, is an extraordinary thing to try to do," Mr. MacGregor said (Erlanger, 2015).

This makes me feel good around my heart. Particular and global: This man can slip into Humboldt's mind and the minds of those around him and before him—a few observers even suspect that he comprehends Germany better than the Germans do. I certainly feel at ease with his way of thinking.

Viewing this from the UK, MacGregor noted that the Germans know us, but we don't know them. "The British, on the whole, don't travel to Germany and read German literature," he told Simon Schama during an interview with the *Financial Times* (Schama, 2014). To him, a museum is more than a storehouse of masterpieces. It should be a space where people reevaluate their place in the world, and where they rediscover, in a friendly way, what it means to be human. The "protean, endlessly mutating thing that is Germany arriving at the status of the senior power in Europe" fascinates him (Schama, 2014). This interest in the language and the history goes back to his childhood in Scotland.

—

Earlier we listened to Sir Halford Mackinder, and his geopolitical heartland theory from the early 1900s. All at once these ideas come back to bounce around in my head again, ready to engage in a bit of whimsical playing. According to Mackinder, I was once a landlocked Heartlander, used to being surrounded by a number of neighbors and languages. Then I crossed the big pond and moved to the U.S. of America, which he counts as a big Offshore Island—with two huge oceans, the Atlantic and the Pacific, protecting its flanks. The people living on the British Isles are also Islanders, and not familiar with having various neighbors and their foreign babbling close to them.

Suppose one accepts Mackinder's teachings, even if only momentarily. Then that would explain some things, wouldn't it? It would show that it is easier for Anglo-Saxons to retain an islander mentality and a certain stand-offish attitude towards non-islanders who come from landlocked locations with shifting borders. These Heartlanders have been living since time immemorial exposed to wildly mixed and mobile neighbors ranging from pagan Goths to nomadic gents on horseback, all communicating in alien tongues. Oh, all right, I am just playing a game.

But it wasn't a game when post-war German youngsters, freshly escaped from the dinosaur war and dwelling in pulverized surroundings, flung themselves on foreign literature, and theater, and film, starved for mental nourishment as much as for food and shelter. It was the only place they could turn to. They needed the world's stories for sanity. Everything they had known and learned was put down, ripped to pieces, made ugly. Their school textbooks were taken away. There was no floor, and no firm ground under their feet. They were lost like in a graphic by M. C. Escher, with false staircases dangling in mid-air and hallways leading to nowhere. First, the young had been indoctrinated about bad art and bad writing (which became good avant-garde art and good writing after 1945), then the reigning regime had prescribed good art and good writing for them. This good stuff included almost all the most valuable names, works, and classics of these students' cultural history, but during the postwar times these Third Reich-approved legacies became, through their forced association, materials of ill repute or, at a minimum, boring old scribblings no longer useful for a new beginning.

So what did the kids do? They soaked up what was not besmirched: Foreign writing. And painting. And music. It was new. It was soul food. They were hungry. At least a few of my friends and I did this. Others did too. And, as I recall the bookstore windows and re-appearing library display shelves, I can see them full of covers and titles from the languages of the world. The translations already existed. So we read our way out of misery, gobbling up French, English, Russian, Italian, Spanish, Danish, Turkish, Persian, even Chinese and Japanese, books and poetry. We discovered humans all across the globe, and life, and joy, and pain.

There was not much rhyme or reason to this haphazard literary consumption, but it was intense, and passionate, and it built up a nutritious layer of sediment. What began with disconnected pieces settling at the bottom of the mind transformed itself very slowly into a big panorama. It showed that there was an amazing, diverse, harsh, dangerous, beautiful, and unforgettable world we could all inhabit. And then, as the years passed, it was even possible to touch and discover the full German inheritance again. After all, if a philosopher or a poet was unfortunate enough to be appropriated by a dictator, that wasn't the philosopher's or poet's failing—both had long been dead.

Today, I am thankful for the self-inflicted deposits gathered in reading everything wildly and without a plan as long as it was foreign and written by *homo sapiens.* This served as a solid vaccination policy that made hatred of the "other" virtually impossible. And what is more, it frequently delivered, and still delivers, delectable examples. The other day there were hyped media reports about large numbers of Americans 100 years and older who still receive their social security checks. Fraud, my dears—except for a few, these ancient persons are long gone. Instantly, synapses snapped to attention, lit up, and delivered the *Dead Souls,* Nicolai Gogol's comical tale from the 1840s. Easy money can be made if dead people are kept on the books—so it was in Russia some 175 years ago, and so it still is in our exceptional United States in the 21st century. Much has changed and changes rapidly all the time, except for our jolly seven cardinal sins: Pride, greed, lust, envy, gluttony, wrath, and sloth. They are our continuity.

—

Another glorious fall is gone, and it is cold and wintry now, with a bright blue sky. Almost always we have these great skies. They are based on illusion and physics, on the diffusion or scattering of light high up on the edge of space, and on wavelength—but it doesn't matter. They create good feelings nevertheless. The Bold Blue is real to me.

It is easy to be glad these days. Small joys will do it. This morning something wild—a roadrunner—found its way into our yard. I observed the large bird searching for hibernating snails, watched how he found two in the evergreens along the northern wall , cleverly cracked their shells open on a rock, had his breakfast, and slowly stalked away.

Simultaneously, ego seems to be dropping off like an outgrown skin. Animals and insects discard their old skins; too bad people can't do it in such a tangible way. Anyway, on hikes in the mountains or along the river, one can sometimes find a delicate dry and brittle outer layer stripped off by a snake.

FIGURE 27. *Peter Schlemihl's Seven-League-Boots. Illustration by George Cruikshank, London,1824.*

For explorations around our state, I don't have to wear my imaginary seven-league-boots. I will do that only for faraway journeys on earth or even in space. My husband was a physicist, and the two of us bantered about quantum leaps, all kinds of particles or waves, and about neutrinos. We fantasized how we would turn into these extremely little guys during our next existence, and how we could then dance happily, and as fast as thought, all through the universe, without barriers.

During the winter months, it is pleasant to travel south. Summers in southern New Mexico are very hot, but winters are usually mild, often more like early spring. When passing near the Trinity test site where the first atom bomb was exploded, I have the eerie notion that here is an axis of our contemporary world. The forces unleashed at this remote location were different from anything else men had invented. From here these powers spread. They are still with us to this day. There are even plans to modernize U.S. nuclear weapons at the cost of $1 trillion over the next 30 years. The limited number of downwinders, however, haven't received much attention since the first blast.

Although I am no longer terrified, nor do I dwell on it, deep down I remain aware that atomic weapons were developed here to be used on the land of my childhood. That country collapsed a few months before the bomb was ready. Japan held out a bit longer and was targeted with these tools of annihilation. No, I don't think much about it—but there is always a note, a low tone that swings inside of me, ever so gently and enduringly. Many species have vanished from our earth, and if our kind is hubris-prone and reckless, we can vanish too.

From time to time I recall *Donald Duck's Atom Bomb,* a 1947 comic strip by Carl Barks. Then I google for it. This little story was given away in Cheerios cereal boxes, but not for long. The strip was quickly censored and taken out of circulation. Today, not many people know about it. That Donald Duck failed to make a bomb, saturated the river with radioactive materials, and bottled this toxic brew for the population that lost its hair due to his atomic experiments, didn't trigger the censorship. Oh, no. What raised eyebrows was the wicked plan to sell the radioactive water for a dollar a flask as a tonic for growing the hair back! Such an unethical business scheme deserved to be censored! It is a hilarious strip with a bite, and now easily found online.

—

La Cruz de Aleman is the cross that marks the spot where the sparse remains of the German trader Bernardo Gruber were found in 1670. He was the fellow we met before. He had been engaged in a prank, was accused of practicing witchcraft, and imprisoned by the Inquisition near Albuquerque. He escaped with the help of his loyal Apache servant. The fleeing men had to cross the desolate tract that was eventually named after the trader—*Jornada del Muerto* (Dead Man's Journey). This was where Gruber perished from thirst and exhaustion, and this also became the location for the explosion of the first atomic bomb. The desert here was the most dangerous 90-mile stretch of the 1800 mile *Camino Real* (Royal Road) between Santa Fe and Mexico City.

Not far from the Aleman Cross is the Aleman Ranch. The main building is an old adobe hacienda, whitewashed, and with additional three-feet thick walls surrounding a large courtyard. The enclosed square served a defensive purpose against attacking Apaches or Navajos, just like the thick-walled, sturdy mission churches of northern New Mexico protected populations during warfare.

Lt. John "Jack" Martin started the place as a homestead in the 1860s. He had been a drummer boy during the Mexican-American War, afterwards tried his luck in the California gold fields, and was later a military escort with the stagecoach and mail delivery service that traveled along the old *Camino Real* and through the *Jornada del Muerto*. He and his wife settled in the location called Aleman, where Jack started to dig the desert's first well. He reached groundwater at a depth of 164 feet. Now the plans for a ranch had a modest chance for success. Soon the couple had cattle, and the cattle had water to drink. I have no idea about their luck with grazing.

In addition, the entrepreneurial Martin charged travelers for using his water, offered free water to the military, and even managed to get soldiers from Fort Selden to protect travelers crossing the death strip. He helped to establish a tiny post office and a small hotel nearby. That spot is now Internet-listed as the Aleman ghost town in Sierra County, but there is not much left to see. It's a fitting monument for the vanished German-American community in the United States.

—

What a strange, vast area of the West this is: neighboring the *Jornada del Muerto* is another desert. This one is icewhite, unsurpassed, and nothing like it is found elsewhere on earth due to special geological conditions. Great dunes of pure white gypsum sand undulate over an area of 275 square miles against our characteristically bold blue sky. This natural jewel is protected as the White Sands National Monument, and open to visitors. The experience is almost otherworldly; it may feel like being on an alien planet. And to enhance the unearthly experience, there is also Virgin Galactic's Spaceport America, which sits gleaming, isolated, and seemingly abandoned in the great emptiness west of White Sands.

If all goes well, this futuristic port will serve within the next few years as the base from which paying civilians fly up into space. Some wealthy people had already signed up at a cost of almost $250,000 per person when an accident happened. It delayed the whole program for years. In October 2014, during a test flight above the Mojave Desert, the rocket ship broke up and killed the pilot. Silence. Finally, during the spring of 2016, there was new activity at the sleeping spaceport in New Mexico. The replacement space ship *White Knight Two* was performing ground and air exercises.

—

Now if I swing around, leave the high deserts of the south and head north for several hours, I will bypass Santa Fe and come to Taos, an ancient settlement of Pueblo Native Americans about a mile north of the town itself. Established Hispanic families have lived in Taos for generations. Nestled in the high-altitude fertile Taos Valley, surrounded by the mountains of the Sangre de Christo range, artists came to visit the town in the late 19th century. The first to look was Joseph Henry Sharp in 1893. Ernest Blumenschein and Bert Phillips arrived in 1898, checked the place out, and became so smitten with the area and its people that they decided to stay. This was the beginning of the Taos art colony. Contacts with friends in New York and Paris spread the word. By 1915, six painters had founded the Taos Society of Artists, which was soon well regarded, even internationally.

Taos Pueblo proper became a UNESCO World Heritage Site in 1992 and looks like a very aged cousin of Montreal's HABITAT 67, a futuristic cubistic housing complex built for the World's Fair Expo 1967. Sometimes called the world's first apartment building, the Pueblo's Bauhaus-style was already many centuries old before the actual Bauhaus arrived on the scene in Europe. Today, the pueblo is still inhabited by several Native American families.

In addition to the studios of the painters, a literary salon developed after the heiress Mabel Dodge Luhan (she was still married to someone with the name Dodge at that time) discovered Taos in 1919. She had gained experience with her salons in New York and Florence. Now war-weary, she wanted to be far away from it all. She bought 12,000 acres of land with a house, married again—this time to the Taos Pueblo Native Tony Luhan—and invited artist friends and international guests to stay with her. Her modest house was transformed into a sprawling adobe mansion and a type of Shangri-La at the end of the United States. D. H. Lawrence painted whimsical things on the glass of her bathroom windows.

Formidable and eccentric as a hostess, Mabel attracted scores of prominent people to come and be her houseguests. Among them were (in no particular order) D. H. Lawrence, Ansel Adams, Mary Hunter Austin, Georgia O'Keeffe, Tennessee Williams, Thomas Wolfe, Greta Garbo, Martha Graham, Robinson Jeffers, Carl Jung, Aldous Huxley, Willa Cather, and Thornton Wilder.

─

I will never come to the end of finding things out about the state and the country. It is just not possible to satisfy one's interest about a landmass and an international population that contains First, Second, and Third Worlds simultaneously. I only have to look around and I can see elements of all these different worlds in our country, region, city, and even in our neighborhood.

In the United States overall, developments happened so rapidly that not all of them could be done properly. Across the West there was so much virgin land, drive, brains, experimentation and brutality, and such a wealth of resources that you didn't have to sweat the small stuff. It was not like in the Netherlands, where they clawed inch by inch of precious new ground from the North Sea, *Mord* Sea (Murder Sea), and are extremely frugal and inventive in making the best of whatever little land they have. They can't afford to be wastefully generous with their terrain, with their human, and with their other limited resources—and so far, the Dutch have handled them quite well.

In the U.S. it was different. If metals or minerals were found, a mine was started. It began producing with breakneck speed. A town sprang up, fast. Workers arrived, fast. The mine ran out of ore or out of whatever. It closed. The people left. The town died. The same process repeated itself somewhat slower with factories, even with whole industries as in the deindustrialized Midwest, and in Rustbelt cities. Detroit is an example. Decaying structures are being torn down, and many gardens have been started. Now the brave urban mini-farmers grow fresh produce and sell it. Parts of the sick city are turning green.

The construction of railroads and of the interstate system produced related results. If you take a leisurely tour on the back roads of the Midwest, you will see small towns, farm houses, and filling stations nearly empty or even abandoned, bleached by the sun and the winds. Their reasons for being in business disappeared, and so did they. The fields of corporate monoculture stretch out to the horizons. Nothing but corn or soybeans. Many family farms have vanished. Bees are threatened with starvation. They are increasingly transported in their hives and by truck over thousands of miles to specific sites around the country, for example, to the huge California almond farms when the trees are in bloom. Once the blooming period is over, the pollinators work is done. But there is nothing left for the bees to live on for the rest of the year. They are now like migrant workers. They must be trucking on. Kind-hearted and forward-looking people and organizations are lately trying to rescue bio-diversity across the Great

Plains by establishing bee-sanctuaries with a plentiful and diverse plant life to feast on. These are first small steps.

At any rate, our huge fly-over country looks empty. The estimated 60 million buffalo are long gone. The cities expanded ever more. Taking all this in can put you in a most melancholic mood. But who knows, perhaps it is a good thing in the end. Maybe slowly, gradually, nature will do her repair work, and a new generation may assist, observe, and do things respectfully. It's impossible to turn the clock back, but with time, and in time, maybe we will manage one day to make, if not 300 marvelous to die-for cheeses like the French from the same simple ingredient—milk—but at least a 100. Free trade is a potentially good thing, but you can also go over the top with your neoliberal fundamentalism, causing much hardship and poverty.

—

Perhaps one day we can make many things at home, as needed, creating work, and stopping to import what doesn't need to be imported, for example so many foodie foods. It's not all high-tech; it's also staples of civilization like quality marmalade, good cheeses, and decent bread. Or faucets for our kitchen sinks, and tools, and eye glasses, and on and on.

I am at present annoyed about my U.S. brand-name printer, which dictates that I use *only* its genuine U.S. brand-name ink cartridges. Hilariously, they are made in China. And there is more: less expensive refills made here in the U.S. are rejected by the machine. Daily life is now overflowing with such absurdities.

It is reckless to ignore that a population without adequate work and income grows angry and restive.

—

Where else in the U.S. could I be content but in this beautiful and comparatively poor state with its perilous symbolism, its warm, resilient people, and a map on which, in the beginning of the book, "I noticed the empty space, / Where there is no map, / Only the theater of man and myth," as the poet Antonio Mares put it (qtd. in Gonzales-Berry, 1989, p.277).

Now the map is alive for me. I was able to add features and fill in some of the empty spaces with markers and stories that add meaning. I named things. People do this. They have to, or they can end up being disoriented. Seasons have passed. I found irrevocable love. And I have also grown a deep, long taproot on a small plot, reaching down into our desert dirt just like many of the plants do it around here. It keeps me anchored in place—but simultaneously wide awake to the world. That is a good thing for someone who is aware of how precarious an at-home notion can be for large numbers of individuals who were born into the 20th century and found themselves tossed about by the powerful and impersonal forces of geopolitics, economics, and war. The new 21st century doesn't look too stable either, especially for those who are fleeing from non-stop conflict, violence, and the related environmental deprivations.

～

The search for Humboldt and for German footprints in our region was an exhilarating task. It was almost like the forensic investigation of a cold case, of looking for something unsolved. I found closure, as they say. I take pleasure in my shadow and live with it, freely. I value all three: the taproot, the small cave, and the seven-league boots. And there is still that song we loved to sing as children: *Die Gedanken sind Frei (Thoughts are Free)*. To me, that is a human birthright—thoughts remain free despite all the political oppressions, nationalistic tall tales, power struggles, snoopings, manipulations, and new-fangled censorships of the digital age. Perhaps some evil geniuses will one day attempt to implant a chip in each infant, attempting to control us like semi-robots. It will not fly.

In the meantime, if things grow too ridiculous in this best of all worlds, I will turn to El Morro, the inscription rock, and to the pageant of human actors it has seen through the ages. This concentrates the mind beautifully. It applies to the entire planet. It is all-important, yet no one should take himself/ herself too seriously. The processions go on. *Paso por aquí.*

REFERENCES

Bailey, L. R. (1998). *Bosque Redondo: The Navajo Internment at Fort Sumner, New Mexico, 1863–68*. Tucson, AZ: Westernlore Press.

Ballantine, G. (1853). *Autobiography of an English Soldier in the United States Army*. New York, NY: Springer & Townsend.

Bank of Canada Museum. (2016). *Currency Museum FAQ [frequently asked questions]*. Retrieved from: http://www.currencymuseum.ca/eng/learning/faq4.html

Borning, B.C. (1962) *The Political and Social Thought of Charles A. Beard*. Seattle: University of Washington Press, p.111

Boorstin, D. J. (1985). *The Discoverers*. New York, NY: Vintage Books/Random House.

Borges, J. L., A. Reid, trans. (1977) *The Gold of the Tigers: Selected Later Poems*. New York: Dutton. p.31.

Botting, D. (1973). *Humboldt and the Cosmos*. New York, NY: Harper & Row.

Braudel, F. (1981). *The Structures of Everyday Life: The Limits of the Possible, Vol. 1*. Trans. from the French. New York, NY: Harper & Row.

Burgum, E. G. (1941). "Romanticism" in The Kenyon Review, 3.4. p. 479–90

Butscher, L. (1942, July). A brief biography of Prince Paul Wilhelm of Württemberg. *New Mexico Historical Review*, 17(3), n.p.

Chamisso, A. von. (1910). *The Shadowless Man*. J. Bowring (Trans.). New York, NY: Frederick Warne.

Christiansen, P. W. (1974). *The Story of Mining in New Mexico*. Socorro, NM: New Mexico Bureau of Mines and Mineral Resources.

Christianson, S. (1998). *With Liberty for Some: 500 Years of Imprisonment in America*. Boston, MA: Northeastern University Press.

Clark, C. (2013). *The Sleepwalkers: How Europe Went to War in 1914*. New York, NY: Harper Perennial.

Conn, S. (Chief 1968, October 17). *Examples of Total War: 149 BC–1945 AD*. Fort Lesley J. McNair, Washington, DC: Office of the Chief of Military History, Dept.oft the Army. Retrieved from: http://www.army.mil/cmh-,pg/documents/misc.ocmh26.htm

Codart: Dutch and Flemish Art in Museums Worldwide. (2009, February 24). *Kaiser Karl V (1500–1558): Macht und Unmacht Europas. [Emperor Charles V (1500–1558): Europe's Power and Weakness]*. Retrieved from http://www.codart.com/exhibitions/details.1965/

Davies, G. (2002). *A History of Money* (3rd ed.). Cardiff, Wales: University of Wales Press.

De Terra, H. (1955). *Humboldt: The Life and Times of Alexander von Humboldt, 1769–1859*. New York, NY: Knopf.

Di Peso, J. (2002, June 25). *Time For Mining Law Reform. Albuquerque Tribune*. Retrieved from http://www.rep.org/opinions/op-eds/25.htm

Ebright, M. (1994). *Land Grants and Lawsuits in Northern New Mexico*. Albuquerque, NM: University of New Mexico Press.

Ehrenberg, H. (1845). [Narrative typescript in German of the Battle of Coleto, 1836, and the Goliad Massacre, 1836]. Austin, TX: Dolph Briscoe Center for American History, University of Texas.

Eco, U. (1988). *Serendipities: Language and Lunacy*. W. Weaver (Trans.). New York, NY: Columbia University Press.

Editorial. (1845), July/Aug. *The United States Magazine and Democratic Review*.

Englehardt, T. (2015, September 10). *TomDispatch*. [Online].

Erlanger, S. (2015, October 16). *British Museum's Director Follows a Fascination to Germany. New York Times*. Retrieved from http://nyti.ms.1jHTbp

Ette, O. (2005). *Alexander von Humboldt Heute*. Potsdam, Germany: University of Potsdam Press. Retrieved from http://verlag.ub.uni-potsdam.de/html/495/html/i53/htm

Farwell, B. (1985). *Queen Victoria's Little Wars*. New York, NY: Norton.

Friedrich, A. M. (2002, October 27). *Alexander von Humboldt as a Pioneer of Western North American Tectonics*. Paper presented at the annual meeting of the Geological Society of America, Denver, CO.

Fussell, P. (1975). *The Great War and Modern Memory*. New York, NY: Oxford University Press.

Gerste, R. D. (2003). Verdoppelung der USA. *Die Zeit, 18*. Retrieved from http://www.zeit.de/2003/18/A-Louisiana/komplettansicht

Gibson, G. R. (1974/1935). *Journal of a Soldier under Kearny and Doniphan, 1846–47*. R. Bieber (Ed.). Philadelphia, PA: Porcupine Press.

Gonzales-Berry, E. (Ed.). (1989). *Paso Por Aquí: Critical Essays on the New Mexican Literary Tradition, 1542–1988*. Albuquerque, NM: University of New Mexico Press.

GreatBasinMineWatch.org. (2002). [Home page]. Reno, NV. Retrieved from www.greatbasinminewatch.org.

Gress, D. (1998). *From Plato to NATO*. New York, NY: Free Press.

Hanke, L., & Fernandez, M. G. (Eds.). (1954). *Bartolome de Las Casas: Bibliografia Critica*. Santiago, Chile: Fondo Histórico y Bibliografico José Toribio Medinahrift.

Healey, G. H. (1955). *Letters of Daniel Defoe*. Oxford, England: Clarendon Press.

Helferich, L. (2004). *Humboldt's Cosmos*. New York, NY: Gotham Books/Penguin.

Hepworth, J. R. (1998). *Stealing Glances: Three Interviews with Wallace Stegner*. Albuquerque, NM: University of New Mexico Press.

Humboldt, A. von. (1811). *Political Essay on the Kingdom of New Spain, Vol. 1:* J. Black (Trans.). London, England: Longman.

Humboldt, A. von. (1838). Über die schwankungen der goldproduction mit rücksicht auf staatswirtschaftliche probleme. In *Deutsche Vierteljahres Schrift*, Vol. 4 (pp. 1–40). Retrieved from http://www.deutschestextarchiv.de/humboldt_schwankungen_1838terial

Humboldt, A. von. (2011). *Researches Concerning the Institutions and Monuments of the Ancient Inhabitants of America.* H. M. Williams (Trans.). New York, NY: Cambridge University Press.

Humboldt Digital Library Project, The Alexander von. (2016). *Humboldt Supplies Precise Details and Evaluation of Areas as Far as the Rio Grande.* Retrieved from http://www.ku.edu/~maxkade/humboldt/sub-washington.htm

Institut für Ur-undFrühgeschichte. (1999). *Mittelalterlicher bergbau.* Freiburg, Germany: Universität Freiburg. Retrieved from http://www2.ufg.uni-freiburg.de/d/publ/zimm1.html

Jaehn, T. (2005). *Germans in the Southwest, 1850–1920,* Albuquerque, NM: University of New Mexico Press.

Jonas, M. (1984). *The United States and Germany: A Diplomatic History.* Ithaca, NY: Cornell University Press.

Kamphoefner et al., W. D., Helbich, W., & Sommer, U. (Eds.). (1993). *News From the Land of Freedom: German Immigrants Write Home: Documents in American Social History.* Ithaca, NY: Cornell University Press.

Karp, W. (1979). *The Politics of War.* New York, NY: Harper & Row.

Kretzmann, J. A. (2001). Santa Fe, NM: Abandoned Mine Land Program, Mining and Minerals Division. Retrieved from http://www.emrd.state.nm.us/EMNRD/Mining/AML/AMLmain.htm

Kukla, J. (2003). *A Wilderness So Immense: The Louisiana Purchase and the Destiny of America.* New York, NY: Knopf.

Limerick, P. N. (2000). *Something in the Soil: Legacies and Reckonings in the New West.* New York, NY: W. W. Norton.

Lindquist, S. (2001). *A History of Bombing.* New York: The New Press.

Ludwig, K. H. (Ed.). (1987). *Bergbau und arbeitsrecht: Die arbeitsverfassung im europäischen bergbau des mittelalters und der frühen neuzeit. Böcksteiner Montanaheft 8.* Vienna, Austria: Bergbau und Arbeitsrecht.

Lynch, J. (2006). *Simon Bolivar: A Life.* New Haven, CT: Yale University Press.

Mackey, C. (1841). *Extraordinary Popular Delusions and the Madness of Crowds.* London, England: Richard Bentley.

Mackinder, H. (1942). *Democratic Ideals and Reality.* New York, NY: Holt.

Marc, F. (1992). *Letters from the War: American University Studies.* New York, NY: Peter Lang.

McDougall, W. A. (1997). *Promised Land, Crusader State.* Boston, MA: Houghton Mifflin.

McKenna, J. A. (1936). Story of the Lost Diggings. In *Black Range Tales: Sixty Years of Life and Adventure in the Southwest.* New York: Wilson-Erickson

Meyer, M. C., & Brescia, M. M. (1998, October). The Treaty of Guadalupe Hidalgo as a Living Document: Water and Land Use Issues in Northern New Mexico. *New Mexico Historical Review,* 73(4), 321–345.

Meyer v. Nebraska, 262 U.S. 390 (1923).

Milford, H. E. (2013). Appendix: Humboldt Supplies Precise Details and Evaluation of Areas as Far as the Rio Grande: Benefaction or refining processes. In *History of the Los Cerrillos Mining Area.* Appendix 1, pp.1–6. Cerillos, NM: Amigos de Cerillos, Hills State Park.

Miller, D. H. (1970). *Balduin Möllhausen: A Prussian's Image of the American West* (Unpublished doctoral dissertation). University of New Mexico, Albuquerque, NM.

Mishra, P. (2016, January 2). *A Generation of Failed Politicians.* Guardian, pp.1–3.

Mitchell, N. (1999). *The Danger of Dreams: German and American Imperialism in Latin America.* Chapel Hill, NC: University of North Carolina Press.

Möllhausen, B. (1861). *Reisen in die Felsengebirge Nord-Amerikas bis zum Hoch-Plateau von Neu-Mexico, unternommen als Mitglied der im Auftrage der Regierung der Vereinigten Staaten ausgesandten Colorado-Expedition, Vol. I.* Leipzig, Germany: Otto Purfürst (und) Hermann Costenoble.

Moyle, B. (Trans.). (1896). *The Institutes of Justinian* (3rd ed.). Oxford, England: Oxford University Press.

New Mexico Mining Museum. (n.d.). *Mining Information Card.* Grants, NM: Author.

Novick, P. (1988). *That Noble Dream.* New York: Cambridge University Press.

Ortiz, S. J. (1994). Destination, seeking [poem]. In *After and Before the Lightning*. Tucson, AZ: University of Arizona Press.

Pagden, A. (Trans.). (1986). *Hernan Cortés: Letters from Mexico*. New Haven, CT: Yale University Press.

Pagden, A. (1995). *Lords of All the World: Ideologies of Empire in Spain, Britain, and France, c. 1500–c. 1800*. New Haven, CT: Yale University Press.

Parsons, J. (2002, Spring). *The 1872 Mining Law and Native Americans*. New Mexico Environmental Law Center Progress Report. Retrieved from http://www.nmenvirolaw.org/

Paz, O. (1961). *The Labyrinth of Solitude: Life and Thought in Mexico*. New York, NY: Grove Press.

Perry, J. W. (2003, June/July). *Noble Islander. Hana Hou Magazine*, 6(3) p.1.

Prieto, C. (1973). *Mining in the New World*. New York, NY: McGraw-Hill.

Public Broadcasting Service (PBS). (2015, January). *Language Matters* [Documentary film].

Reed, C. (1999, May/June). *The Damn'd South Sea. Harvard Magazine*, Retrieved from: http://www.harvard-magazine.com/issues/mj99/damnd.html

Rosengarten, F. (1988). *Thomas Gage: The English-American traveler*. Princeton, NJ: Princeton University Press.

Rowan, S. W. (2012). *The Baron in the Grand Canyon: Friedrich Wilhelm von Egloffstein in the West*. St. Louis, MO: University of Missouri Press.

Sachs, A. (2006). *The Humboldt Current: Nineteenth-Century Exploration and the Roots of American Environmentalism*. New York, NY: Viking.

Schama, S. (2014, September 14). Neil MacGregor talks to Simon Schama. *Financial Times* (London). Retrieved from http://www.ft.com/intl/cms/s/2/da6bd362-3efa-11e4-a861-00144feabdc0.html

Schwarz, I. (n.d.). Äußerungen A. v. Humboldts über sich selbst [Alexander von Humboldt's sociopolitical views of the Americas]. Potsdam, Germany: University of Potsdam. Retrieved from http://www.uni-potsdam.de/u/romanistik/humboldt/frames/inh57.htm

Semmel, B. (1968). *Imperialism and SocialReform: English Social-Imperial Thought, 1895–1914*. Garden City, NY: Anchor Books.

Shäfer, E. (1936–1937). Johann Tetzel, ein deutscher Bergmann in Westindia zur Zeit Karl V. *Ibero-Amerikanisches Archiv, 10*, 160–170.

Slotkin, R. (1994). *Fatal Environment: The Myth of the Frontier in the Age of Industrialization, 1800–1890*. New York, NY: Harper Perennial.

Smith, G. W., & Judah, C. (Eds.). (1968). *Chronicles of the Gringos: The U.S. Army in the Mexican War, 1846–1848*. Albuquerque, NM: University of New Mexico Press.

Smithsonian Institution. (2002). *Corridos Sin Fronteras: Cancionero [Songbook]*. Washington, DC: Author.

Southwest Parks and Monuments Association. (1998). *El Morro Trails*. San Antonio, TX: Author.

Steck, M. (Ed.). (1981). *Duerer schriften, tagebuecher, briefe*. Stuttgart, Germany: W. Kohlhammer.

Stevens, H. (Ed.). (1893). *The New Laws of the Indies*. London, England: Chiswick Press.

Stevens, P. F. (1999). *The Rogues' march: John Riley and the St. Patrick's Battalion, 1846–48*. Washington, DC: Brassey's.

Sunseri, A. S. (1979). *Seeds of Discord: New Mexico in the Aftermath of the American Conquest, 1846–1861*. Chicago, IL: Nelson-Hall.

Thrapp, D. L. (2012). *Al Sieber, Chief of Scouts*. Norman, OK: University of Oklahoma Press.

Thubron, C. (2015, September 27). Review of *The Invention of Nature*, by Andrea Wulf. *New York Times*.

Twitchell, R. E. (1863). *Old Santa Fe: The story of New Mexico's Ancient Capital*. Chicago, IL: Rio Grande Press.

U.S. Army. (1917). Poster. [Located in Washington, DC: Library of Congress.]

U.S. Census Bureau. (2004, June). *Census Brief 2000*. Washington, DC: Author.

Virginia Military Institute (VMI). (n.d.). *Stonewall Jackson Papers*. Lexington, VA: VMI Archives. Retrieved from http://www.vmi.edu/archives/jackson/tj480410.html

von-Humboldt Forschungsstelle [Alexander von Humboldt Digital Library Project]. (n.d.). Retrieved from http://www.uni-potsdam.de/u/romanistic/humboldt/frames/inh57.htm

Vonnegut, K. (2005). *A Man Without a Country*. New York, NY: Seven Stories Press.

Webster, H. T. (1917, September). *Cartoon Magazine*. Bisbee Deportation Online Exhibit, Tucson, AZ: University of Arizona. Retrieved from http://www.library.arizona.edu/exhibits/bisbee,index.html

Wilson, G. (2003, Spring). The Louisiana Purchase. *Monticello* [Newsletter], *14*(1), 1–5.

Zeh, F. (1995). *An Immigrant Aoldier in the Mexican War*. W. J. Orr (Trans.). College Station, TX: Texas A&M University Press.

Zimmermann, U. (1999). *Mittelalterlicher bergbau auf eisen, blei und silber*. Freiburg, Germany: University of Freiburg Press. Retrieved from http://www.2.ufg.uni-freiburg.de/publ/zimm1.html

ACKNOWLEDGEMENTS

My special thanks go to Frederick T. Courtright of the Permissions Company, Inc. in Pennsylvania for his expertise in working with the manuscript. His company obtained the following necessary permissions:

Carl Blümner and Carl Blümner, Jr., excerpts from letters from *News from the Land of Freedom: German Immigrants Write Home: Documents in American Social History* edited by Walter D. Kamphoefner, Wolfgang Helbich, and Ulrike Sommer, translated by Susan C. Vogel. Copyright © 1988 by C. H. Beck'sche Verlagbuchhandlung (Oscar Beck) Munich. Translation copyright © 1990 by Cornell University. Reprinted with the permission of Cornell University Press.

"To the German Language" 31 (30 lines) by Jorge Luis Borges, translated by Alistair Reid, copyright 1999 by Maria Kodama, translation copyright 1999 by Alistair Reid; from SELECTED POEMS by Jorge Luis Borges, edited by Alexander Colemann. Used by permission of Viking Books, an imprint of Penguin Publishing Group; a division of Penguin Random House LLC.

All rights reserved. Arctic Ocean First Non-stop World Record Challenge Completed by Guo Chuan Racing, September 15, 2015. Source: http://www.sailingscuttlebutt.com/2015/09/15/arctic-ocean-world-record ©—photo reprint permission granted by Dr. Lingling Lui, lingling@chinasport-business.com

INDEX

Made in the USA
Middletown, DE
29 October 2021